The St. Martin's Pocket Guide to Research and Documentation

Fifth Edition

The St. Martin's Pocket Guide to Research and Documentation

Fifth Edition

ADAPTED FROM

The St. Martin's Handbook
Seventh Edition

ANDREA A. LUNSFORD
MARCIA MUTH

BEDFORD / ST. MARTIN'S
Boston ♦ New York

Manufactured in the United States of America.

6 5 4 3 2 1
f e d c b a

For information, write: Bedford/St. Martin's, 75 Arlington Street, Boston, MA 02116   (617-399-4000)

ISBN: 978-0-312-66192-2

Acknowledgments

Acknowledgments and copyrights are continued at the back of the book on page 287, which constitutes an extension of the copyright page. It is a violation of the law to reproduce these selections by any means whatsoever without the written permission of the copyright holder.

Contents

The St. Martin's Pocket Guide to Research and Documentation

Fifth Edition

Introduction

The St. Martin's Pocket Guide to Research and Documentation, Fifth Edition, is small enough to fit in your pocket but big enough to provide all the speedy and reliable help you'll need with research assignments from across the disciplines, including advice for planning, conducting, and documenting your research. Specifically, this guide provides

- general advice on the research process:
    - narrowing and focusing a topic
    - finding and evaluating sources in the library and on the Web
    - taking notes
    - acknowledging sources and avoiding plagiarism
- general resource materials useful in many fields
- specialized resources useful in particular disciplines
- documentation guidelines for five styles:
    - MLA (Modern Language Association)
    - *Chicago* (*Chicago Manual of Style*)
    - APA (American Psychological Association)
    - CSE (Council of Science Editors)
    - AIP (American Institute of Physics)

- sample student research assignments that show how to incorporate research materials and document sources
- innovative new source maps that annotate sample sources, giving step-by-step guidelines to help you evaluate and cite print and electronic materials
- integrated library research coverage to help you navigate today's wired libraries
- guidelines for avoiding plagiarism and knowing how to quote, paraphrase, and summarize sources

1

Preparing for a Research Project

Narrowing a Topic

Any topic you choose to research must be manageable — it must suit the scope, audience, length, and time limits of your assignment. Making a topic manageable often requires narrowing it, but you may also need to find a particular slant and look for a question to guide your research. To arrive at such a question, you might first generate a series of questions about your topic. You can then evaluate them and choose one or two that are both interesting and manageable. The result of the narrowing process is a research question that can be tentatively answered by a hypothesis, a statement of what you anticipate your research will show.

Like a working thesis, a hypothesis must be manageable, interesting, and specific. In addition, it must be arguable, a debatable proposition that you can prove or disprove with a reasonable amount of research evidence. For example, a statement like this one is not arguable since it merely states a widely known fact: "Senator Joseph McCarthy attracted great attention with his anti-Communist crusade during the 1950s." On the other hand, this statement is an arguable hypothesis because evidence for or against it can be found: "Roy Cohn's biased research while he was an assistant to Senator Joseph

McCarthy was partially responsible for McCarthy's anti-Communist crusade."

In moving from a general topic of interest, such as Senator Joseph McCarthy's anti-Communist crusade of the 1950s, to a useful hypothesis, such as the one in the previous paragraph, you first narrow the topic to a single manageable issue: Roy Cohn's role in the crusade, for instance. After background reading, you then raise a question about that issue ("To what extent did Cohn's research contribute to McCarthy's crusade?") and devise a possible answer, your hypothesis. The hypothesis, which tentatively answers your research question, must be precise enough to be supported or challenged by a manageable amount of research.

As you gather information and begin reading and evaluating sources, you will probably refine your research question and change your hypothesis significantly. Only after you have explored your hypothesis, tested it, and sharpened it by reading, writing, and talking with others does it become a working thesis.

In doing your own research, you may find that your interest shifts, that a whole line of inquiry is unproductive, or that your hypothesis is simply wrong. In each case, the process of research pushes you to learn more about your hypothesis, to make it more precise, to become an expert on your topic.

Determining What You Know

Once you have formulated a hypothesis, determine what you already know about your topic. Here are some strategies for doing so:

- *Brainstorming.* Take five minutes to list everything you think of or wonder about your hypothesis. You may find it helpful to do this in a group with other students.

- *Freewriting about your hypothesis.* For five minutes, write about every reason for believing your hypothesis is true. Then for another five minutes, write down every argument you can think of, no matter how weak, that someone opposed to your hypothesis might make.

- *Freewriting about your audience.* Write for five minutes about your readers, including your instructor. What do you think they currently believe about your topic? What sorts of evidence will convince them to accept your hypothesis? What sorts of sources will they respect?

- *Tapping your memory for sources.* List everything you can remember about *where* you learned about your topic: Web sites, email, books, magazines, courses, conversations, television. What you know comes from somewhere, and that "somewhere" can serve as a starting point for research.

Preliminary Research Plan

Once you've considered what you already know about your topic, you can develop a research plan. To do so, answer the following questions:

- What kinds of sources (books, journal articles, databases, Web sites, government documents, specialized reference works, images, videos, and so on) will you need to consult? How many sources should you consult?

- How current do your sources need to be? (For topical issues, especially those related to science, current sources are usually most important. For historical subjects, older sources may offer the best information.)

- How can you determine the location and availability of the kinds of sources you need?

- Do you need to consult sources contemporary with an event or a person's life? If so, how will you get access to those sources?

One goal of your research plan is to begin building a strong working bibliography (Chapter 3). Carrying out systematic research and keeping careful notes on your sources will make developing your works-cited list or bibliography (Chapters 5–8) easier later on.

2

Conducting
Research

Differentiating Kinds of Sources

Sources can include data from interviews and surveys, books and articles in print and online, Web sites, film, video, audio, images, and more. Consider these important differences among sources.

Primary and Secondary Sources

Primary sources provide firsthand knowledge, while secondary sources report on or analyze the research of others. Primary sources are basic sources of raw information, including your own field research; films, works of art, or other objects you examine; literary works you read; and eyewitness accounts, photographs, news reports, and historical documents (such as letters and speeches). Secondary sources are descriptions or interpretations of primary sources, such as researchers' reports, reviews, biographies, and encyclopedia articles. Often what constitutes a primary or secondary source depends on the purpose of your research. A critic's evaluation of a film, for instance, serves as a secondary source if you are writing about the film but as a primary source if you are studying the critic's writing.

Most research projects draw on both primary and secondary sources. A research-based essay on the effects of steroid use on major

league baseball, for example, might draw on primary sources, such as the players' testimony to Congress, as well as secondary sources, such as articles or books by baseball experts.

Scholarly and Popular Sources

While nonacademic sources like magazines and personal Web sites can help you get started on a research project, you will usually want to depend more heavily on authorities in a field, whose work generally appears in scholarly journals in print or online. The following list will help you distinguish scholarly and popular sources:

SCHOLARLY

- Title often contains the word *Journal*
- Source available mainly through libraries and library databases
- Few commercial advertisements
- Authors identified with academic credentials
- Summary or abstract appears on first page of article; articles are fairly long
- Articles cite sources and provide bibliographies

POPULAR

- *Journal* usually does not appear in title
- Source generally available outside of libraries (at newsstands or from a home Internet connection)
- Many advertisements
- Authors are usually journalists or reporters hired by the publication, not academics or experts
- No summary or abstract; articles are fairly short
- Articles may include quotations but do not cite sources or provide bibliographies

Older and More Current Sources

Most projects can benefit from both older, historical sources and more current ones. Some older sources are classics in their fields, essential for understanding the scholarship that follows them. Others are simply dated, though even these works can be useful to researchers who want to see what people wrote and read about a topic in the past. Depending on your purpose, you may rely primarily on recent sources (for example, if you are writing about a new scientific discovery), primarily on historical sources (if your project discusses a nineteenth-

century industrial accident), or on a mixture of both. Whether a source appeared hundreds of years ago or this morning, evaluate it carefully to determine how useful it will be for you (Chapter 3).

Using the Library to Get Started

Even when you have a general idea of what kinds of sources exist and which kinds you need for your research project, you still have to locate these sources. Many beginning researchers are tempted to assume that all the information they could possibly need is readily available on the Internet from a home connection. However, it is a good idea to begin almost any research project with the sources available in your college library.

Reference Librarians

You might start by getting to know one particularly valuable resource, your library staff — especially reference librarians. You can make an appointment to talk with a librarian — or with the subject specialist for your discipline — about your research project and get specific recommendations about databases and other helpful places to begin your research. In addition, many libraries have online chat environments where students can ask questions about their research and have them answered, in real time, by a reference librarian. To get the most helpful advice, whether online or in person, pose *specific* questions — not "Where can I find information about computers?" but "Where can I find information on the history of messaging technologies?" If you are having difficulty asking precise questions, you probably need to do some background research on your topic and formulate a sharper hypothesis. A librarian may be helpful in this regard as well.

Catalogs and Databases

Your library's computers hold many resources not available on the Web or not accessible to students except through the library's system. One of these resources is the library's own catalog of books

and other holdings, but most college libraries also subscribe to a large number of databases — electronic collections of information, such as indexes to journal and magazine articles, texts of news stories and legal cases, lists of sources on particular topics, and compilations of statistics — that students can access for free. Many of these databases have been screened or compiled by editors, librarians, or other scholars. Your library may also have metasearch software that allows you to search several databases at once.

Reference Works

Consulting general reference works is another good way to get started on a research project. These works are especially helpful for getting an overview of a topic, identifying subtopics, finding more specialized sources, and identifying useful keywords for electronic searches.

The following guides to reference works can help you identify those that suit your purpose:

Gale Directory of Databases. 2 vols. 1993–; annual. This two-volume resource is the most comprehensive index and guide to databases available.

Guide to Reference. This online resource (which replaces the *Guide to Reference Books*, 11th ed.) supplies annotated lists of general reference works and specialized bibliographies and is divided into six sections: General Reference; Humanities; Social and Behavioral Sciences; History and Area Studies; Science, Technology, and Medicine; and Interdisciplinary Fields. Each section is further subdivided into areas and then into special approaches.

The New Walford: Guide to Reference Resources. 8th ed. 3 vols. 2005–2010. *The New Walford*'s three volumes deal with Science, Technology, and Medicine; the Social Sciences; and Arts, Humanities, and General Reference.

GENERAL ENCYCLOPEDIAS

For general background on a subject, encyclopedias are a good place to begin, particularly because many include bibliographies that

can point you to more specialized sources. A librarian can direct you to such reference works. Remember that encyclopedias will serve as a place to start your research — not as major sources for a research project.

SPECIALIZED ENCYCLOPEDIAS

Compared with general encyclopedias, specialized encyclopedias, on subjects ranging from ancient history to world drama usually provide more detailed articles by authorities in the field as well as extensive bibliographies. Again, you should rely on these works more for background material than as major sources of information. Many specialized encyclopedias are available online as well as in print. For more information on specialized encyclopedias in particular fields, see Chapters 5–8.

BIOGRAPHICAL RESOURCES

The lives and historical settings of famous people are the topics of biographical dictionaries and indexes. Here are a few examples of biographical reference works; many others, particularly volumes specialized by geographic area or field, are available.

African American Biographies: Profiles of 909 Current Men and Women. 2009. Profiles over nine hundred notable African Americans.

American Men and Women of Science. 29th ed. 2011. Formerly *American Men of Science.* Provides biographical information on notable scientists alive today.

American National Biography. 1999; supplements 2002. Contains biographies of over seventeen thousand deceased Americans from all phases of public life from colonial days to 1980. Entries include bibliographies of sources.

Contemporary Authors. 1962–; annual. Supplies short biographies of authors who have published works during the year.

Current Biography. 1940–; monthly, with annual cumulations. Provides informative articles on people in the news. Includes photographs and short biographies.

International Who's Who. 1935–; annual. Contains biographies of persons of international status.

Merriam Webster's Biographical Dictionary. 1995. Provides biographical information on important deceased people of the last five thousand years.

Notable American Women: 1607–1950. 3 vols. 1972. Supplement, *Notable American Women: The Modern Period.* 1980. Supplement, *Notable American Women: A Biographical Dictionary Completing the Twentieth Century.* 2004. Contains biographies (with bibliographies) of women who contributed to North American society. The supplements cover women who died between 1951 and 1975, and the remaining years of the twentieth century.

Oxford Dictionary of National Biography. 2004. Covers deceased notables from Great Britain and its colonies (excluding the postcolonial United States).

Who's Who. 1849–; annual. Covers well-known living British people. *Who Was Who,* with volumes covering about a decade each, lists British notables who died between 1897 and the present.

Who's Who in America. 1899–; annual. Covers famous living North Americans. Notable Americans no longer living are in *Who Was Who in America,* covering 1607 to the present. Similar specialized works include *Who's Who of American Women, Who's Who in the World, Who's Who in Asia,* and so on.

BIBLIOGRAPHIES

Bibliographies are collections of resources available on a subject—for example, Shakespeare or World War II. Bibliographies may be databases or bound collections, and they may list books alone, both books and articles, or media such as film or video. A bibliography may simply list or describe each resource it includes, or it may include analysis of the resources.

ALMANACS, YEARBOOKS, AND NEWS DIGESTS

Almanacs, yearbooks, and news digests provide information on current events and statistical data.

Facts on File: World News Digest. 1940–; twice weekly. Summarizes and indexes facts about current events.

The Statesman's Yearbook. 1863–; annual. Contains current facts and statistics about the agriculture, government, population, development, religion, and so on of the countries of the world.

Statistical Abstract of the United States. 1878–; annual. Published by the Bureau of the Census; provides government data on U.S. population, business, immigration, and other subjects. (online at www .census.gov/compendia/statab)

The Time Almanac. 1947–; annual. Includes many charts, facts, and lists as well as short summaries of the year's events and accomplishments in various fields. (online at www.infoplease.com/almanacs.html)

World Almanac and Book of Facts. 1868–; annual. Presents data and statistics on business, education, sports, government, population, and other topics. Includes institutional names and addresses and reviews important annual public events.

ATLASES

In addition to physical maps of all parts of the world, the following atlases contain maps showing population, food distribution, mineral concentrations, temperature and rainfall, and political borders, among other facts and statistics.

Atlas of World Cultures: A Geographical Guide to Ethnographic Literature. 2004.

Hammond World Atlas. 2007.

National Geographic Atlas of the World. 2005.

The Rand McNally Commercial Atlas and Marketing Guide. 2010.

The Times Comprehensive Atlas of the World. 2007.

Finding Library Resources

The library is one of a researcher's best friends, especially in an age of electronic communication. Your college library houses a great

number of print materials and gives you access to electronic catalogs, indexes, and databases. But the library may seem daunting to you, especially on your first visit. Experienced student researchers will tell you that the best way to make the library a friend is to get to know it: a good starting place is its Web site, where you can find useful information, including its hours of operation, its floor plan, its collections, and so on; many libraries also have a virtual tour and other tutorials on their Web sites that give you a first-rate introduction to the library's resources.

Search Options

The most important tools your library offers are its online catalog and databases. Searching these tools will always be easier and more efficient if you use carefully chosen words to limit the scope of your research.

SUBJECT WORD SEARCHING

Catalogs and databases usually index their contents not only by author and title, but also by subject headings — standardized words and phrases used to classify the subject matter of books and articles. (For books, most U.S. academic libraries use the *Library of Congress Subject Headings,* or LCSH, for this purpose.) When you search the catalog by subject, you need to use the exact subject words.

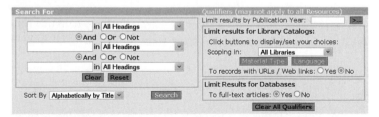

Advanced search page from a library catalog that incorporates Boolean operators

KEYWORD SEARCHING

Searches using keywords, on the other hand, make use of the computer's ability to look for any term in any field of the electronic record, including not just subject but also author, title, series, and notes. In article databases, a keyword search will look in abstracts and summaries of articles as well. Keyword searching is less restrictive, but it requires you to put some thought into choosing your search terms in order to get the best results.

ADVANCED SEARCHING

Many library catalogs and database search engines offer advanced search options (sometimes on a separate page) to help you combine keywords, search for an exact phrase, or exclude items containing particular keywords. Often they let you limit your search in other ways as well, such as by date, language, country of origin, or location of the keyword within a site.

Many catalogs and databases offer a search option using the Boolean operators AND, OR, and NOT, and some allow you to use parentheses and quotation marks to refine your search or wildcards to expand it. Note that much Boolean decision making is done for you when you use an advanced search option (as on the advanced search page shown on page 14). Note, too, that search engines vary in the exact terms and symbols they use to refine searches, so check before you search.

- AND *limits your search.* If you enter the terms *messaging* AND *language* AND *literacy*, the search engine will retrieve only those items that contain all the terms. Some search engines use a plus sign (+) instead of AND.

- OR *expands your search.* If you enter the terms *messaging* OR *language,* the computer will retrieve every item that contains the term *messaging* and every item that contains the term *language.*

- NOT *limits your search.* If you enter the terms *messaging* NOT *language,* the search engine will retrieve every item that contains *messaging*

except those that also contain the term *language*. Some search engines use a minus sign (–) or AND NOT instead of NOT.

- *Parentheses customize your search.* Entering *messaging* AND (*literacy* OR *linguistics*), for example, will locate items that mention either of those terms in connection with instant messaging.

- *Wildcards expand your search.* Use a wildcard, usually an asterisk (*) or a question mark (?), to find related words that begin with the same letters. Entering *messag** will locate *message, messages,* and *messaging.*

- *Quotation marks narrow your search.* Most search engines interpret words within quotation marks as a phrase that must appear with the words in that exact order.

Books

CATALOG INFORMATION

The library catalog lists all the library's books. Library catalogs follow a standard pattern of organization, with each holding identified by three kinds of entries: one headed by the *author's name,* one by the *title,* and one or (usually) more by the *subject.* If you can't find a particular source under any of these headings, you can search the catalog by using a combination of subject headings and keywords. Such searches may turn up other useful titles as well.

Following are a search page, a page of results for noted linguist and author David Crystal, and a catalog entry for one of his books from a university library catalog. Note that many electronic catalogs indicate whether a book has been checked out and, if so, when it is due to be returned. Sometimes, as in this case, you must click on a link to check the availability of the book.

Catalog entries for books list not only the author, title, subject, and publication information but also a call number that indicates how the book is classified and where it is shelved. Like many online catalogs, the catalog used for the following examples allows you to save the information about the book while you continue searching and then retrieve the call numbers for all of the books you want to find in one list. Once you have the call number for a book, look for a

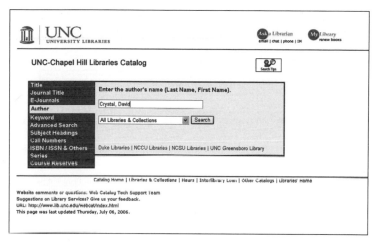

Library catalog search page

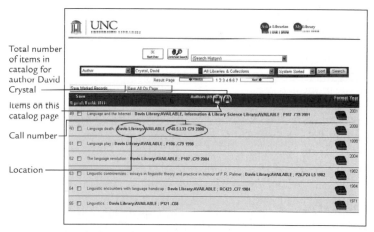

Results for author search in library catalog database

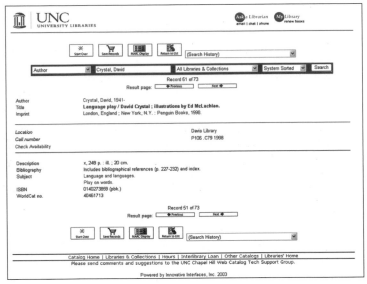

Catalog entry for a book chosen from author search

library map or shelving plan to tell you where the book is housed. Take the time to browse through the books near the call number you are looking for. Often you will find other books related to your topic in the immediate area.

INDEXES TO BOOKS AND REVIEWS

Book indexes can be helpful for quickly locating complete information on a book when you know only one piece of it — the author's last name, perhaps, or the title. These sources can also alert you to other works by a particular author or on a particular subject. Although book indexes are generally available online, if you are looking for an older book you may need to consult the print version of an index rather than an electronic database.

Books in Print. 1948–; annual. Lists by author, subject, and title all books distributed in the United States that are currently in print.

Cumulative Book Index. 1898–; monthly. Lists by author, subject, and title books in English distributed in the United States and internationally.

Consider also using a review index to check the relevance of a source or to get a thumbnail sketch of its contents. Be sure to check not only the year of a book's publication but also the next year.

Annual Bibliography of English Language and Literature (ABELL). 1921–; annual. Lists monographs, periodical articles, critical editions, book reviews, and essay collections related to literary works.

Book Review Digest. 1905–; annual. Contains excerpts from reviews of books along with information for locating the full reviews in popular and scholarly periodicals.

Book Review Index. 1965–; annual. Identifies dates and locations for finding full reviews in several hundred popular and scholarly periodicals; organizes entries by the name of the book's author.

International Bibliography of Book Reviews (IBR). 1985–; monthly. Lists book reviews published in scholarly journals, primarily in the social sciences and humanities.

Periodical Articles

Titles of periodicals held by a library appear in its catalog, but the titles of individual articles do not. To find the contents of periodicals, you will need to use an index source.

PERIODICAL INDEXES

Periodical indexes are databases or print volumes that hold information about articles published in newspapers, magazines, and scholarly journals. Different indexes cover different groups of periodicals; articles written before 1990 may be indexed only in a print volume. Ask a reference librarian for guidance about the most likely index for the subject of your research.

Electronic periodical indexes come in different forms, with some offering the full text of articles and some offering abstracts (short summaries) of the articles. Be sure not to confuse an abstract with a complete article. Full-text databases can be extremely convenient — you can read and print out articles directly from the computer, without the extra step of tracking down the periodical in question. However, don't limit yourself to full-text databases, which may not contain graphics and images that appeared in the print version of the periodical — and which may not include the sources that would benefit your research most. Take advantage of databases that offer abstracts, which give you an overview of the article's contents that can help you decide whether you need to spend time finding and reading the full text.

GENERAL AND SPECIALIZED INDEXES

General indexes of periodicals list articles from general-interest magazines (such as *Time*), newspapers, and perhaps some scholarly

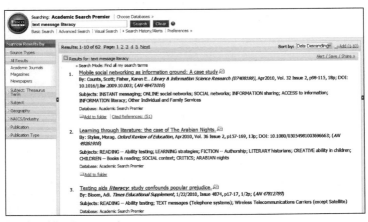

Results of database search

journals. General indexes are useful for finding current sources on a topic, but you may need to look further for in-depth articles. Online access to general indexes is usually available through your library. Ask a reference librarian for details.

Access: The Supplementary Index to Periodicals. 1979–; monthly. Indexes magazines not covered by the *Readers' Guide to Periodical Literature* (see following), such as regional and particular-interest magazines (the environment, women's issues).

Alternative Press Index. 1970–; monthly. Indexes alternative and radical publications.

InfoTrac College Edition. Updated daily. Covers over six thousand academic and general-interest publications, incorporating the *Magazine Index* and including the *New York Times, Time, Newsweek,* and the *Wall Street Journal.* Some entries include a summary or even the entire article. See infotrac.thomsonlearning.com.

LexisNexis Academic. 1974–. LexisNexis contains legal, legislative, and regulatory information. LexisNexis contains full texts and abstracts of newspapers, magazines, wire services, newsletters, company and industry analyst reports, and broadcast transcripts.

NewsBank. 1970–; updated monthly. Includes articles from more than two thousand newspapers.

New York Times Index. 1851–; bimonthly with annual cumulations. Lists by subject every article that has appeared in the *New York Times.* For most articles of any length, short summaries are given as well.

Nineteenth Century Readers' Guide to Periodical Literature. 1890–1899. (See also *Readers' Guide,* following.)

Periodical Abstracts PlusText. 1986–. Contains abstracts of articles in over one thousand periodicals and journals in science, social science, humanities, and business.

Poole's Index to Periodical Literature. 1802–1907. Indexes nineteenth-century British and American periodicals.

ProQuest Historical Newspapers. Ongoing project. Offers full-text digitized articles with images from thirty-six sources dating back to the 1700s.

Readers' Guide to Periodical Literature. 1900–; semimonthly with quarterly and annual cumulations. Indexes articles from nearly four hundred

magazines. Particularly helpful for social trends, popular scientific questions, and contemporary political issues. Entries are arranged by author and subject with cross-references to related topics.

Times Index (London). 1913–; bimonthly. Lists articles and summaries of stories published in the London *Times*.

Specialized indexes, which tend to include mainly scholarly periodicals, may focus on one discipline (as the education index ERIC does) or on a group of related disciplines (as Social Sciences Abstracts does). For more information on specialized indexes and abstracts in particular fields, see Chapters 5–8. Ask a reference librarian for help choosing an appropriate index for your topic and purpose.

LOCATING INDEXED PERIODICAL ARTICLES

To locate an indexed article that seems promising for your research project, you can check the library catalog to see whether the periodical is available electronically and, if so, whether your library

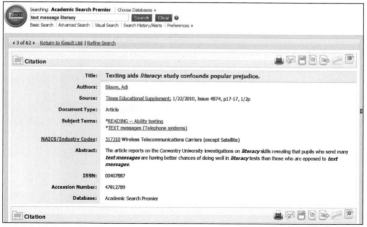

Article page with abstract

has access to it. Using the library computer network for access can help you avoid paying to view the text of an article that is available online only for subscribers or for a fee.

If the periodical is not available electronically (some scholarly journals, for example, are not), the library catalog also will tell you whether a print version is available in your library's periodicals room. This room probably has recent issues of hundreds or even thousands of newspapers, magazines, and scholarly journals, and it may also contain bound volumes of past issues and microfilm copies of older newspapers. If you're searching for an old issue, ask a librarian if you can find that issue in the library stacks or offsite.

Bibliographies

Look at any bibliographies (lists of sources) in books or articles you are using for your research; they can lead you to other valuable resources. In addition, check with a reference librarian to find out whether your library has more extensive bibliographies devoted to the area of your research.

Other Library Resources

In addition to books and periodicals, libraries give you access to many other useful materials that might be appropriate for your research.

- *Special collections and archives.* Your library may house archives (collections of valuable papers) and other special materials that are often available to student researchers. Ask a special collections librarian whether the archives contain possible sources on your topic.

- *Audio, video, multimedia, and art collections.* Many libraries have areas devoted to media and art where they collect films, videos, paintings, and sound recordings. Some libraries also let students check out laptops and other equipment for classroom presentations.

- *Government documents.* Many libraries have collections of historical documents produced by local or state government offices. Check with a librarian if government publications would be useful sources

for your topic. You can also look at the online version of the U.S. Government Printing Office, known as GPO Access (www.gpoaccess .gov), for electronic versions of government publications from the past decade or so.

• *Interlibrary loans.* To borrow books, videos, or audio materials from another library, use an interlibrary loan. You can also request copies of journal articles from other libraries. Some loans — especially of books — can take time, so plan ahead.

Internet Research

The Internet is many college students' favorite way of accessing information, and it's true that much information — including authoritative sources identical to those your library provides — can be found online, sometimes for free. However, information in library databases comes from identifiable and professionally edited sources; because no one is responsible for regulating information on the Web, you need to take special care to find out which information online is reliable and which is not. (See Chapter 3 for more on evaluating sources.)

Internet Searches

Most search tools allow keyword searches as well as subject directory searches. With a search engine, you simply type in keywords and get results; some metasearch tools use several search engines at once and compile their findings. In a subject directory, on the other hand, you start with general categories and then click on increasingly narrow subcategories. At any point, you can switch to a keyword search to look for specific terms and topics.

If you decide to use a keyword search in an Internet search engine, you will need to choose keywords carefully in order to get a reasonable number of hits. For example, if you're searching for information on legal issues regarding the Internet and enter *Internet* and *law* as keywords in a Google search, you will get over six hundred million possible sources — a number too huge to be helpful for a researcher. To be useful, then, the keywords you choose — names, titles, authors,

concepts — need to lead you to more specific sources. A Google search for *"text message language"* in quotation marks yields a more manageable hundred thousand results. Look for a search engine's search tips or advanced search options for help with refining and limiting a keyword search.

Although Yahoo! and Google are probably the most popular online search engines, the following list covers a broad range of search tools and their unique features.

AltaVista
www.altavista.com
> Lets you search the entire Web using either a single keyword or multiple keywords.

Ask
www.ask.com
> Ranks results based on the number of same-subject pages that refer to it, not just general popularity.

Google search yielding too many results

Excite
www.excite.com
> Allows keyword and subject directory searches.

Google
www.google.com
> A popular search tool and a favorite among students; offers keyword and subject directory searches.

HotBot
www.hotbot.com
> Allows you to search one of several search engines and to narrow a search by specific dates, media, and other criteria. Offers keyword and subject directory searches.

Ixquick
www.ixquick.com
> A speedy metasearch tool that searches fourteen other engines or directories simultaneously using keywords.

Lycos
www.lycos.com
> Lets you search a huge catalog of Web sites as well as multimedia documents. Offers keyword and subject directory searches.

WebCrawler
www.webcrawler.com
> Searches several engines (including some that return sponsored listings) and subject directories.

Yahoo!
www.yahoo.com
> Allows you either to search directories of sites related to particular subjects (such as entertainment or education) or to enter keywords that Yahoo! gives to a search engine, which sends back the results.

Zworks
www.zworks.com
> Calls itself "the metasearch loved by parents and webmasters alike" because it can be filtered. Ranks results for relevancy.

Bookmarking Tools

Today's powerful bookmarking tools can help you browse, sort, and track resources online. Social bookmarking sites, such as Delicious

and Digg, allow users to tag information and share it with others. Once you register on a social bookmarking site, you can tag an online resource with any words you choose. Users' tags are visible to all other users. If you find a helpful site, you can check to see how others have tagged it and quickly browse similar tags to find related information. You can sort and group information according to your tags. Fellow users whose tagged sites you like and trust can become part of your network so that you can follow their sites of interest.

Web browsers can also help you bookmark and return to online resources that you have found. However, unlike the bookmarking tools in a Web browser, which are tied to one machine, social bookmarking tools are available from any computer with an Internet connection.

Authoritative Sources Online

You can find many sources online that are authoritative and reliable. For example, the Internet enables you to enter virtual libraries that allow access to some collections in libraries other than your own. Online collections housed in government sites can also be reliable and useful sources.

Bureau of Labor Statistics
www.bls.gov
> Provides information by region and allows keyword searches.

The Library of Congress
www.loc.gov
> Offers a vast array of information on government legislation and copyright and intellectual property; a library catalog; and collections such as American Memory, which contains more than nine million digital items from over a hundred historical collections. Allows searches by title, author/creator, subject, and keyword.

National Institutes of Health
www.nih.gov
> Provides data on health and medical issues; allows keyword searches.

Statistical Abstract of the United States
www.census.gov/compendia/statab
> Provides information on social and economic trends; allows searches by keyword or place.

U.S. Census Bureau
www.census.gov
> Provides population and other demographic data; allows searches
> by keyword, place, and region.

For current national news, consult online versions of reputable
newspapers such as the *New York Times,* the *Washington Post,* the *Los
Angeles Times,* or the *Chicago Tribune* or electronic sites for news services such as CNN and C-SPAN. You can also use a search tool like
Yahoo!, which has a "News and Media" category you can click on
from the main page.

Some scholarly journals (such as those from Berkeley Electronic
Press) and general-interest magazines (including Slate and Salon)
are published only on the Web, and many other publications, like
Newsweek, the *New Yorker,* and the *New Republic,* make at least some of
their contents available online for free.

Internet Resources

The following general Web sites provide access to a wide range of
information and more specialized sites.

American Library Association: Links to Library Web Resources
www.ala.org/library/weblinks.html
> Supplies links to notable library-related organizations and resources.

Infomine: Scholarly Internet Resource Collections
infomine.ucr.edu
> Supplies indexed and annotated links to more than ninety-five
> hundred databases and other resources of academic interest,
> grouped in interdisciplinary categories; also includes resources on
> using the Internet, maps, and teaching materials.

ipl2
www.ipl.org
> Selects worthwhile sources and organizes information by subject
> categories; a highly recommended site with many references,
> exhibits, and useful resources. Includes general reference informa-
> tion, topics of popular interest (as varied as automobiles, food,

government, health, music, and recreation), and subjects ranging from the arts to world cultures.

RefDesk
www.refdesk.com
> Supplies access to reference materials, a variety of news organizations, and sites related to topics of current interest.

The Webliography: Internet Subject Guides
www.lib.lsu.edu/weblio.html
> Provides extensive annotated guides and access to academic and government resources in the humanities, sciences, and social sciences.

The WWW Virtual Library
vlib.org
> Provides links to information on a wide variety of topics.

3

Evaluating Sources and Taking Notes

Keeping a Working Bibliography

A working bibliography is a list of sources that you may ultimately use for your project. As you find and begin to evaluate research sources — articles, books, Web sites, and so on — you should record source information for every source you think you might use. (Relevant information includes everything you need to find the source again and cite it correctly; the information you will need varies based on the type of source, whether you found it in a library or not, and whether you consulted it in print or online.) The emphasis here is on *working* because the list will probably include materials that end up not being useful. For this reason, you don't absolutely need to put all entries into the documentation style you will use (see Chapters 5–8). If you do follow the required documentation style, however, that part of your work will be done when you prepare the final draft.

The following chart will help you keep track of the sorts of information you should try to find:

Type of Source	Information to Collect (if applicable)
Print book	Library call number, author(s) or editor(s), title and subtitle, place of publication, publisher, year of publication, any other information (translator, edition, volume)
Part of a book	Call number, author(s) of part, title of part, author(s) or editor(s) of book, title of book, place of publication, publisher, year of publication, inclusive page numbers for part
Print periodical article	Call number of periodical, author(s) of article, title of article, name of periodical, volume number, issue number, date of issue, inclusive page numbers for article
Electronic source	Author(s), title of document, title of site, editor(s) of site, sponsor of site, publication information for print version of source, name of database or online service, date of electronic publication or last update, date you accessed the source, URL

For other kinds of sources (films, recordings, visuals), you should also list the information required by the documentation style you are using (see Chapters 5–8) and note where you found the information.

Evaluating Usefulness and Credibility

Since you want the information and ideas you glean from sources to be reliable and persuasive, you must evaluate each potential source carefully. The following guidelines can help you assess the usefulness and credibility of sources you are considering:

- *Your purpose.* What will this source add to your research project? Does it help you support a major point, demonstrate that you have thoroughly researched your topic, or help establish your own credibility through its authority?

- *Relevance.* How closely related is the source to the narrowed topic you are pursuing? You may need to read beyond the title and opening paragraph to check for relevance.

- *Level of specialization and audience.* General sources can be helpful as you begin your research, but you may then need the authority or

currency of more specialized sources. On the other hand, extremely specialized works may be very hard to understand. Who was the source originally written for — the general public? experts in the field? advocates or opponents? How does this fit with your concept of your own audience?

- *Credentials of the publisher or sponsor.* What can you learn about the publisher or sponsor of the source you are using? For example, is it a major newspaper known for integrity in reporting, or is it a tabloid? Is it a popular source, whether in print or electronic, or is it sponsored by a professional organization or academic institution? If you're evaluating a book, is the publisher one you recognize or can find described on its own Web site? If you are evaluating a Web site, is the site's sponsor a commercial (.com), educational (.edu), governmental (.gov), military (.mil), network (.net), or nonprofit (.org) entity? No hard and fast rules exist for deciding what kind of source to use. But knowing the sponsor's or publisher's credentials can help you determine whether a source is appropriate for your research project.

- *Credentials of the author.* As you do your research, note names that come up from one source to another, since these references may indicate that the author is influential in the field. An author's credentials may also be presented in the article, book, or Web site, or you can search the Internet for information about the author. In U.S. academic writing, experts and those with significant experience in a field have more authority on the subject than others.

- *Date of publication.* Recent sources are often more useful than older ones, particularly in the sciences or other fields that change rapidly. However, in some fields — such as the humanities — the most authoritative works may be older ones. The publication dates of Internet sites can often be difficult to pin down. And even for sites that include dates of posting, remember that the material posted may have been composed sometime earlier. Sites that list recent updates may be more reliable.

- *Accuracy of the source.* How accurate and complete is the information in the source? How thorough is the bibliography or list of works cited that accompanies the source? Can you find other sources that corroborate what your source is saying?

- *Stance of the source.* Identify the source's point of view or rhetorical stance, and scrutinize it carefully. Does the source present facts, or does it interpret or evaluate them? If it presents facts, what is included and what is omitted, and why? If it interprets or evaluates information that is not disputed, the source's stance may be obvious, but at other times, you will need to think carefully about the source's goals. What does the author or sponsoring group want? to convince you of an idea? sell you something? call you to action in some way?

- *Cross-references to the source.* Is the source cited in other works? If you see your source cited by others, notice how they cite it and what they say about it to find additional clues to its credibility.

For more on evaluating Web sources and periodical articles, see the source maps on pp. 34–37.

Reading and Interpreting Sources

For those sources that you want to analyze more closely, reading with a critical eye can make your research process more efficient. Use the tips on pp. 38–41 to guide your critical reading.

YOUR RESEARCH QUESTION

As you read, keep your research question in mind, and ask yourself the following questions:

- How does this material address your research question and support your hypothesis?
- What quotations from this source might help support your thesis?
- Does the source include counterarguments to your hypothesis that you will need to answer? If so, what answers can you provide?

THE AUTHOR'S STANCE AND TONE

Even a seemingly factual report, such as an encyclopedia article, is filled with judgments, often unstated. Read with an eye for the

SOURCE MAP: Evaluating Web sources

Is the sponsor credible?

(1)   Who is the **sponsor or publisher** of the source? See what information you can get from the URL. The domain names for government sites may end in *.gov* or *.mil* and for educational sites in *.edu*. The ending *.org* may—but does not always—indicate a nonprofit organization. If you see a tilde (~) or percent sign (%) followed by a name, or if you see a word such as *users* or *members*, the page's creator may be an individual, not an institution. In addition, check the header and footer, where the sponsor may be identified. The page shown here, from the domain **niemanwatchdog.org**, is from a site sponsored by the nonprofit Nieman Foundation for Journalism at Harvard University.

(2)   Look for an *About* **page** or a link to a home page for background information on the sponsor. Is a mission statement included? What are the sponsoring organization's purpose and point of view? Does the mission statement seem balanced? What is the purpose of the site (to inform, to persuade, to advocate for a cause, to advertise, or something else)? Does the information on the site come directly from the sponsor, or is the material reprinted from another source? If it is reprinted, check the original.

Is the author credible?

(3)   What are the **author's credentials**? Look for information accompanying the material on the page. You can also run a search on the author to find out more. Does the author seem qualified to write about this topic?

Is the information credible and current?

(4)   When was the information **posted or last updated**? Is it recent enough to be useful?

(5)   Does the page document sources with **footnotes or links**? If so, do the sources seem credible and current? Does the author include any additional resources for further information? Look for ways to corroborate the information the author provides.

④ **Posted or Last Updated**

② *About* Page

① **Sponsor or Publisher**

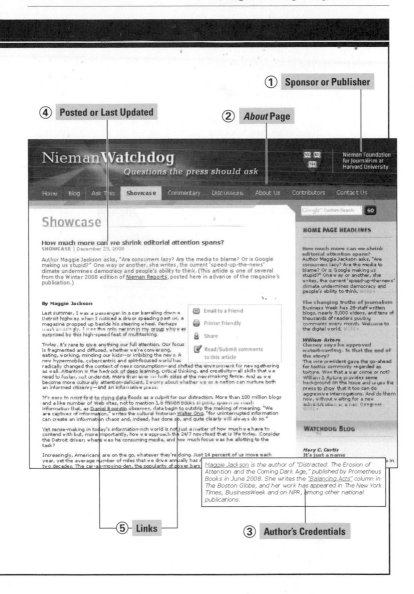

Nieman**Watchdog**
Questions the press should ask

Nieman Foundation
for Journalism at
Harvard University

Home   Blog   Ask This   **Showcase**   Commentary   Discussions   About Us   Contributors   Contact Us

Showcase

Google™ Custom Search   GO

How much more can we shrink editorial attention spans?
SHOWCASE | December 23, 2008

Author Maggie Jackson asks, "Are consumers lazy? Are the media to blame? Or is Google making us stupid?" One way or another, she writes, the current 'speed-up-the-news' climate undermines democracy and people's ability to think. (This article is one of several from the Winter 2008 edition of *Nieman Reports*, posted here in advance of the magazine's publication.)

By Maggie Jackson

Last summer, I was a passenger in a car barreling down a Detroit highway when I noticed a driver speeding past us, a magazine propped up beside his steering wheel. Perhaps not amazingly, I was the only person in my group who was surprised by this high-speed feat of multitasking.

Today, it's rare to give anything our full attention. Our focus is fragmented and diffused, whether we're conversing, eating, working, minding our kids—or imbibing the news. A new hypermobile, cybercentric and split-focused world has radically changed the context of news consumption—and shifted the environment for newsgathering as well. Attention is the bedrock of deep learning, critical thinking, and creativity—all skills that we need to foster, not undercut, more than ever on both sides of the newsmaking fence. And as we become more culturally attention-deficient, I worry about whether we as a nation can nurture both an informed citizenry—and an informative press.

✉ Email to a Friend
🖨 Printer Friendly
📎 Share
📝 Read/Submit comments to this article

It's easy to point first to rising data floods as a culprit for our distraction. More than 100 million blogs and a like number of Web sites, not to mention 1.8 million books in print, span so much information that, as Daniel Boorstin observes, data begin to outstrip the making of meaning. "We are captives of information," writes the cultural historian Walter Ong, "for uninterrupted information can create an information chaos and, indeed, has done so, and quite clearly will always do so."

Yet sense-making in today's information-rich world is not just a matter of how much we have to contend with but, more importantly, how we approach the 24/7 newsfeed that is life today. Consider the Detroit driver; where was he consuming media, and how much focus was he allotting to the task?

Increasingly, Americans are on the go, whatever they're doing. Just 14 percent of us move each year, yet the average number of miles that we drive annually has risen ... in two decades. The car-as-moving-den, the popularity of power bars ...

HOME PAGE HEADLINES

How much more can we shrink editorial attention spans?
Author Maggie Jackson asks, "Are consumers lazy? Are the media to blame? Or is Google making us stupid?" One way or another, she writes, the current 'speed-up-the-news' climate undermines democracy and people's ability to think. MORE ›

The changing truths of journalism
Business Week has 28-staff written blogs, nearly 5,000 videos, and tens of thousands of readers posting comments every month. Welcome to the digital world. MORE ›

William Astore
Cheney says he approved waterboarding. Is that the end of the story?
The vice president gave the go-ahead for tactics commonly regarded as torture. Was that a war crime or not? William J. Astore provides some background on the issue and urges the press to show that it too can do aggressive interrogations. And do them now, without waiting for a new administration or a new Congress. MORE ›

WATCHDOG BLOG

Mary C. Curtis
It's just a name

Maggie Jackson *is the author of "Distracted: The Erosion of Attention and the Coming Dark Age," published by Prometheus Books in June 2008. She writes the "Balancing Acts" column in The Boston Globe, and her work has appeared in The New York Times, BusinessWeek and on NPR, among other national publications.*

⑤ **Links**

③ **Author's Credentials**

SOURCE MAP: Evaluating articles

Determine the relevance of the source.

① Look for an **abstract**, which provides a summary of the entire article. Is this source directly related to your research? Does it provide useful information and insights? Will your readers consider it persuasive support for your thesis?

Determine the credibility of the publication.

② Consider the publication's **title**. Words in the title such as *Journal, Review*, and *Quarterly* may indicate that the periodical is a scholarly source. Most research projects rely on authorities in a particular field, whose work usually appears in scholarly journals. For more on distinguishing between scholarly and popular sources, see Differentiating Kinds of Sources on p. 6.

③ Try to determine the **publisher or sponsor**. This journal is published by Johns Hopkins University Press. Academic presses such as this one generally review articles carefully before publishing them and bear the authority of their academic sponsors.

Determine the credibility of the author.

④ Evaluate the **author's credentials**. In this case, they are given in a note, which indicates that the author is a college professor and has written at least two books on related topics.

Determine the currency of the article.

⑤ Look at the **publication date**, and think about whether your topic and your credibility depend on your use of very current sources.

Determine the accuracy of the article.

⑥ Look at the **sources cited** by the author of the article. Here, they are documented in footnotes. Ask yourself whether the works the author has cited seem credible and current. Are any of these works cited in other articles you've considered?

In addition, consider the following questions:

- What is the article's stance or point of view? What are the author's goals? What does the author want you to know or believe?

- How does this source fit in with your other sources? Does any of the information it provides contradict or challenge other sources?

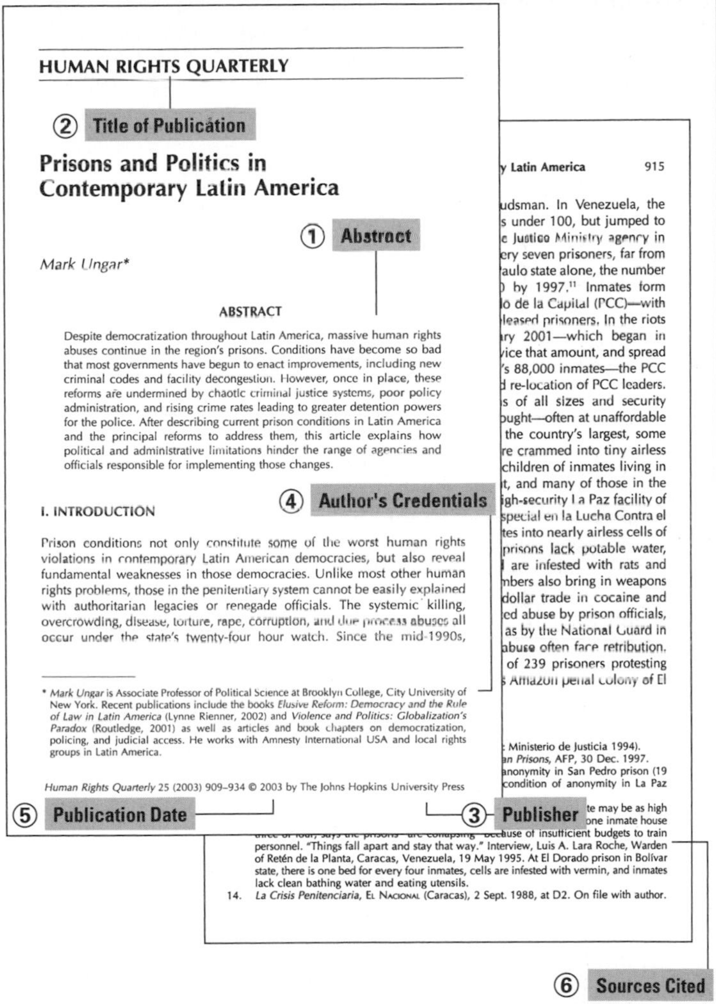

HUMAN RIGHTS QUARTERLY

(2) **Title of Publication**

Prisons and Politics in Contemporary Latin America

(1) **Abstract**

Mark Ungar*

ABSTRACT

Despite democratization throughout Latin America, massive human rights abuses continue in the region's prisons. Conditions have become so bad that most governments have begun to enact improvements, including new criminal codes and facility decongestion. However, once in place, these reforms are undermined by chaotic criminal justice systems, poor policy administration, and rising crime rates leading to greater detention powers for the police. After describing current prison conditions in Latin America and the principal reforms to address them, this article explains how political and administrative limitations hinder the range of agencies and officials responsible for implementing those changes.

I. INTRODUCTION

(4) **Author's Credentials**

Prison conditions not only constitute some of the worst human rights violations in contemporary Latin American democracies, but also reveal fundamental weaknesses in those democracies. Unlike most other human rights problems, those in the penitentiary system cannot be easily explained with authoritarian legacies or renegade officials. The systemic killing, overcrowding, disease, torture, rape, corruption, and due process abuses all occur under the state's twenty-four hour watch. Since the mid-1990s,

* *Mark Ungar* is Associate Professor of Political Science at Brooklyn College, City University of New York. Recent publications include the books *Elusive Reform: Democracy and the Rule of Law in Latin America* (Lynne Rienner, 2002) and *Violence and Politics: Globalization's Paradox* (Routledge, 2001) as well as articles and book chapters on democratization, policing, and judicial access. He works with Amnesty International USA and local rights groups in Latin America.

Human Rights Quarterly 25 (2003) 909–934 © 2003 by The Johns Hopkins University Press

(5) **Publication Date**

Right column (page 915)

...udsman. In Venezuela, the ...s under 100, but jumped to ...e Justice Ministry agency in ...ery seven prisoners, far from ...aulo state alone, the number ... by 1997.[11] Inmates form ...o de la Capital (PCC)—with ...leased prisoners. In the riots ...ry 2001—which began in ...vice that amount, and spread ...'s 88,000 inmates—the PCC ...d re-location of PCC leaders. ...s of all sizes and security ...ught—often at unaffordable ... the country's largest, some ...re crammed into tiny airless ...children of inmates living in ...t, and many of those in the ...gh-security La Paz facility of ...special en la Lucha Contra el ...tes into nearly airless cells of ...prisons lack potable water, ... are infested with rats and ...mbers also bring in weapons ...dollar trade in cocaine and ...ed abuse by prison officials, ...as by the National Guard in ...abuse often face retribution. ... of 239 prisoners protesting ...s Amazon penal colony of El

...: Ministerio de Justicia 1994). ...n Prisons, AFP, 30 Dec. 1997. ...anonymity in San Pedro prison (19 ...condition of anonymity in La Paz

(3) **Publisher** ...te may be as high
...one inmate house

...ince or four, says the prisons are collapsing—because of insufficient budgets to train personnel. "Things fall apart and stay that way." Interview, Luis A. Lara Roche, Warden of Retén de la Planta, Caracas, Venezuela, 19 May 1995. At El Dorado prison in Bolívar state, there is one bed for every four inmates, cells are infested with vermin, and inmates lack clean bathing water and eating utensils.

14. *La Crisis Penitenciaria*, EL NACIONAL (Caracas), 2 Sept. 1988, at D2. On file with author.

(6) **Sources Cited**

GUIDELINES FOR EXAMINING POTENTIAL SOURCES

Looking quickly at the various parts of a source can provide useful information and help you decide whether to explore that particular source more thoroughly. You are already familiar with some of these basic elements: title and subtitle, title page and copyright page, home page, table of contents, index, footnotes, and bibliography. Be sure to check other items as well.

- *Abstracts* — concise summaries of articles and books — routinely precede journal articles and are often included in indexes and databases.

- A *preface* or *foreword* generally discusses the writer's purpose and thesis.

- *Subheadings* within the text can alert you to how much detail is given on a topic.

- A *conclusion* or *afterword* may summarize or draw the strands of an argument together.

- For an electronic source, click on some of the *links* to see if they're useful, and see if the overall *design* of the site is easy to navigate.

author's overall rhetorical stance, or perspective, as well as for facts or explicit opinions. Also pay attention to the author's tone, the way his or her attitude toward the topic and audience is conveyed. The following questions can help:

- Is the author a strong advocate or opponent of something? a skeptical critic? a specialist in the field?

- Are there any clues to why the author takes this stance? Is professional affiliation a factor?

- How does this stance affect the author's presentation and your reaction to it?

- What facts does the author include? Can you think of any important fact that is omitted?

- What is the author's tone? Is it cautious, angry, flippant, serious, impassioned? What words indicate this tone?

THE AUTHOR'S ARGUMENT AND EVIDENCE

Every piece of writing takes a position. Even a scientific report implicitly "argues" that we should accept it and its data as reliable. As you read, look for the main point or the main argument the author is making. Try to identify the reasons the author gives to support his or her position. Then try to determine *why* the author takes this position. Consider these questions:

- What is the author's main point, and what evidence supports it?
- How persuasive is the evidence? Can you think of a way to refute it?
- Can you detect any questionable logic or fallacious thinking?
- Does this author disagree with arguments you have read elsewhere? If so, what causes the disagreements—differences about facts or about how to interpret facts?

Synthesizing Sources

When you read and interpret a source—for example, when you consider its purpose and relevance, its author's credentials, its accuracy, and the kind of argument it is making—you are analyzing the source. Analysis requires you to take apart something complex (such as an article in a scholarly journal) and look closely at the parts to understand the whole better. For academic writing you also need to *synthesize*—group similar pieces of information together and look for patterns—so you can put your sources (and your own knowledge and experience) together in an original argument. Synthesis is the flip side of analysis: you already understand the parts, so your job is to assemble them into a new whole.

To synthesize sources for a research project, try the following tips.

- *Read the material carefully.*

- *Determine the important ideas in each source.* Take notes on each source. Identify and summarize the key ideas of each piece.

- *Formulate a position.* Review the key ideas of each source and figure out how they fit together. Look for patterns: discussions of causes and effects, specific parts of a larger issue, background information, and so on. Be sure to consider the complexity of the issue, and demonstrate that you have considered more than one perspective.

- *Summon evidence to support your position.* You might use paraphrases, summaries, or direct quotations from your sources as evidence or you might draw on your personal experience or prior knowledge. Integrate quotations properly and keep your ideas central to the piece of writing.

- *Deal with counterarguments.* You don't have to use every idea or every source available—some will be more useful than others. However, ignoring evidence that opposes your position makes your argument weaker. You should acknowledge the existence of valid opinions that differ from yours and try to explain why they are incorrect or incomplete.

- *Combine your source materials effectively.* Be careful to avoid simply summarizing or listing your research. Think carefully about how the ideas in your reading support your argument. Try to weave the various sources together rather than discussing your sources one by one.

For more information on synthesis, see the chart on p. 41.

Taking Notes and Annotating Sources

Note-taking methods vary greatly from one researcher to another, so you may decide to use a computer file, a notebook, or index cards. Regardless of the method, however, you should (1) record enough information to help you recall the major points of the source; (2) put the information in the form in which you are most likely to incorporate it into your research essay, whether a summary, a paraphrase, or a quotation; and (3) note all the information you will need to cite the source accurately. The following example shows the major items a note should include (numbered explanations are on p. 42):

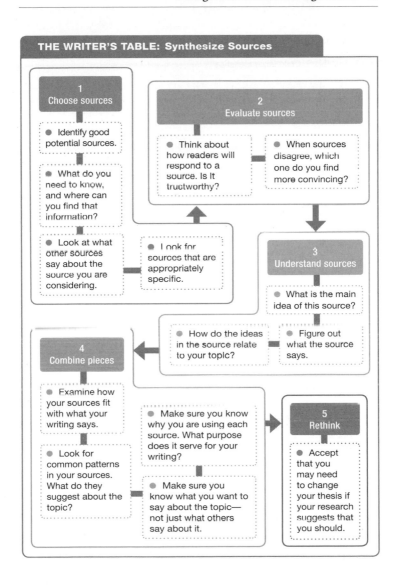

THE WRITER'S TABLE: Synthesize Sources

1 Choose sources

- Identify good potential sources.

- What do you need to know, and where can you find that information?

- Look at what other sources say about the source you are considering.

- Look for sources that are appropriately specific.

2 Evaluate sources

- Think about how readers will respond to a source. Is it trustworthy?

- When sources disagree, which one do you find more convincing?

3 Understand sources

- What is the main idea of this source?

- How do the ideas in the source relate to your topic?

- Figure out what the source says.

4 Combine pieces

- Examine how your sources fit with what your writing says.

- Look for common patterns in your sources. What do they suggest about the topic?

- Make sure you know why you are using each source. What purpose does it serve for your writing?

- Make sure you know what you want to say about the topic—not just what others say about it.

5 Rethink

- Accept that you may need to change your thesis if your research suggests that you should.

ELEMENTS OF AN ACCURATE NOTE

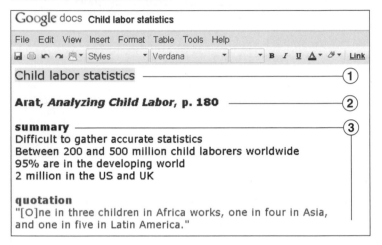

① *Use a subject heading.* Label each note with a brief but descriptive subject heading so that you can group similar subtopics together.

② *Identify the source.* List the author's name and a shortened title of the source, and a page number, if available. Your working-bibliography entry for the source will contain the full bibliographic information, so you don't need to repeat it in each note.

③ *Indicate whether the note is a direct quotation, paraphrase, or summary* (see p. 43). Make sure quotations are copied accurately. Put square brackets around any change you make, and use ellipses if you omit material.

Taking complete notes will help you digest the source information as you read and incorporate the material into your text without inadvertently plagiarizing the source (see Chapter 4). Be sure to reread each note carefully, and recheck it against the source to make sure quotations, statistics, and specific facts are accurate.

The box on p. 43 will help you determine whether to quote, paraphrase, or summarize various types of information. The guidelines that follow it offer note-taking strategies for all three types of notes.

DECIDING TO QUOTE, PARAPHRASE, OR SUMMARIZE

QUOTE

- wording that is so memorable or powerful or expresses a point so perfectly that you cannot change it without weakening the meaning you need

- authors' opinions you wish to emphasize

- authors' words that show you are considering varying perspectives

- respected authorities whose opinions support your ideas

- authors whose opinions challenge or vary greatly from those of others in the field

PARAPHRASE

- passages you do not wish to quote but whose details are important to your point

SUMMARIZE

- long passages whose main point is important to your point but whose details are not

Quotations

Some of the notes you take will contain quotations, which give the *exact words* of a source.

GUIDELINES FOR QUOTATIONS

- Copy quotations carefully, with punctuation, capitalization, and spelling *exactly* as in the original.

- Enclose the quotation in quotation marks; don't rely on your memory to distinguish your own words from those of the source.

(Continued)

- Use square brackets if you introduce words of your own into a quotation or make changes in it, and use ellipses if you omit material. If you later incorporate the quotation into your essay, copy it faithfully — brackets, ellipses, and all.

- Record the author's name, the shortened title, and the page number(s) on which the quotation appears. If the note refers to more than one page, use a slash (/) within the quotation to indicate where one page ends and another begins. For sources without page numbers, record the paragraph or other section number(s), if any.

- Make sure you have a corresponding working-bibliography entry with complete source information.

- Label the note with a subject heading, and identify it as a quotation.

Paraphrases

A paraphrase accurately states all the relevant information from a passage *in your own words and sentence structures,* without any additional comments or elaborations. A paraphrase is useful when the main points of a passage, their order, and at least some details are important but — unlike passages worth quoting — the particular wording is not. Unlike a summary, a paraphrase always restates *all* the main points of a passage in the same order and often in about the same number of words.

GUIDELINES FOR PARAPHRASES

- Include all main points and any important details from the original source, in the same order in which the author presents them.

(Continued)

- State the meaning in your own words and sentence structures. If you want to include especially memorable language from the original, enclose it in quotation marks.

- Save your comments, elaborations, or reactions on another note.

- Record the author's name, the shortened title, and the page number(s) on which the original material appears. For sources without page numbers, record the paragraph or other section number(s), if any.

- Make sure you have a corresponding working-bibliography entry with complete source information.

- Label the note with a subject heading, and identify it as a paraphrase.

Summaries

A summary is a significantly shortened version of a passage or even of a whole chapter or work that captures main ideas *in your own words*. Unlike a paraphrase, a summary uses just enough information to record the main points you wish to emphasize. Your goal is to keep the summary as brief as possible, capturing only the main idea of the original and not distorting the author's meaning.

GUIDELINES FOR SUMMARIES

- Include just enough information to recount the main points you wish to cite. A summary is usually far shorter than the original.

- Use your own words. If you include any language from the original, enclose it in quotation marks.

(Continued)

- Record the author's name, the shortened title, and the page number(s) on which the original material appears. For sources without page numbers, record the paragraph, screen, or other section number(s), if any.

- Make sure you have a corresponding working-bibliography entry with complete source information.

- Label the note with a subject heading, and identify it as a summary.

Annotations

Sometimes you may photocopy or print out a source you intend to use. In such cases, you can annotate the photocopies or printouts with your thoughts and questions and highlight interesting quotations and key terms.

If you take notes in a computer file, you may be able to copy online sources electronically, paste them into the file, and annotate them there. Try not to rely too heavily on copying or printing out whole pieces, however; you still need to read the material very carefully. Also resist the temptation to treat copied material as notes, an action that could lead to inadvertent plagiarizing. (In a computer file, using a different color for text pasted from a source will help prevent this problem.)

4

Acknowledging Sources and Avoiding Plagiarism

Knowing Which Sources to Acknowledge

As you carry out research, you should understand the distinction between materials that require acknowledgment and those that do not.

Materials That Do Not Require Acknowledgment

Information does not need to be credited to a source if it is well known or if you gathered the data yourself.

- *Common knowledge.* If most readers know a fact, you probably do not need to cite a source for it. You do not need to credit a source to say that Barack Obama was elected in 2008, for example.

- *Facts available in a wide variety of sources.* If a number of encyclopedias, almanacs, reputable Web sites, or textbooks include a certain piece of information, you usually need not cite a specific source for it. For instance, you would not need to cite a source if you write that the Japanese bombed Pearl Harbor on December 7, 1941.

- *Findings from field research.* If you conduct observations or surveys, announce your findings as your own. Acknowledge people you interview as individuals rather than as part of a survey.

If you are not sure whether a fact, an observation, or a piece of information requires acknowledgment, err on the side of safety and cite the source.

AVOIDING PLAGIARISM

- Maintain an accurate and thorough working bibliography.
- Establish a consistent note-taking system, listing sources and page numbers and clearly identifying all quotations, paraphrases, summaries, statistics, and visuals.
- Identify all quotations with quotation marks — both in your notes and in your essay.
- Be sure your summaries and paraphrases use your own words and sentence structures.
- Give a citation or note for each quotation, paraphrase, summary, arguable assertion or opinion, statistic, and visual from a source, including an online source.
- Prepare an accurate and complete list of sources cited according to the required documentation style. (See Chapters 5 through 8.)
- Plan ahead on writing assignments so that you can avoid the temptation to take shortcuts.

Materials That Require Acknowledgment

For material that does not fall under the preceding categories, credit sources as fully as possible. Follow the conventions of the citation style you are using (see Chapters 5–8), and include each source in a bibliography or list of works cited.

- *Quotations, paraphrases, and summaries.* Whenever you use another person's words, ideas, or opinions, credit the source. Even though the

wording of a paraphrase or summary is your own, you should still
acknowledge the source.

- *Facts that aren't widely known or claims that are arguable.* If your readers
would be unlikely to know a fact, or if an author presents as fact a
claim that may or may not be true, cite the source. To claim, for
instance, that Switzerland is amassing an offensive nuclear arsenal
would demand the citation of a source because Switzerland has long
been an officially neutral state. If you are not sure whether a fact will
be familiar to your readers or whether a statement is arguable, go
ahead and cite the source.

- *Images, statistics, charts, tables, graphs, and other visuals from any source.*
Credit all visual and statistical material not derived from your own
field research, even if you create your own graph or table from the
data provided in a source.

- *Help provided by others.* If an instructor gave you a good idea or if
friends responded to your draft or helped you conduct surveys, give
credit — usually in a footnote that says something like "Thanks to
Kiah Williams, who first suggested this connection."

Here is a quick-reference chart to guide you in deciding whether
or not you need to acknowledge a source:

NEED TO ACKNOWLEDGE	DON'T NEED TO ACKNOWLEDGE
quotations	your own words, observations, surveys, and so on
paraphrases or summaries of a source	
ideas you glean from a source	common knowledge
facts that aren't widely known	facts available in many sources
graphs, tables, and other statistical information from a source	drawings or other visuals you create on your own
photographs, visuals, video, or sound taken from sources	
experiments conducted by others	
interviews that are not part of a survey	
organization or structure taken from a source	
help or advice from an instructor or another student	

Maintaining Academic Integrity and Avoiding Plagiarism

The principle of academic integrity in intellectual work allows you to trust the sources you use and to demonstrate that your own work is equally trustworthy. While there are many ways to damage your ethos and academic integrity, two that are especially important are inaccurate or incomplete citation of sources — also called unintentional plagiarism — and plagiarism that is deliberately intended to pass off one writer's work as another's.

Inaccurate or Incomplete Citation of Sources

If your paraphrase is too close to the original wording or sentence structure of the source (even if you identify the source); if you do not identify the source of a quotation (even if you include the quotation marks); or if you fail to indicate clearly the source of an idea that you obviously did not come up with on your own, you may be accused of plagiarism even if your intent was not to plagiarize. Inaccurate or incomplete acknowledgment of sources often results either from carelessness or from not learning how to borrow material properly in the first place. Still, because the costs of even unintentional plagiarism can be severe, it's important to understand how it can happen and how you can guard against it.

As a writer of academic integrity, you will want to take responsibility for your research and for acknowledging all sources accurately. One easy way to keep track is to keep photocopies, printouts, or unaltered electronic copies of every source as you do your research; then you can identify needed quotations by highlighting them on each source.

Deliberate Plagiarism

Deliberate plagiarism — handing in an essay written by a friend or purchased (or simply downloaded) from an essay-writing company;

cutting and pasting passages directly from source materials without marking them with quotation marks and acknowledging your sources; failing to credit the source of an idea or concept in your text—is what most people think of when they hear the word *plagiarism*. This form of plagiarism is particularly troubling because it represents dishonesty and deception: those who intentionally plagiarize present the hard thinking and hard work of someone else as their own, and they deceive readers by claiming knowledge they don't really have.

Deliberate plagiarism is also fairly simple to spot: your instructor will be well acquainted with your writing and likely to notice any sudden shifts in the style or quality of your work. In addition, by typing a few words from an essay into a search engine, your instructor can identify "matches" very easily.

5

Research in the Humanities

Resources in the Humanities

INDEXES AND DATABASES FOR THE HUMANITIES

Arts and Humanities Citation Index. Philadelphia: Institute for Scientific Information, 1975–. Indexes citations in articles from over a thousand periodicals in the humanities and arts; entries allow tracing influence through later citations of books and periodicals.

Essay and General Literature Index. New York: Wilson, 1900–. Indexes authors and subjects of separate essays published in collections. (Essays are not usually listed separately in library catalogs.)

Humanities Index. New York: Wilson, 1984–. Formerly *Social Sciences and Humanities Index,* 1965–1974, and *International Index,* 1907–1965. Indexes and abstracts articles and book reviews from about three hundred periodicals covering literature, history, the arts, the classics, and other topics in the humanities.

WEB RESOURCES FOR THE HUMANITIES

EDSITEment
www.edsitement.neh.gov
Links to nearly two hundred high-quality humanities Web sites, selected under the auspices of the National Endowment for the Humanities.

Infomine: Scholarly Internet Resource Collections
www.infomine.ucr.edu

> Supplies indexed and annotated links to databases and other resources of academic interest in the humanities, performing arts, and visual arts.

Voice of the Shuttle: Web Site for Humanities Research
vos.ucsb.edu

> Includes highlights, top sites, and links to extensive research essay resources for general or specialized research in the humanities.

The Webliography: Internet Subject Guides
www.lib.lsu.edu/subjectguides/humanities.html

> Provides extensive annotated guides to Web resources in many fields in the humanities, including art, film, theater, literature, history, music, classics, and others.

Art and Architecture

GENERAL REFERENCE SOURCES FOR ART AND ARCHITECTURE

Encyclopedia of Architecture: Design, Engineering, and Construction. Ed. Robert T. Packer. 5 vols. Hoboken: Wiley-Interscience, 1988-1990. Supplies articles, including bibliographies, on architectural history, technology, construction, and design.

Encyclopedia of Artists. Ed. William Vaughn. 6 vols. New York: Oxford University Press, 2000. Provides an illustrated introduction to Western art, with entries on artists, works, and major periods from the Middle Ages through the present.

Encyclopedia of World Art. 15 vols., plus supplements. New York: McGraw-Hill, 1959-1968; 1983; 1987. Includes articles, many illustrated, on artists, art history, art in other cultures and societies, and related topics.

The Grove Dictionary of Art. Ed. Jane Turner. 34 vols. New York: Oxford University Press, 1996. Examines all the visual arts except film, with fifteen thousand illustrations.

Oxford Dictionary of Art. 2004. Provides entries on the Western fine and decorative arts, including artists, terms, and institutions.

INDEXES AND DATABASES FOR ART AND ARCHITECTURE

ARTBibliographies Modern. Bethesda: Cambridge Scientific Abstracts, 1969–. Lists and abstracts articles, books, and catalogs about art.

Art Index. New York: Wilson, 1929–. *Art Index Retrospective* covers 1929–1984. Indexes articles from about 250 periodicals on the fine arts, archaeology, architecture, interior design, city planning, photography, film, and other topics.

Avery Index to Architectural Periodicals. Ann Arbor: ProQuest, 1941–. Available in print and online. Contains citations to articles in architecture and design, archaeology, city planning, interior design, and historic preservation.

Bibliography of the History of Art (BHA). Santa Monica: John Paul Getty Trust, 1973–. Last print edition, 1999. Formerly *RILA (Répertoire internationale de la littérature de l'art),* 1975–1989, and *RAA (Répertoire d'art et d'archéologie),* 1910–1963. Lists articles from about four thousand periodicals plus books, papers, and other materials about the arts.

Grove Art Online. A continuously updated online version of *The Dictionary of Art* (34 vols., 1996) and *The Oxford Companion to Western Art* (2001); includes articles on artists, movements, and works in the fine and decorative arts worldwide, as well as image links and a search engine.

WEB RESOURCES FOR ART AND ARCHITECTURE

Architecture and Building
library.nevada.edu/arch/rsrce/webresources
> Organizes extensive topical and alphabetical listings of Web resources on architecture and related issues.

The Art History Research Centre
www.harmsen.net/ahrc
> Introduces Internet research in art history and links to many resources such as Internet art collections, library catalogs, periodical indexes, newsgroups, and other art history servers.

Art History Resources on the Web
witcombe.sbc.edu/ARTHLinks.html
> Provides an extraordinarily detailed set of chronologically organized links to art history sources, from prehistoric through modern.

Art Museum Network
www.artmuseumnetwork.com
> Free access to information about collections, exhibitions, and services of the world's largest and most prestigious art museums.

The Getty Research Institute
www.getty.edu/research
> Provides access to major databases and indexes on art and cultural history, including specialized search tools and numerous graphic images with reference pages.

National Gallery of Art
www.nga.gov/
> Supplies images from the collection and news about current displays and educational opportunities.

Virtual Library Museums Pages
archives.icom.museum/vlmp/
> Includes a large number of links to recent and current exhibitions at many major museums, by country.

World Art Treasures
www.bergerfoundation.ch/
> Offers in-depth links to selected artists' works and areas of art, with good links to other sites.

World Wide Arts Resources
wwar.com/
> Contains extensive links and search capability to artists, art history, museums, and other art-related topics.

The World Wide Web Virtual Library: History of Art
www.chart.ac.uk/vlib
> Includes links to art history sites, museums, galleries, art history organizations, and university art departments.

The WWW Virtual Library — Art
vlib.org/Art
> Provides an excellent collection of links to both art and literature sites, including links to other virtual libraries.

Classics

GENERAL REFERENCE SOURCES FOR THE CLASSICS

The Oxford Classical Dictionary. Ed. Simon Hornblower and Anthony
    Spawnforth. New York: Oxford University Press, 2003. Supplies
    articles with bibliographies on classical figures, literature, places,
    and events.

The Oxford Companion to Classical Civilization. Ed. M. C. Howaston. New
    York: Oxford University Press, 2004. Includes articles on classical
    writers, major works and characters, literary forms, and mythology,
    as well as background information on classical history, geography,
    religion, politics, and social context.

INDEXES AND DATABASES FOR THE CLASSICS

L'Année Philologique. Paris: Société Internationale de Bibliographic Clas-
    sique (SIBC), 1928–. Indexes periodical articles, books, and other
    resources about classical language, literature, history, law, science,
    culture, and other topics.

WEB RESOURCES FOR THE CLASSICS

Classics and Mediterranean Archaeology
www.gzg.fn.bw.schule.de/faecher/links/classic.html
    Provides links to widely varied resources on texts, field sites, proj-
    ects, images, archaeological excavations, exhibitions, museums, aca-
    demic institutions, maps, publications, and other information on
    classical studies.

Classics at Oxford
www.classics.ox.ac.uk/
    Provides links to many resources in the classics and ancient history;
    has search capability.

The Perseus Digital Library
www.perseus.tufts.edu
    Supplies extensive information on the ancient world, including
    background information, Greek texts and translations, maps,
    descriptions, and over thirteen thousand images of vases, coins,
    buildings, sculptures, and site plans.

History

GENERAL REFERENCE SOURCES FOR HISTORY

The Cambridge Ancient History. 19 vols. Cambridge: Cambridge University Press, 2006. Includes articles, illustrations, maps, and other supporting materials in volumes on early civilization in Europe and the Middle East; additional volumes supply illustrations and appendices.

The Cambridge Encyclopedia of Latin America and the Caribbean. Cambridge: Cambridge University Press, 1992. Supplies articles on the history, politics, economics, and culture of the region.

The Cambridge History of Africa. 8 vols. Cambridge: Cambridge University Press, 1986. Covers African history chronologically from early times through the mid-1970s.

The Cambridge Medieval History. 9 vols. Cambridge: Cambridge University Press, 1999. Covers the major events and changes in medieval history, including government, religion, and cultural background.

Chambers Dictionary of World History. Edinburgh: Chambers Harrap, 2005. Contains over seventy-five hundred entries on key figures and events of world history, with an in-depth focus on the period between AD 1000 and 2000; includes maps, tables, and family trees.

Dictionary of Concepts in History. Westport: Greenwood Press, 1986. Supplies articles on major historical concepts, including definitions, histories of the concepts, and additional sources of information.

Dictionary of the Middle Ages. Ed. Joseph R. Strainer. 13 vols. New York: Scribner, 1982–1989, with 2004 supplement. Provides authoritative articles with bibliographies on many people and topics relating to the culture, politics, and religion of the medieval period (AD 500–1500).

Encyclopedia of American Social History. Ed. Mary Clayton et al. 3 vols. New York: Scribner, 1993. Includes articles and bibliographies on aspects of ordinary life, work, and leisure.

Encyclopedia of Asian History. Ed. Robin Lewis and Ainslee Embree. 4 vols. New York: Macmillan Library Resource, 1988. Supplies articles, often with bibliographies for further research in English, including major figures and wide-ranging topics about Asian history and civilization from early times on.

Encyclopedia of the Renaissance. Ed. Paul F. Grendler. New York: Scribner, 1999. Offers brief entries on the Renaissance, including historical, political, and other topics.

Encyclopedia of World History. Ed. Peter N. Stearns. Boston: Houghton Mifflin, 1999. Contains entries on events, figures, and concepts from prehistoric through modern times; includes cross-references, maps, portraits, and engravings.

The Oxford Companion to British History. Ed. John Cannon. New York: Oxford University Press, 2002. Provides entries on social, political, cultural, economic, and scientific events, both national and local, from 55 BCE to the 1990s; includes maps and genealogical charts.

The Oxford Companion to United States History. Ed. Paul S. Boyer. New York: Oxford University Press, 2004. Examines major figures, events, ideologies, and developments in technology, the economy, immigration, and urbanization from before 1492 to the end of the twentieth century.

The Oxford Dictionary of World History. Ed. Jonathon Law. New York: Oxford University Press, 2003. Covers key figures, subjects, and events from prehistoric to modern times in concise entries; includes detailed maps on particular events and topics.

United States History: A Selective Guide to Information Sources. Ed. Anna H. Perrault and Ron Blazek. Westport: Libraries Unlimited, 1994. Offers a topically arranged annotated list of the reference works published in the previous two hundred years on the subject of U.S. history, including print sources, online databases, and CD-ROMs.

INDEXES AND DATABASES FOR HISTORY

America: History and Life. Santa Barbara: ABC-CLIO, 1964–2005. Formerly in *History Abstracts* (1954–1963). Indexes and abstracts articles from more than two thousand periodicals on the history and culture of North America (United States and Canada), including local, regional, and national coverage.

Handbook for Research in American History: A Guide to Bibliographies and Other Reference Books. Lincoln: University of Nebraska Press, 1994. Lists reference sources covering many aspects of American history.

Harvard Guide to American History. 2 vols. Cambridge: Harvard University Press, 1974. Supplies research guidance and lists major sources about notable people and topics as diverse as social context, religion, and law; vol. 2 chronologically surveys U.S. history.

Historical Abstracts. 1954–2005. Indexes and abstracts articles from more than two thousand periodicals and books on history, culture, historical research methods, and regional, national, and worldwide topics from 1450 on, excluding North America.

Reference Sources in History: An Introductory Guide. 2004. Lists and annotates resources for studying history worldwide in all periods.

WEB RESOURCES FOR HISTORY

Bedford/St. Martin's: Make History
bcs.bedfordstmartins.com/makehistory2e
    Provides an annotated list of links to history sites.

Eurodocs
eurodocs.lib.byu.edu/
    Offers primary historical documents from western Europe; organized by country.

Historical Text Archive
historicaltextarchive.com/
    Provides access to many world history texts; organized by both area and topic.

The History Net
www.theHistoryNet.com/
    A project of the National Historical Society; provides a historical magazine as well as a search service.

Internet History Sourcebooks Project
www.fordham.edu/halsall
    Collections of public domain and copy-permitted historical texts for educational use.

The Library of Congress: American Memory
memory.loc.gov
    An extensive site with text and links to millions of primary-source

items (including maps, photos, and documents) from the Library of
Congress and other collections; has excellent search capabilities.

World History Archives
www.hartford-hwp.com/archives/
Offers access to actual versions of important texts in world history
and many links to contemporary writings.

The WWW Virtual Library — History
vlib.org/History
Provides links to history servers by research subject, eras and ep-
ochs, historical topics, and countries and regions; includes search
capability.

Literature

GENERAL REFERENCE SOURCES FOR LITERATURE

The Cambridge History of American Literature. Ed. Sacvan Bercovitch. 8 vols.
Cambridge: Cambridge Univeristy Press, 2006–. Covers poetry, prose,
and literary criticism from 1590 to the present in multiple volumes
that include thematically arranged entries on works of writers, critics,
and scholars.

Dictionary of Literary Biography (DLB). 25 vols. Detroit: Gale Group, 1978–.
Supplies articles, including bibliographies and photographs, on the
major writers representing each period or topic covered.

Encyclopedia of Folklore and Literature. Ed. Mary Ellen Brown and Bruce A.
Rosenberg. Santa Barbara: ABC-CLIO, 1998. Includes entries about
authors, works, scholars, and movements of folklore and literature
throughout the world.

Harper Handbook to Literature. New York: Longman, 1997. Provides a dictionary of literary terms, concepts, genres, and movements with a
mixture of brief entries and longer entries with bibliographies.

The Oxford Companion to American Literature. Ed. James D. Hart and Phillip
Leininger. New York: Oxford Universty Press, 1995. Supplies articles
on authors, works, characters, and other literary topics, as well as on
related background topics.

The Oxford Companion to English Literature. Ed. Dinah Birch. 7th ed. New
York: Oxford University Press, 2009. Supplies articles on literary

topics, terms, authors, works, characters, movements, trends, and influences.

Reader's Guide to Literature in English. Ed. Mark Hawkins-Dady. Chicago: Fitzroy Dearborn, 1996. Includes entries on writers, literary devices, genres, movements, criticism, and the literatures of various groups, regions, and time periods.

INDEXES AND DATABASES FOR LITERATURE

MLA International Bibliography of Books and Articles on the Modern Languages and Literature. New York: Modern Language Association, 1921-. Indexes articles from over three thousand periodicals plus books and dissertations on literature and language, including literary works, authors, national literatures, literary movements and themes, literary theory and criticism, linguistics, and related topics.

Reference Works in British and American Literature. Ed. James K. Bracken. 2 vols. Englewood: Libraries Unlimited, 1998. Lists and annotates publications and other resources for studying literary topics and specific authors.

WEB RESOURCES FOR LITERATURE

American Studies Web
lamp.georgetown.edu/asw/
    Provides links to many elements of American studies, with an emphasis on literary texts, authors, approaches, genres, and associations.

In Other Words: A Lexicon of the Humanities
web.mac.com/radney/humanities/
    Provides an interesting hyperlinked lexicon and glossary of major terms in literary criticism, rhetoric, and linguistics.

International Gay & Lesbian Review
gaybookreviews.info
    Provides abstracts and reviews of many books related to lesbian, gay, bisexual, and transgender studies.

Literary Resources on the Net
ethnicity.rutgers.edu/~jlynch/Lit/
    Allows you to search for online literary materials and provides a list of periodicals and genre-based categories to explore.

Project Gutenberg
promo.net/pg
> Offers the best current index to PG texts, most of which are now in the public domain.

Resources for Russian and Slavic Languages and Literature
www.library.vanderbilt.edu/central/russian.html
> Provides links to Web sites, dictionaries, literary sites, e-journals, e-texts, departments, and professional organizations.

Romance Languages Resources Page
rll.uchicago.edu/undergraduate/resources/
> Offers links to cultural and textual resources and to sites that help those studying Romance languages.

Music

GENERAL REFERENCE SOURCES FOR MUSIC

The New Grove Dictionary of Music and Musicians. Ed. Stanley Sadie. 2nd ed. 29 vols. New York: Grove, 2001. Supplies entries on thousands of musicians and music topics, including bibliographies, lists of works, maps, family trees, and illustrations of instruments.

New Oxford History of Music. 10 vols. New York: Oxford University Press, 1954–2001. Covers music, ancient through modern, including bibliographies and music examples.

The Oxford Companion to Music. Ed. Alison Latham. New York: Oxford University Press, 2002. Provides entries defining musical terms, types of music, aspects of music history, and related topics. Primarily covers Western classical music.

INDEXES AND DATABASES FOR MUSIC

Music Index: A Subject-Author Guide to Current Music Periodical Literature. Detroit: Information Coordinators, 1949–. Indexes articles from over three hundred periodicals on music and musicians.

Music Reference and Research Materials: An Annotated Bibliography. New York: Schirmer, 1997. Lists standard reference sources about music.

RILM Abstracts of Music Literature. New York: RILM, 1967–. Indexes and abstracts articles, books, and other sources.

WEB RESOURCES FOR MUSIC

Classical Music on the Web
classicalusa.com
> Offers an "organized jumpstation" to the best classical music sites on the Web.

Loeb Music Library
hcl.harvard.edu/libraries/loebmusic/
> Contains links, with search capability, to databases, journals, and many other music-related sites.

Sibelius Academy Music Resources
www2.siba.fi/kulttuuripalvelut/music.html
> Provides links to every aspect of music appreciation, production, and education.

Worldwide Internet Music Resources
www.music.indiana.edu/music_resources/
> Includes a general list of links to musicians, composers, performance sites, genres, research, industry, and journals.

Philosophy and Religion

GENERAL REFERENCE SOURCES FOR PHILOSOPHY AND RELIGION

The Cambridge Dictionary of Philosophy. Ed. Robert Audi. Cambridge: Cambridge University Press, 1999. Surveys key concepts and figures in both Western and non-Western philosophy, with extensive coverage of contemporary philosophers and new fields of thought.

Encyclopedia of Philosophy. Ed. Donald M. Borchert. 2nd ed. 10 vols. New York: Macmillan, 2006. Includes articles and bibliographies on philosophers and topics of significance in the field.

Encyclopedia of Religion. Ed. Lindsay Jones. 2nd ed. 16 vols. New York: Macmillan, 2005. Provides articles and bibliographies on both historical and present-day religions worldwide, including beliefs, practices, and major figures and groups.

The Oxford Dictionary of Philosophy. By Simon Blackburn. 2nd ed. New York: Oxford University Press, 2008. Supplies entries on key terms and notable philosophers.

The Routledge Encyclopedia of Philosophy. 10 vols. London: Routledge, 1998. Contains entries on concepts, scholarship, schools, and themes of world philosophy and religion.

INDEXES AND DATABASES FOR
PHILOSOPHY AND RELIGION

Philosopher's Index. Bowling Green: Philosophy Documentation Center, 1967–. Indexes and abstracts books and articles from about three hundred periodicals.

Philosophy: A Guide to the Reference Literature. Santa Barbara: Libraries Unlimited, 2006. Supplies annotated entries on reference works in philosophy.

Religion Index One: Periodicals; Religion Index Two: Multi-Author Works. Evanston: American Theological Library Association, 1949–. Annual. Indexes and abstracts books and articles from several hundred periodicals. (online as ATLA Religion Database)

Religious Information Sources: A Worldwide Guide. New York: Garland, 1992. Lists sources for all world religions.

WEB RESOURCES FOR PHILOSOPHY AND RELIGION

American Philosophical Association
www.apaonline.org
> Includes Web resources with guides to philosophy, philosophers, texts, journals, and academic organizations.

Guide to Philosophy on the Internet
www.earlham.edu/~peters/philinks.htm
> Includes links to sites with philosophy guides (in various languages), philosophers, journals, organizations, dictionaries, and many topics dealing with philosophy.

Noesis: Philosophical Research On-line
hippias.evansville.edu
> Provides keyword searches as well as links to associated sites and search tools.

Religion (Humanities): Galaxy
www.galaxy.com/dir18174/Religion

Supplies access to collections of resources and directories for the study of religion.

Religious Studies Resources
www.bu.edu/religion/resources
Offers selected annotated links to resources on philosophy and religion, including Christianity, Judaism, Islam, and Asian religions.

The WWW Virtual Library — Philosophy
www.bristol.ac.uk/philosophy/department/resources/virtual.html
Provides links to thousands of sources, including articles, journals, books, databases, and discussion groups; allows searches.

Theater and Film

GENERAL REFERENCE SOURCES FOR THEATER AND FILM

The Concise Oxford Companion to the Theatre. Ed. Phyllis Hartnoll and Peter Found. New York: Oxford University Press, 1992. Supplies essays on theater history and style, buildings, dramatists, performers, directors, festivals, and technology.

Film Encyclopedia. By Ephraim Katz and Ronald Dean Nolen. 6th ed. New York: HarperCollins, 2008. Supplies biographical and topical entries on many aspects of film.

McGraw-Hill Encyclopedia of World Drama. 2nd ed. 5 vols. New York: McGraw-Hill, 1984. Supplies extensive articles, including bibliographies, on playwrights, theaters, genres, dramatic terms, regional drama, and related topics.

INDEXES AND DATABASES FOR THEATER AND FILM

Film and Television Literature Index. Albany: Film and Television Documentation Center, SUNY Albany, 1975-. Indexes articles from several hundred periodicals on film, television, and video.

International Index to Film Periodicals. Brussels: FIAF, 1972-. Indexes articles, interviews, and reviews from more than eighty-five periodicals, with entries divided into three sections: general subjects, individual films, and biography.

WEB RESOURCES FOR THEATER AND FILM

McCoy's Brief Guide to Internet Resources in Theatre and Performance Studies
www2.stetson.edu/csata/thr_guid.html
> Supplies useful research resources on topics such as acting, stage-craft, playwrights, and plays, as well as an annotated list of especially helpful sites.

Playbill On-line
www.playbill.com
> Covers theater news, awards, and listings, and provides links through Theatre Central to a directory of resources on playwrights, stage-craft, Shakespeare, theater companies, casting calls, publications, and other varied topics.

World Wide Arts Resources: Theater
wwar.com/categories/Theater
> Provides numerous links, by category, to most aspects of theater, including acting, choreography, plays, Broadway theater, and opera; has search capability.

The WWW Virtual Library: Theatre and Drama
vl-theatre.com
> Provides international theater resources (including studies, collections of images, events, companies, and academic institutions) and also indexes plays available online.

MLA Style

This section discusses the Modern Language Association (MLA) style of formatting manuscripts and documenting sources, which is widely used in literature, languages, and other fields in the humanities.

For more information on the Modern Language Association style, consult the *MLA Handbook for Writers of Research Papers,* Seventh Edition (2009).

In-Text Citations

MLA style requires documentation in the text of an essay for every quotation, paraphrase, summary, or other material requiring

documentation. In-text citations document material from other sources with both signal phrases and parenthetical references. Parenthetical references should include the information your readers need to locate the full reference in the list of works cited at the end of the text. An in-text citation in MLA style aims to give the reader two kinds of information: (1) it indicates *which source* on the works-cited page the writer is referring to, and (2) it explains *where in the source* the material quoted, paraphrased, or summarized can be found, if the source has page numbers or other numbered sections.

The basic MLA in-text citation includes the author's last name either in a signal phrase introducing the source material or in parentheses at the end of the sentence. It also includes the page number in parentheses at the end of the sentence.

CITATION USING A SIGNAL PHRASE

In his discussion of Monty Python routines, Crystal notes that the group relished "breaking the normal rules" of language (107).

PARENTHETICAL CITATION

A noted linguist explains that Monty Python humor often relied on "bizarre linguistic interactions" (Crystal 108).

Note in the following examples where punctuation is placed in relation to the parentheses.

1. AUTHOR NAMED IN A SIGNAL PHRASE

The MLA recommends using the author's name in a signal phrase to introduce the material and citing the page number(s) in parentheses.

Lee claims that his comic-book creation, Thor, was "the first regularly published superhero to speak in a consistently archaic manner" (199).

2. AUTHOR NAMED IN A PARENTHETICAL REFERENCE

When you do not mention the author in a signal phrase, include the author's last name before the page number(s) in the parentheses. Use no punctuation between the author's name and the page number(s).

The word *Bollywood* is sometimes considered an insult because it implies that Indian movies are merely "a derivative of the American film industry" (Chopra 9).

3. TWO OR THREE AUTHORS

Use all the authors' last names in a signal phrase or in parentheses.

Gortner, Hebrun, and Nicolson maintain that "opinion leaders" influence other people in an organization because they are respected, not because they hold high positions (175).

4. FOUR OR MORE AUTHORS

Use the first author's name and *et al.* ("and others"), or name all the authors in a signal phrase or in parentheses.

Similarly, as Belenky et al. assert, examining the lives of women expands our understanding of human development (7).

Similarly, as Belenky, Clinchy, Tarule, and Goldberger assert, examining the lives of women expands our understanding of human development (7).

5. ORGANIZATION AS AUTHOR

Give the group's full name or a shortened form of it in a signal phrase or in parentheses.

Any study of social welfare involves a close analysis of "the impacts, the benefits, and the costs" of its policies (Social Research Corporation iii).

6. UNKNOWN AUTHOR

Use the full title, if it is brief, in your text — or a shortened version of the title in parentheses.

One analysis defines *hype* as "an artificially engendered atmosphere of hysteria" ("Today's Marketplace" 51).

7. AUTHOR OF TWO OR MORE WORKS CITED IN THE SAME PROJECT

If your list of works cited has more than one work by the same author, include a shortened version of the title of the work you are citing in a signal phrase or in parentheses to prevent reader confusion.

Gardner shows readers their own silliness in his description of a "pointless, ridiculous monster, crouched in the shadows,

stinking of dead men, murdered children, and martyred cows"
(*Grendel* 2).

8. TWO OR MORE AUTHORS WITH THE SAME LAST NAME

Include the author's first *and* last names in a signal phrase or
first initial and last name in a parenthetical reference.

Children will learn to write if they are allowed to choose their own
subjects, James Britton asserts, citing the Schools Council study of
the 1960s (37-42).

9. INDIRECT SOURCE (AUTHOR QUOTING SOMEONE ELSE)

Use the abbreviation *qtd. in* to indicate that you are quoting from
someone else's report of a source.

As Arthur Miller says, "When somebody is destroyed everybody
finally contributes to it, but in Willy's case, the end product would
be virtually the same" (qtd. in Martin and Meyer 375).

10. MULTIVOLUME WORK

In a parenthetical reference, note the volume number first and
then the page number(s), with a colon and one space between them.

Modernist writers prized experimentation and gradually even sought to
blur the line between poetry and prose, according to Forster (3: 150).

If you name only one volume of the work in your list of works cited,
include only the page number in the parentheses.

11. LITERARY WORK

Because literary works are often available in many different editions, cite the page number(s) from the edition you used followed by

a semicolon, and then give other identifying information that will lead readers to the passage in any edition. Indicate the act and/or scene in a play (*37; sc. 1*). For a novel, indicate the part or chapter (*175; ch. 4*).

> In utter despair, Dostoyevsky's character Mitya wonders aloud
> about the "terrible tragedies realism inflicts on people" (376;
> bk. 8, ch. 2).

For a poem, cite the part (if there is one) and line(s), separated by a period. If you are citing only line numbers, use the word *line(s)* in the first reference (*lines 33–34*).

> Whitman speculates, "All goes onward and outward, nothing
> collapses, / And to die is different from what anyone supposed,
> and luckier" (6.129-30).

For a verse play, give only the act, scene, and line numbers, separated by periods.

> The witches greet Banquo as "Lesser than Macbeth, and greater"
> (1.3.65).

12. WORK IN AN ANTHOLOGY OR COLLECTION

For an essay, short story, or other piece of prose reprinted in an anthology, use the name of the author of the work, not the editor of the anthology, but use the page number(s) from the anthology.

> Narratives of captivity play a major role in early writing by women
> in the United States, as demonstrated by Silko (219).

13. SACRED TEXT

To cite a sacred text such as the Qur'an or the Bible, give the title of the edition you used, the book, and the chapter and verse (or their equivalent) separated by a period. In your text, spell out the names of

books. In parenthetical references, use abbreviations for books with names of five or more letters (*Gen.* for *Genesis*).

> He ignored the admonition "Pride goes before destruction, and a haughty spirit before a fall" (*New Oxford Annotated Bible*, Prov. 16.18).

14. ENCYCLOPEDIA OR DICTIONARY ENTRY

An entry from a reference work — such as an encyclopedia or dictionary — without an author will appear on the works-cited list under the entry's title. Enclose the title in quotation marks and place it in parentheses. Omit the page number for reference works that arrange entries alphabetically.

> The term *prion* was coined by Stanley B. Prusiner from the words *proteinaceous* and *infectious* and a suffix meaning *particle* ("Prion").

15. GOVERNMENT SOURCE

Because entries for sources from government agencies will appear on your list of works cited under the name of the country (see model 71, p. 111), your in-text citation should include the name of the country as well as the name of the agency responsible for the source.

> To reduce the agricultural runoff into the Chesapeake Bay, the United States Environmental Protection Agency argued that "[h]igh nutrient loading crops, such as corn and soybean, should be replaced with alternatives in environmentally sensitive areas" (2-26).

16. ELECTRONIC OR NONPRINT SOURCE

Give enough information in a signal phrase or in parentheses for readers to locate the source in your list of works cited. Many works found online or in electronic databases lack stable page numbers; you

can omit the page number in such cases. However, if you are citing a work with stable pagination, such as an article in PDF format, include the page number in parentheses.

> As a *Slate* analysis has noted, "Prominent sports psychologists get praised for their successes and don't get grief for their failures" (Engber).

In the example above, the source, an article on a Web site, does not have stable pagination.

> According to Whitmarsh, the British military had experimented with using balloons for observation as far back as 1879 (328).

The source, an online PDF of a print article, includes stable page numbers.

If the source includes numbered sections, paragraphs, or screens, include the abbreviation (*sec.*), paragraph (*par.*), or screen (*scr.*) and the number in parentheses.

> Sherman notes that the "immediate, interactive, and on-the-spot" nature of Internet information can make nondigital media seem outdated (sec. 32).

17. ENTIRE WORK

Include the reference in the text, without any page numbers.

> Jon Krakauer's *Into the Wild* both criticizes and admires the solitary impulses of its young hero, which end up killing him.

18. TWO OR MORE SOURCES IN ONE PARENTHETICAL REFERENCE

Separate the information with semicolons.

> Economists recommend that *employment* be redefined to include unpaid domestic labor (Clark 148; Nevins 39).

19. VISUALS INCLUDED IN THE TEXT

When you include an image in your text, number it and include a parenthetical reference in your text (*see Fig. 2*). Number figures (photos, drawings, cartoons, maps, graphs, and charts) and tables separately. Each visual should include a caption with the figure or table number and information about the source.

This trend is illustrated in a chart distributed by the College Board as part of its 2002 analysis of aggregate SAT data (see Fig. 1).

Soon after the preceding sentence, readers find the following figure and caption:

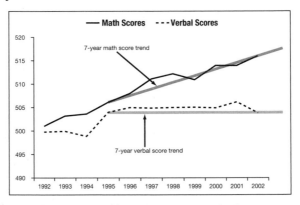

Fig. 1. Comparison of SAT math and verbal scores (1992-2002). Trend lines added. Source: Kristin Carnahan and Chiara Coletti, *Ten-Year Trend in SAT Scores Indicates Increased Emphasis on Math Is Yielding Results; Reading and Writing Are Causes for Concern.* New York: College Board, 2002; print; 9.

An image that you create might appear with a caption like this:

Fig. 4. Young woman reading a magazine. Personal photograph by author.

MLA Style for Explanatory and Bibliographic Notes

MLA style recommends explanatory notes for information or commentary that would not readily fit into your text but is needed for clarification or further explanation. In addition, MLA style permits bibliographic notes for citing several sources for one point and for offering thanks to, information about, or evaluation of a source. Use superscript numbers in the text to refer readers to the notes, which may appear as endnotes (typed under the heading *Notes* on a separate page after the text but before the list of works cited) or as footnotes at the bottom of the page (typed four lines below the last text line).

SUPERSCRIPT NUMBER IN TEXT

Stewart emphasizes the existence of social contacts in Hawthorne's life so that the audience will accept a different Hawthorne, one more attuned to modern times than the figure in Woodberry [3]

NOTE

[3] Woodberry does, however, show that Hawthorne *was* often an unsociable individual. He emphasizes the seclusion of Hawthorne's mother, who separated herself from her family after the death of her husband, often even taking meals alone (28). Woodberry seems to imply that Mrs. Hawthorne's isolation rubbed off onto her son.

MLA Style for a List of Works Cited

A list of works cited is an alphabetical list of the sources you have referred to in your essay. (If your instructor asks you to list everything

you have read as background, call the list *Works Consulted*.) Here are some guidelines for preparing such a list:

- Start your list on a separate page after the text of your essay and any notes.

- Continue the consecutive numbering of pages.

- Center the heading *Works Cited* (not italicized or in quotation marks) one inch from the top of the page.

- Start each entry flush with the left margin, indent subsequent lines for the entry one-half inch. Double-space the entire list.

- List sources alphabetically by the first word. Start with the author's name, if available; if not, use the editor's name, if available. If no author or editor is given, start with the title.

- List the author's last name first, followed by a comma and the first name. If a source has multiple authors, subsequent authors' names appear first name first (see model 2).

- Italicize titles of books and long works, but put titles of articles and other short works in quotation marks.

- In general, use a period and a space after each element of the entry; look at the models in this chapter for information on punctuating particular kinds of entries.

- For a book, list the city of publication (add a country abbreviation for non-U.S. cities that may be unfamiliar). Follow it with a colon and a shortened form of the publisher's name — omit *Co.* or *Inc.*, shorten names such as *Simon & Schuster* to *Simon*, and abbreviate *University Press* to *UP*.

- List dates of periodical publication or of access to electronic items in day, month, year order, and abbreviate months except for May, June, and July.

- Give a medium, such as *Print* or *Web*, for each entry.

- List inclusive page numbers for a part of a larger work. For numbers 1–99, give all digits of the second number. For numbers larger than 99, give the last two digits of the second number (*115–18, 1378–79*) and any other digits that change in the second number (*296–301*).

Guidelines for Author Listings

The list of works cited is arranged alphabetically. The in-text citations in your writing point readers toward particular sources on the list.

NAME CITED IN SIGNAL PHRASE IN TEXT

Crystal explains . . .

NAME IN PARENTHETICAL CITATION IN TEXT

. . . (Crystal 107).

BEGINNING OF ENTRY ON LIST OF WORKS CITED

Crystal, David.

Models 1–5 below explain how to arrange author names. The information that follows the name of the author depends on the type of work you are citing—a book (models 6–27); a print periodical (models 28–34); a written text from an electronic source, such as an article from a Web site or database (models 35–54); sources from art, film, radio, or other media, including online versions (models 55–69); and other kinds of sources (models 70–78). Consult the model that most closely resembles the kind of source you are using.

1. ONE AUTHOR

Put the last name first, followed by a comma, the first name (and initial, if any), and a period.

Crystal, David.

2. MULTIPLE AUTHORS

List the first author with the last name first (see model 1). Give the names of any other authors with the first name first. Separate

authors' names with commas, and include the word *and* before the last person's name.

Martineau, Jane, Desmond Shawe-Taylor, and Jonathan Bate.

For four or more authors, either list all the names, or list the first author followed by a comma and *et al.* ("and others").

Lupton, Ellen, Jennifer Tobias, Alicia Imperiale, Grace Jeffers, and
    Randi Mates.

Lupton, Ellen, et al.

3. ORGANIZATION OR GROUP AUTHOR

Give the name of the group, government agency, corporation, or other organization listed as the author.

Getty Trust.

United States. Government Accountability Office.

4. UNKNOWN AUTHOR

When the author is not identified, begin the entry with the title, and alphabetize by the first important word. Italicize titles of books and long works, but put titles of articles and other short works in quotation marks.

"California Sues EPA over Emissions."

New Concise World Atlas.

5. TWO OR MORE WORKS BY THE SAME AUTHOR

Arrange the entries alphabetically by title. Include the author's name in the first entry, but in subsequent entries, use three hyphens followed by a period. (For the basic format for citing a book, see model

6. For the basic format for citing an article from an online newspaper, see model 38.)

> Chopra, Anupama. "Bollywood Princess, Hollywood Hopeful." *New York Times*. New York Times, 10 Feb. 2008. Web. 13 Feb. 2008.
>
> ---. *King of Bollywood: Shah Rukh Khan and the Seductive World of Indian Cinema*. New York: Warner, 2007. Print.

Note: Use three hyphens only when the work is by *exactly* the same author(s) as the previous entry.

Books

6. BASIC FORMAT FOR A BOOK

Begin with the author name(s). (See models 1–5.) Then include the title and subtitle, the city of publication, the publisher, and the publication date. End with the medium of publication. The source map on pp. 82–83 shows where to find this information in a typical book.

> Crystal, David. *Language Play*. Chicago: U of Chicago P, 1998. Print.

Note: Place a period and a space after the name, title, and date. Place a colon after the city and a comma after the publisher, and shorten the publisher's name — omit *Co.* or *Inc.*, and abbreviate *University Press* to *UP*.

7. AUTHOR AND EDITOR BOTH NAMED

> Bangs, Lester. *Psychotic Reactions and Carburetor Dung*. Ed. Greil Marcus. New York: Knopf, 1988. Print.

Note: To cite the editor's contribution instead, begin the entry with the editor's name.

> Marcus, Greil, ed. *Psychotic Reactions and Carburetor Dung*. By Lester Bangs. New York: Knopf, 1988. Print.

MLA SOURCE MAP: Citing books

Take information from the book's title page and copyright page (on the reverse side of the title page), not from the book's cover or a library catalog.

(1) **Author**. List the last name first. End with a period. For variations, see models 2–5.

(2) **Title.** Italicize the title and any subtitle; capitalize all major words. End with a period.

(3) **City of publication.** If more than one city is given, use the first one listed. For foreign cities, add an abbreviation of the country or province (*Cork, Ire.*). Follow it with a colon.

(4) **Publisher.** Give a shortened version of the publisher's name (*Oxford UP* for *Oxford University Press*). Follow it with a comma.

(5) **Year of publication.** If more than one copyright date is given, use the most recent one. End with a period.

(6) **Medium of publication.** End with the medium (*Print*) followed by a period.

A citation for the book on p. 83 would look like this:

Kingsolver, Barbara. *Small Wonder*. New York: Harper, 2002. Print.
    ①   ②   ③   ④   ⑤   ⑥

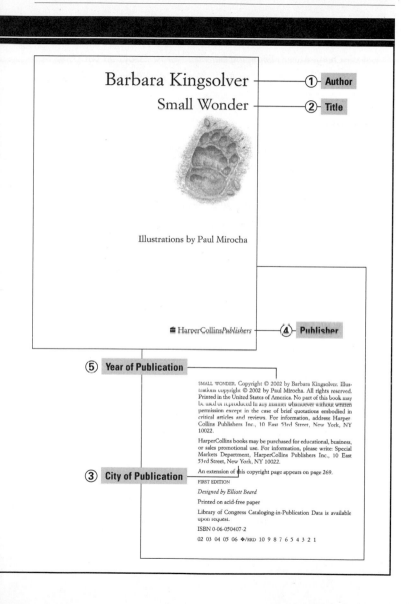

Barbara Kingsolver — (1)- **Author**

Small Wonder — (2)- **Title**

Illustrations by Paul Mirocha

≡ HarperCollins*Publishers* — (4)- **Publisher**

(5) **Year of Publication**

(3) **City of Publication**

8. EDITOR, NO AUTHOR NAMED

Wall, Cheryl A., ed. *Changing Our Own Words: Essays on Criticism,
    Theory, and Writing by Black Women*. New Brunswick: Rutgers
    UP, 1989. Print.

9. ANTHOLOGY

Cite an entire anthology the same way you would cite a book
with an editor and no named author (see model 8).

Walker, Dale L., ed. *Westward: A Fictional History of the American
    West*. New York: Forge, 2003. Print.

10. WORK IN AN ANTHOLOGY OR CHAPTER IN A BOOK WITH AN EDITOR

List the author(s) of the selection or chapter; its title, in quotation marks; the title of the book, italicized; *Ed.* and the name(s) of the
editor(s); publication information; and the selection's page numbers.

Komunyakaa, Yusef. "Facing It." *The Seagull Reader*. Ed. Joseph
    Kelly. New York: Norton, 2000. 126-27. Print.

Note: Use the following format to provide original publication information for a reprinted selection:

Byatt, A. S. "The Thing in the Forest." *New Yorker* 3 June 2002:
    80-89. Rpt. in *The O. Henry Prize Stories 2003*. Ed. Laura
    Furman. New York: Anchor, 2003. 3-22. Print.

11. TWO OR MORE ITEMS FROM THE SAME ANTHOLOGY

List the anthology as one entry (see model 9). Also list each selection separately with a cross-reference to the anthology.

Estleman, Loren D. "Big Tim Magoon and the Wild West." Walker
    391-404.

Salzer, Susan K. "Miss Libbie Tells All." Walker 199-212.

12. TRANSLATION

Bolaño, Robert. *2666*. Trans. Natasha Wimmer. New York: Farrar,
    2008. Print.

13. BOOK WITH BOTH TRANSLATOR AND EDITOR

List the editor's and translator's names after the title, in the
order they appear on the title page.

Kant, Immanuel. *"Toward Perpetual Peace" and Other Writings on
    Politics, Peace, and History*. Ed. Pauline Kleingeld. Trans. David
    L. Colclasure. New Haven: Yale UP, 2006. Print.

14. TRANSLATION OF A SECTION OF A BOOK

If different translators have worked on various parts of the book,
identify the translator of the part you are citing.

García Lorca, Federico. "The Little Mad Boy." Trans. W. S. Merwin.
    The Selected Poems of Federico García Lorca. Ed. Francisco García
    Lorca and Donald M. Allen. London: Penguin, 1969. Print.

15. TRANSLATION OF A BOOK BY AN UNKNOWN AUTHOR

Grettir's Saga. Trans. Denton Fox and Hermann Palsson. Toronto:
    U of Toronto P, 1974. Print.

16. BOOK IN A LANGUAGE OTHER THAN ENGLISH

Include a translation of the title in brackets, if necessary.

Benedetti, Mario. *La borra del café [The Coffee Grind]*. Buenos Aires:
    Sudamericana, 2000. Print.

17. GRAPHIC NARRATIVE

If the words and images are created by the same person, cite a graphic narrative just as you would a book (model 6).

Bechdel, Alison. *Fun Home: A Family Tragicomic*. New York: Houghton, 2006. Print.

If the work is a collaboration, indicate the author or illustrator who is most important to your research before the title of the work. List other contributors after the title, in the order of their appearance on the title page. Label each person's contribution to the work.

Stavans, Ilan, writer. *Latino USA: A Cartoon History*. Illus. Lalo Arcaraz. New York: Basic, 2000. Print.

18. EDITION OTHER THAN THE FIRST

Walker, John A. *Art in the Age of Mass Media*. 3rd ed. London: Pluto, 2001. Print.

19. ONE VOLUME OF A MULTIVOLUME WORK

Give the number of the volume cited after the title. Including the total number of volumes after the publication date is optional.

Ch'oe, Yong-Ho, Peter Lee, and William Theodore De Barry, eds. *Sources of Korean Tradition*. Vol. 2. New York: Columbia UP, 2000. Print. 2 vols.

20. TWO OR MORE VOLUMES OF A MULTIVOLUME WORK

Ch'oe, Yong-Ho, Peter Lee, and William Theodore De Barry, eds. *Sources of Korean Tradition*. 2 vols. New York: Columbia UP, 2000. Print.

21. PREFACE, FOREWORD, INTRODUCTION, OR AFTERWORD

After the writer's name, describe the contribution. After the title, indicate the book's author (with *By*) or editor (with *Ed.*).

Atwan, Robert. Foreword. *The Best American Essays 2002*. Ed.
Stephen Jay Gould. Boston: Houghton, 2002. viii-xii. Print.

22. ENTRY IN A REFERENCE BOOK

For a well-known encyclopedia, note the edition (if identified) and year of publication. If the entries are alphabetized, omit publication information and page number.

Judge, Erica. "Foreign-Language Daily Newspapers in New York City."
The Encyclopedia of New York City. Ed. Kenneth T. Jackson. New
Haven: Yale UP, 1995. Print.

Kettering, Alison McNeil. "Art Nouveau." *World Book Encyclopedia*.
2002 ed. Print.

23. BOOK THAT IS PART OF A SERIES

Cite the series name (and number, if any) from the title page.

Nichanian, Marc, and Vartan Matiossian, eds. *Yeghishe Charents:*
Poet of the Revolution. Costa Mesa: Mazda, 2003. Print.
Armenian Studies Ser. 5.

24. REPUBLICATION (MODERN EDITION OF AN OLDER BOOK)

Indicate the original publication date after the title.

Austen, Jane. *Sense and Sensibility*. 1813. New York: Dover, 1996.
Print.

25. PUBLISHER'S IMPRINT

If the title page gives a publisher's imprint, hyphenate the imprint and the publisher's name.

> Hornby, Nick. *About a Boy*. New York: Riverhead-Penguin Putnam, 1998. Print.

26. BOOK WITH A TITLE WITHIN THE TITLE

Do not italicize a book title within a title. For an article title within a title, italicize as usual and place the article title in quotation marks.

> Mullaney, Julie. *Arundhati Roy's* The God of Small Things: *A Reader's Guide*. New York: Continuum, 2002. Print.

> Rhynes, Martha. *"I, Too, Sing America": The Story of Langston Hughes*. Greensboro: Morgan, 2002. Print.

27. SACRED TEXT

To cite individual published editions of sacred books, begin the entry with the title. If you are not citing a particular edition, do not include sacred texts in the list of works cited.

> *Qur'an: The Final Testament (Authorized English Version) with Arabic Text*. Trans. Rashad Khalifa. Fremont: Universal Unity, 2000. Print.

Print Periodicals

Begin with the author name(s). (See models 1–5.) Then include the article title, the title of the periodical, the date or volume information, and the page numbers. The source map on pp. 90–92 shows where to find this information in a sample periodical.

28. ARTICLE IN A JOURNAL

Follow the journal title with the volume number, a period, the issue number (if given), and the year (in parentheses).

Gigante, Denise. "The Monster in the Rainbow: Keats and the
Science of Life." *PMLA* 117.3 (2002): 433-48. Print.

29. ARTICLE IN A MAGAZINE

Provide the date from the magazine cover instead of volume or
issue numbers.

Surowiecki, James. "The Stimulus Strategy." *New Yorker* 25 Feb.
2008: 29. Print.

Taubin, Amy. "All Talk?" *Film Comment* Nov.-Dec. 2007: 45-47. Print.

30. ARTICLE IN A NEWSPAPER

Include the edition (if listed) and the section number or letter (if
listed).

Bernstein, Nina. "On Lucille Avenue, the Immigration Debate." *New
York Times* 26 June 2006, late ed.: A1+. Print.

Note: For locally published newspapers, add the city in brackets after
the name if it is not part of the name: *Globe and Mail [Toronto]*.

31. ARTICLE THAT SKIPS PAGES

When an article skips pages, give only the first page number and
a plus sign.

Tyrnauer, Matthew. "Empire by Martha." *Vanity Fair* Sept. 2002:
364+. Print.

32. EDITORIAL OR LETTER TO THE EDITOR

Include the writer's name, if given, and the title, if any, followed
by a label for the work.

"California Dreaming." Editorial. *Nation* 25 Feb. 2008: 4. Print.

MLA SOURCE MAP: Citing articles in print periodicals

① **Author.** List the last name first. End with a period. For variations, see models 2–5.

② **Article title.** Put the title and any subtitle in quotation marks; capitalize all major words. Place a period inside the closing quotation mark.

③ **Periodical title.** Italicize the title; capitalize all major words. Omit any initial *A, An,* or *The.*

④ **Volume and issue / Date of publication.** For journals, give the volume number and issue number (if any), separated by a period; then list the year in parentheses and follow it with a colon. For magazines, list the day (if given), month, and year.

⑤ **Page numbers.** List inclusive page numbers. If the article skips pages, give the first page number and a plus sign. End with a period.

⑥ **Medium.** Give the medium (*Print*). End with a period.

A citation for the journal article on p. 91 would look like this:

   ①   ②   ③   ④

Marcoplos, Lucas. "Drafting Away from It All." *Southern Cultures* 12.1 (2006):

    33-41. Print.
     ⑤   ⑥

A citation for the magazine article on p. 92 would look like this:

   ①   ②

Quart, Alissa. "Lost Media, Found Media: Snapshots from the Future of Writing."

    Columbia Journalism Review May/June 2008: 30-34. Print.
            ③   ④   ⑤   ⑥

④ Publication Information   ③ Periodical Title

Southern cultures
SPRING 2006

Julian Bond finds a bullet
hole. Judy Garland throws

② Article Title

ESSAY

Drafting Away from It All

by Lucas Marcoplos   ① Author

*Author Lucas Marcoplos fit just about every other stereotype of white southern identity,
and felt duty-bound to journey into the world of NASCAR—like these veteran fans at
the Nashville Superspeedway. All photographs courtesy of Douglas Conway.*

⑤ Page Numbers

COLUMBIA
JOURNALISM REVIEW ③ Periodical Title

May / June 2008 • cjr.org ④ Date of Publication

The Futur...
Writi...

Nonfiction's disqui...
ALISSA QUART

Kindle isn't it, but ...
EZRA KLEIN

UNDER THE SHI...
A reporter recalls ...
that got him throu...
CAMERON MCWHIRT...

LOVE THY NEIGH...
The religion beat it...
TIM TOWNSEND

② Article Title

Lost Media, Found Media

Snapshots from the future of writing

BY ALISSA QUART

① Author

If there were an ashram for people who worship contemplative long-form journalism, it would be the Nieman Conference on Narrative Journalism. This March, at the Sheraton Boston Hotel, hundreds of journalists, authors, students, and aspirants came for the weekend event. Seated on metal chairs in large conference rooms, we learned about muscular storytelling (the Q-shaped narrative structure—who knew?). We sipped cups of coffee and ate bagels and heard about reporting history through letters and public documents and how to evoke empathy for our subjects, particularly our most marginal ones. As we listened to reporters discussing great feats—exposing Walter Reed's fetid living quarters for wounded soldiers, for instance—we also renewed our pride in our profession. In short, the conference exemplified the best of the older media models, the ones that have so recently fallen into economic turmoil.

Yet even at the weekend's strongest lectures on interview techniques or the long-form profile, we couldn't ignore the digital elephant in the room. We all knew as writers that the kinds of pieces we were discussing require months of work to be both deep and refined, and that we were all hard-pressed for the time and the money to do that. It was always hard for nonfiction writers, but something seems to have changed. For those of us who believed in the value of the journalism and literary nonfiction of the past, we had

become like the people at the ashram after the guru has died.

Right now, journalism is more or less divided into two camps, which I will call Lost Media and Found Media. I went to the Nieman conference partially because I wanted to see how the forces creating this new division are affecting and afflicting the Lost Media world that I love best, not on the institutional level, but for reporters and writers themselves. This world includes people who write for all the newspapers and magazines that are currently struggling with layoffs, speedups, hiring freezes, buyouts, the death or shrinkage of film- and book-review sections, limits on expensive investigative work, the erasure of foreign bureaus, and the general narrowing of institutional ambition. It includes freelance writers competing with hordes of ever-younger competitors willing to write and publish online for free, the fade-out of established journalistic career paths, and, perhaps most crucially, a muddled sense of the meritorious, as blogs level and scramble the value and status of print publications, and of professional writers. The glamour and influence once associated with a magazine elite seem to have faded, becoming a sort of pasticche of winsome articles about yearning and boxers and dinners at Elaine's.

Found Media-ites, meanwhile, are the bloggers, the contributors to Huffington Post-type sites that aggregate blogs, as well as other work that somebody else paid for, and the new nonprofits and pay-per-article schemes that aim to save journalism from 20 percent profit-margin demands. Although these elements are often disparate, together they compose the new media landscape. In economic terms, I mean all the outlets for nonfiction writing that seem to be thriving in the new era or striving to fill niches that Lost Media is giving up in a new order. Stylistically, Found Media tends to feel spontaneous, almost accidental. It's a domain dominated by the young, where writers get points not for following traditions or burnishing them but for amateur and hybrid vigor, for creating their own venues and their own genres. It is about public expression and community—not quite John Dewey's Great Community, which the critic Eric Alterman alluded to in a recent *New Yorker* article on newspapers, but rather a fractured form of Dewey's ideal: call it Great Communities.

To be a Found Media journalist or pundit, one need not be elite, expert, or trained; one must simply produce punchy intellectual property that is in conversation with groups of

Illustration by Tomer Hanuka

⑤ Page Numbers

Galbraith, James K. "JFK's Plans to Withdraw." Letter. *New York Review of Books* 6 Dec. 2007: 77-78. Print.

33. REVIEW

Franklin, Nancy. "Teen Spirit." Rev. of *Glee,* by Ryan Murphy, Brad Falchuk, and Ian Brennan. *New Yorker* 10 May 2010: 72-73. Print.

34. UNSIGNED ARTICLE

"Performance of the Week." *Time* 6 Oct. 2003: 18. Print.

Electronic Sources

Electronic sources such as Web sites differ from print sources in the ease with which they can be — and frequently are — changed, updated, or even eliminated. In addition, the various electronic media do not organize their works the same way. The most commonly cited electronic sources are documents from Web sites and databases. The entry for an electronic source may include up to six basic elements.

- *Author.* For variations on author, see models 1–5.
- *Title.* Italicize the titles of books or entire sites. Put shorter titles in quotation marks. Capitalize all important words.
- *Print publication information.* For an online book or journal article from a database that provides information about the work's publication in print, include the volume and issue number with the year in parentheses, then a colon and the inclusive page numbers, or *n. pag.* if no page numbers are listed. (For articles taken from online newspapers and magazines, however, omit the print publication information.)
- *Electronic publication information.* For a work from a Web site, including online magazines and newspapers, list all of the following that you can find: the title of the site, italicized; the site's editor(s), if given, preceded by *Ed.*; and the name of any sponsor. (The sponsor's name usually appears at the bottom of the home page.) Then add the date of electronic publication or latest update. For a work from

a database such as InfoTrac or LexisNexis, give the name of the database, italicized.

- *Medium of publication.* List the medium (*Web*).
- *Date of access.* Give the most recent date you accessed the source.

The *MLA Handbook* does not usually require a URL. If you think your readers will have difficulty finding the source without one, put it after the period following the date of access, enclosed in angle brackets. Put a period after the closing bracket.

35. WORK FROM A DATABASE

The basic format for citing a work from a database appears on pp. 96–97.

For a periodical article that you access in an online database, including a work you find in a library subscription service such as Academic Search Premier, begin with the author's name (if given); the title of the work, in quotation marks; and publication information for the print version of the work (see models 28–34). Include the page numbers from the print version; if no page numbers are available, use *n. pag.* Then give the name of the online database, italicized; the medium (*Web*); and your most recent date of access.

> Collins, Ross F. "Cattle Barons and Ink Slingers: How Cow Country
> Journalists Created a Great American Myth." *American
> Journalism* 24.3 (2007): 7-29. *Communication and Mass Media
> Complete.* Web. 7 Feb. 2010.

36. ARTICLE IN AN ONLINE JOURNAL

Cite an online journal article as you would a print journal article (see model 28). If an online article does not have page numbers, use *n. pag.* End with the medium consulted (*Web*) and the date of access.

> Gallagher, Brian. "Greta Garbo Is Sad: Some Historical Reflections
> on the Paradoxes of Stardom in the American Film Industry,

1910-1960." *Images: A Journal of Film and Popular Culture* 3 (1997): n. pag. Web. 7 Aug. 2009.

37. ARTICLE IN AN ONLINE MAGAZINE

See model 29 for print publication information if the article also appears in print. After the name of the magazine, give the sponsor of the Web site, followed by a comma and the date of publication. Then give the medium (*Web*), and the date of access.

Shapiro, Walter. "The Quest for Universal Healthcare." *Salon*. Salon Media Group, 21 Feb. 2008. Web. 2 Mar. 2008.

38. ARTICLE IN AN ONLINE NEWSPAPER

After the name of the newspaper, give the publisher, publication date, medium (*Web*), and access date.

Bustillo, Miguel, and Carol J. Williams. "Old Guard in Cuba Keeps Reins." *Los Angeles Times*. Los Angeles Times, 25 Feb. 2008. Web. 26 Feb. 2010.

39. ONLINE BOOK

Provide information as for a print book (see models 6–27), then give the electronic publication information, the medium, and the date of access.

Euripides. *The Trojan Women*. Trans. Gilbert Murray. New York: Oxford UP, 1915. *Internet Sacred Text Archive*. Web. 12 Oct. 2010.

Note: Cite a part of an online book as you would a part of a print book (see models 10 and 21). Give the print (if any) and electronic publication information, the medium (*Web*), and the date of access.

Riis, Jacob. "The Genesis of the Gang." *The Battle with the Slum*. New York: Macmillan, 1902. *Bartleby.com: Great Books Online*. 2000. Web. 31 Mar. 2010.

MLA SOURCE MAP: Citing articles from databases

Library subscriptions—such as EBSCOhost and Academic Search Premier—provide access to huge databases of articles.

(1) **Author.** List the last name first.

(2) **Article title.** Enclose the title and any subtitle in quotation marks.

(3) **Periodical title.** Italicize it. Exclude any initial *A, An,* or *The.*

(4) **Print publication information.** List the volume and issue number, if any; the date of publication, including the day (if given), month, and year, in that order; and the inclusive page numbers. If an article has no page numbers, write *n. pag.*

(5) **Database name.** Italicize the name of the database.

(6) **Medium.** For an online database, use *Web.*

(7) **Date of access.** Give the day, month, and year, then a period.

A citation for the article on p. 97 would look like this:

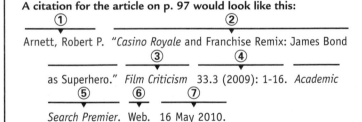

Arnett, Robert P. "*Casino Royale* and Franchise Remix: James Bond as Superhero." *Film Criticism* 33.3 (2009): 1-16. *Academic Search Premier*. Web. 16 May 2010.

③ **Periodical Title**

② **Article Title**

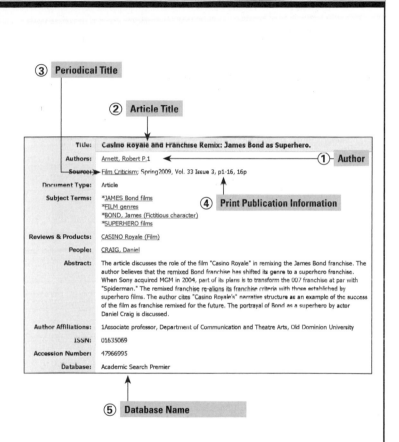

Title:	Casino Royale and Franchise Remix: James Bond as Superhero.
Authors:	Arnett, Robert P.1 ◄——————————————— ①— **Author**
Source: ►	Film Criticism; Spring2009, Vol. 33 Issue 3, p1-16, 16p
Document Type:	Article
Subject Terms:	*JAMES Bond films ④ **Print Publication Information**
	*FILM genres
	*BOND, James (Fictitious character)
	*SUPERHERO films
Reviews & Products:	CASINO Royale (Film)
People:	CRAIG, Daniel
Abstract:	The article discusses the role of the film "Casino Royale" in remixing the James Bond franchise. The author believes that the remixed Bond franchise has shifted its genre to a superhero franchise. When Sony acquired MGM in 2004, part of its plans is to transform the 007 franchise at par with "Spiderman." The remixed franchise re-aligns its franchise criteria with those established by superhero films. The author cites "Casino Royale's" narrative structure as an example of the success of the film as franchise remixed for the future. The portrayal of Bond as a superhero by actor Daniel Craig is discussed.
Author Affiliations:	1Associate professor, Department of Communication and Theatre Arts, Old Dominion University
ISSN:	01635069
Accession Number:	47966995
Database:	Academic Search Premier

⑤ **Database Name**

40. ONLINE POEM

Include the poet's name, the title of the poem, and the print publication information (if any). End with the electronic publication information, the medium (*Web*), and the date of access.

> Dickinson, Emily. "The Grass." *Poems: Emily Dickinson*. Boston,
>   1891. U of Michigan. *Humanities Text Initiative: American
>   Verse Project*. Web. 6 Jan. 2006.

41. ONLINE EDITORIAL OR LETTER

Include the word *Editorial* or *Letter* after the author (if given) and title (if any). End with the periodical name, the sponsor of the Web site, the date of electronic publication, the medium, and the access date.

> "The Funding Gap." Editorial. *Washington Post*. Washington Post, 5
>   Nov. 2003. Web. 19 Oct. 2009.

> Moore, Paula. "Go Vegetarian." Letter. *New York Times*. New
>   York Times, 25 Feb. 2008. Web. 25 Feb. 2010.

42. ONLINE REVIEW

Cite an online review as you would a print review (see model 33). End with the name of the Web site, the sponsor, the date of electronic publication, the medium, and the date of access.

> O'Hehir, Andrew. "Parity or Party?" Rev. of *Iron Man 2*, dir. Jon
>   Favreau. *Salon*. Salon Media Group, 7 May 2010. Web. 24
>   May 2010.

43. ENTRY IN AN ONLINE REFERENCE WORK

Cite the entry as you would an entry from a print reference work (see model 22). Follow with the name of the Web site, the sponsor, date of publication, medium, and date of access.

"Tour de France." *Encyclopaedia Britannica Online*. Encyclopaedia
    Britannica, 2006. Web. 21 May 2006.

44. WORK FROM A WEB SITE

For basic information on citing a work from a Web site, see pp.
100–101. Include all of the following elements that are available: the
author; the title of the document, in quotation marks; the name of
the Web site, italicized; the name of the publisher or sponsor (if none
is available, use *N.p.*); the date of publication (if not available, use
n.d.); the medium consulted (*Web*), and the date of access.

"America: A Center-Left Nation." *Media Matters for America*.
    Media Matters for America, 27 May 2009. Web. 31 May 2009.

Stauder, Ellen Keck. "Darkness Audible: Negative Capability
    and Mark Doty's 'Nocturne in Black and Gold.'" *Romantic
    Circles Praxis Series*. U of Maryland, 2003. Web. 28 Sept.
    2003.

45. ENTIRE WEB SITE

Follow the guidelines for a specific work from the Web, beginning with the name of the author, editor, compiler, or director (if
any), followed by the title of the Web site, italicized; the name of the
sponsor or publisher (if none, use *N p*); the date of publication or last
update; the medium of publication (*Web*); and the date of access.

Bernstein, Charles, Kenneth Goldsmith, Martin Spinelli, and Patrick
    Durgin, eds. *Electronic Poetry Corner*. SUNY Buffalo, 2003. Web.
    26 Sept. 2006.

Weather.com. Weather Channel Interactive, 2010. Web. 13 Mar.
    2010.

For a personal Web site, include the name of the person who created
the site; the title in quotation marks if it is part of a larger work or

MLA SOURCE MAP: Citing works from Web sites

You may need to browse other parts of a site to find some of the following elements, and some sites may omit elements. Uncover as much information as you can.

1. **Author.** List the last name first, followed by a comma, the first name, and the middle initial (if given). End with a period. If no author is given, begin with the title.

2. **Title of work.** Enclose the title and any subtitle of the work in quotation marks.

3. **Title of Web site.** Give the title of the entire Web site, italicized.

4. **Publisher or sponsor.** Look for the sponsor's name at the bottom of the home page. If no information is available, write *N.p.* Follow it with a comma.

5. **Date of publication or latest update.** Give the most recent date, followed by a period. If no date is available, use *n.d.*

6. **Medium.** Use *Web* and follow it with a period.

7. **Date of access.** Give the date you accessed the work. End with a period.

A citation for the work on p. 101 would look like this:

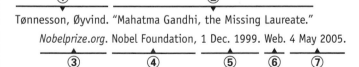

Tønnesson, Øyvind. "Mahatma Gandhi, the Missing Laureate."

Nobelprize.org. Nobel Foundation, 1 Dec. 1999. Web. 4 May 2005.

① **Author**

② **Title of Work**

③ **Title of Web Site**

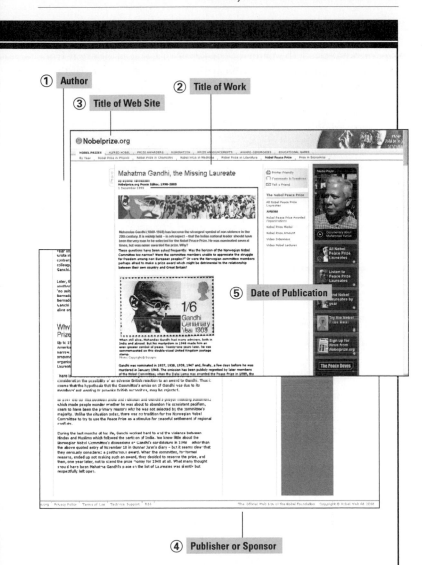

⑤ **Date of Publication**

④ **Publisher or Sponsor**

italicized if it is not, or (if there is no title) a description such as *Home page*, not italicized; the name of the larger site, if it is different from the personal site's title; the publisher or sponsor of the site (if none, use *N.p.*); the date of the last update; the medium of publication (*Web*); and the date of access.

> Ede, Lisa. Home page. *Oregon State*. Oregon State U, 2010. Web.
>
> 17 May 2010.

46. ACADEMIC COURSE OR DEPARTMENT WEB SITE

For a course site, include the name of the instructor, the title of the course in quotation marks, the title of the site in italics, the department (if relevant) and institution sponsoring the site, the medium consulted (*Web*), and the access information.

> Creekmur, Corey K., and Philip Lutgendorf. "Topics in Asian
>
> Cinema: Popular Hindi Cinema." *University of Iowa*. Depts.
>
> of English, Cinema, and Comparative Literature, U of Iowa.
>
> Web. 13 Mar. 2007.

For a department Web site, give the department name, the description *Dept. home page,* the institution (in italics), the site sponsor, the medium (*Web*), and the access information.

> English Dept. home page. *Amherst College,* n.d. Web. 5 Apr. 2006.

47. BLOG

For an entire blog, give the author's name; the title of the blog, italicized; the sponsor or publisher of the blog (if there is none, use *N.p.*); the date of the most recent update; the medium (*Web*); and the date of access.

> *Little Green Footballs*. Little Green Footballs, 5 Mar. 2010. Web.
>
> 5 Mar. 2010.

Note: To cite a blogger who writes under a pseudonym, begin with the pseudonym, then put the writer's real name (if you know it) in square brackets.

> Atrios [Duncan Black]. *Eschaton*. N.p., 27 June 2010. Web.
>
> > 27 June 2010.

48. POST OR COMMENT ON A BLOG

Give the author's name; the title of the post or comment, in quotation marks (if there is no title, use the description *Web log post* or *Web log comment*, not italicized); the title of the blog, italicized; the sponsor of the blog (if there is none, use *N.p.*); the date of the most recent update; the medium (*Web*); and the date of access.

> Marcotte, Amanda. "Rights without Perfection." *Pandagon*. N.p.,
>
> > 16 May 2010. Web. 16 May 2010.

49. ENTRY IN A WIKI

Because wiki content is collectively edited, do not include an author. Treat a wiki as you would a work from a Web site (see model 44). Include the title of the entry; the name of the wiki, italicized; the sponsor or publisher of the wiki (use *N.p.* if there is no sponsor); the date of the latest update; the medium (*Web*); and the date of access. Check with your instructor before using a wiki as a source.

> "Fédération Internationale de Football Association." *Wikipedia*.
>
> > Wikimedia Foundation, 27 June 2010. Web. 27 June 2010.

50. POSTING TO A DISCUSSION GROUP OR NEWSGROUP

Begin with the author's name and the title of the posting in quotation marks (or the words *Online posting*). Follow with the name of the Web site, the sponsor or publisher of the site (use *N.p.* if there is no sponsor), the date of publication, the medium (*Web*), and the date of access.

> Daly, Catherine. "Poetry Slams." *Poetics Discussion List*. SUNY
>   Buffalo, 29 Aug. 2003. Web. 1 Oct. 2003.

51. POSTING TO A SOCIAL NETWORKING SITE

To cite a message or posting on Facebook or another social networking site, include the writer's name, a description of the posting that mentions the recipient, the date it was written, and the medium of delivery. (The MLA does not provide guidelines for citing postings or messages on such sites; this model is based on the MLA's guidelines for citing email.)

> Ferguson, Sarah. Message to the author. 6 Mar. 2008. Facebook
>   message.

52. EMAIL

Include the writer's name; the subject line, in quotation marks; *Message to* (not italicized or in quotation marks) followed by the recipient's name; the date of the message; and the medium of delivery (*E-mail*). (MLA style hyphenates *e-mail*.)

> Harris, Jay. "Thoughts on Impromptu Stage Productions." Message to
>   the author. 16 July 2006. E-mail.

53. COMPUTER SOFTWARE OR ONLINE GAME

Include the author name (if given); the title, italicized; the version number (if given); the publisher or sponsor; and the publication date (or *n.d.* if no date is given). End with the medium and the date of access.

> *Web Cache Illuminator*. Vers. 4.02. NorthStar Solutions, n.d. Web.
>   12 Nov. 2003.

54. CD-ROM OR DVD-ROM

Include the medium.

Cambridge Advanced Learner's Dictionary. 3rd ed. Cambridge: Cambridge UP, 2008. CD-ROM.

Grand Theft Auto: San Andreas. New York: Rockstar Games, 2004. DVD-ROM.

Video and Audio Sources (Including Online Versions)

55. FILM OR DVD

If you cite a particular person's work, start with that name. If not, start with the title; then name the director, distributor, and year of release. Other contributors, such as writers or performers, may follow the director. If you cite a DVD instead of a theatrical release, include the original film release date and the label *DVD*. For material found on a Web site, give the name of the site or database, the medium (*Web*), and access date.

Spirited Away. Dir. Hayao Miyazaki. 2001. Walt Disney Video, 2003. DVD.

The Hurt Locker. Dir. Kathryn Bigelow. Perf. Jeremy Renner. Summit Entertainment, 2009. Film.

56. ONLINE VIDEO CLIP

Cite an online video as you would a work from a Web site (model 44).

Weber, Jan. "As We Sow, Part 1: Where Are the Farmers?" *YouTube*. YouTube, 15 Mar. 2008. Web. 27 Sept. 2010.

57. TELEVISION OR RADIO PROGRAM

In general, begin with the title of the program, italicized. Then list important contributors (narrator, writer, director, actors); the network; the local station and city, if any; the broadcast date; and the medium. To cite a particular person's work, begin with that name. To cite a particular episode from a series, begin with the episode title, in quotation marks.

The American Experience: Buffalo Bill. Writ., dir., prod. Rob Rapley.
PBS. WNET, New York, 25 Feb. 2008. Television.

"The Fleshy Part of the Thigh." *The Sopranos*. Writ. Diane Frolov and
Andrew Schneider. Dir. Alan Taylor. HBO. 2 Apr. 2006. Television.

Note: For a streaming version online, give the name of the Web site,
italicized. Then give the publisher or sponsor, a comma, and the date
posted. End with the medium (*Web*) and the access date. (For downloaded versions, see models 64–65.)

Komando, Kim. "E-mail Hacking and the Law." *CBSRadio.com*. CBS
Radio, 28 Oct. 2003. Web. 11 Nov. 2003.

58. BROADCAST INTERVIEW

List the person interviewed and then the title, if any. If the interview has no title, use the label *Interview* and name the interviewer, if
relevant. Then identify the source. To cite a broadcast interview, end
with information about the program, the date(s) the interview took
place, and the medium.

Revkin, Andrew. Interview with Terry Gross. *Fresh Air*. Natl. Public
Radio. WNYC, New York, 14 June 2006. Radio.

Note: If you listened to an archived version online, provide the site's
sponsor (if known), the date of the interview, the medium (*Web*), and
the access date. For a podcast interview, see model 64.

Revkin, Andrew. Interview with Terry Gross. *Fresh Air*. *NPR.org*. NPR,
14 June 2006. Web. 12 Jan. 2009.

59. UNPUBLISHED OR PERSONAL INTERVIEW

List the person interviewed; the label *Telephone interview*, *Personal
interview*, or *E-mail interview*; and the date the interview took place.

Freedman, Sasha. Personal interview. 10 Nov. 2006.

60. SOUND RECORDING

List the name of the person or group you wish to emphasize (such as the composer, conductor, or band); the title of the recording or composition; the artist, if appropriate; the manufacturer; and the year of issue. Give the medium (such as *CD, MP3 file*, or *LP*). If you are citing a particular song or selection, include its title, in quotation marks, before the title of the recording.

Bach, Johann Sebastian. *Bach: Violin Concertos*. Perf. Itzhak Perlman

and Pinchas Zukerman. English Chamber Orch. EMI, 2002. CD.

Sonic Youth. "Incinerate." *Rather Ripped*. Geffen, 2006. MP3 file.

Note: If you are citing instrumental music that is identified only by form, number, and key, do not underline, italicize, or enclose it in quotation marks.

Grieg, Edvard. Concerto in A minor, op. 16. Cond. Eugene Ormandy.

Philadelphia Orch. RCA, 1989. LP.

61. MUSICAL COMPOSITION

When you are not citing a specific published version, first give the composer's name, followed by the title.

Mozart, Wolfgang Amadeus. *Don Giovanni*, K527.

Mozart, Wolfgang Amadeus. Symphony no. 41 in C major, K551.

Note: Cite a published score as you would a book. If you include the date the composition was written, do so immediately after the title.

Schoenberg, Arnold. *Chamber Symphony No. 1 for 15 Solo*

Instruments, Op. 9. 1906. New York: Dover, 2002. Print.

62. LECTURE OR SPEECH

List the speaker; title, in quotation marks; sponsoring institution or group; place; and date. If the speech is untitled, use a label such as *Lecture*.

Colbert, Stephen. Speech. White House Correspondents' Association
Dinner. *YouTube*. YouTube, 29 Apr. 2006. Web. 20 May 2010.

Eugenides, Jeffrey. Portland Arts and Lectures. Arlene Schnitzer
Concert Hall, Portland, OR. 30 Sept. 2003. Lecture.

63. LIVE PERFORMANCE

List the title, appropriate names (such as writer or performer),
the place, and the date. To cite a particular person's work, begin the
entry with that name.

Anything Goes. By Cole Porter. Perf. Klea Blackhurst. Shubert
Theater, New Haven. 7 Oct. 2003. Performance.

64. PODCAST

Include all of the following that are relevant and available: the
speaker, the title of the podcast, the title of the program, the host
or performers, the title of the site, the site's sponsor, the date of
posting, the medium (such as *MP3* file or *Web*), and the access date.
(This model is based on MLA guidelines for a short work from a
Web site.)

"Seven Arrested in U.S. Terror Raid." *Morning Report*. Host Krishnan
Guru-Murthy. *4 Radio*. Channel 4 News, 23 June 2006. MP3 file.
27 June 2006.

65. DIGITAL FILE

A citation for a file that you can download — one that exists
independently, not only on a Web site — begins with citation information required for the type of source (photograph, sound recording, etc.). For the medium, indicate the type of file (*MP3 file*, *JPEG
file*, etc.).

Officers' Winter Quarters, Army of Potomac, Brandy Station. Mar.
1864. Prints and Photographs Div., Lib. of Cong. TIFF file.

"Return to the Giant Pool of Money." *This American Life*. Narr. Ira
Glass. NPR, 25 Sept. 2009. MP3 file.

66. WORK OF ART OR PHOTOGRAPH

List the artist or photographer; the work's title, italicized; the
date of composition (if unknown, use *n.d.*); and the medium of composition (*Oil on canvas, Bronze*). Then cite the name of the museum
or other location and the city. To cite a reproduction in a book, add
the publication information. To cite artwork found online, omit the
medium of composition, and after the location, add the title of the
database or Web site, italicized; the medium consulted (*Web*); and
the date of access.

Chagall, Marc. *The Poet with the Birds*. 1911. Minneapolis Inst. of
Arts. *artsmia.org*. Web. 6 Oct. 2003.

General William Palmer in Old Age. 1810. Oil on canvas. National
Army Museum, London. *White Mughals: Love and Betrayal in
Eighteenth-Century India*. William Dalrymple. New York:
Penguin, 2002. 270. Print.

Kahlo, Frida. *Self-Portrait with Cropped Hair*. 1940. Oil on canvas.
Museum of Mod. Art, New York.

67. MAP OR CHART

Cite a map or chart as you would a book or a short work within
a longer work and include the word *Map* or *Chart* after the title. Add
the medium of publication. For an online source, end with the date
of access.

"Australia." Map. *Perry-Castaneda Library Map Collection*. U of Texas,
1999. Web. 4 Nov. 2003.

California. Map. Chicago: Rand, 2002. Print.

68. CARTOON OR COMIC STRIP

List the artist's name; the title (if any) of the cartoon or comic
strip, in quotation marks; the label *Cartoon* or *Comic strip*; and the
usual publication information for a print periodical (see models
28–34) or a work from a Web site (model 44).

Johnston, Lynn. "For Better or Worse." Comic strip. *FBorFW.com*.
Lynn Johnston Publications, 30 June 2006. Web. 20 July 2006.

Lewis, Eric. "The Unpublished Freud." Cartoon. *New Yorker*
11 Mar. 2002: 80. Print.

69. ADVERTISEMENT

Include the label *Advertisement* after the name of the item or organization being advertised.

Microsoft. Advertisement. *Harper's* Oct. 2003: 2-3. Print.

Microsoft. Advertisement. *New York Times*. New York Times, 11 Nov.
2003. Web. 11 Nov. 2003.

Other Sources (Including Online Versions)

If an online version is not shown here, use the appropriate model
for the source and then end with the medium and date of access.

70. REPORT OR PAMPHLET

Follow the guidelines for a print book (models 6–27) or an online
book (model 39).

Allen, Katherine, and Lee Rainie. *Parents Online*. Washington: Pew
    Internet and Amer. Life Project, 2002. Print.

Environmental Working Group. *Dead in the Water*. Washington:
    Environmental Working Group, 2006. Web. 24 Apr. 2010.

71. GOVERNMENT PUBLICATION

Begin with the author, if identified. Otherwise, start with the
name of the government, followed by the agency. For congressional
documents, cite the number, session, and house of Congress (*S* for
Senate, *H* for House of Representatives); the type (*Report, Resolution,
Document*) in abbreviated form; and the number. End with the publication information. The print publisher is often the Government
Printing Office (GPO). For online versions, follow the models for a
work from a Web site (model 44) or an entire Web site (model 45).

Gregg, Judd. *Report to Accompany the Genetic Information Act of
    2003*. US 108th Cong., 1st sess. S. Rept. 108-22. Washington:
    GPO, 2003. Print.

Kinsella, Kevin, and Victoria Velkoff. *An Aging World: 2001*. US
    Bureau of the Census. Washington: GPO, 2001. Print.

United States. Environmental Protection Agency. Office of
    Emergency and Remedial Response. *This Is Superfund*. Jan.
    2000. *Environmental Protection Agency*. Web. 16 Aug. 2002.

72. PUBLISHED PROCEEDINGS OF A CONFERENCE

Cite proceedings as you would a book.

Cleary, John, and Gary Gurtler, eds. *Proceedings of the Boston Area
    Colloquium in Ancient Philosophy 2002*. Boston: Brill Academic,
    2003. Print.

73. DISSERTATION

Enclose the title in quotation marks. Add the label *Diss.*, the school, and the year the work was accepted.

> Paris, Django. "Our Culture: Difference, Division, and Unity in
>   Multicultural Youth Space." Diss. Stanford U, 2008. Print.

Note: Cite a published dissertation as a book, adding the identification *Diss.* and the university after the title.

74. DISSERTATION ABSTRACT

Cite as you would an unpublished dissertation (see model 73). For the abstract of a dissertation using *Dissertation Abstracts International (DAI)*, include the *DAI* volume, year, and page number.

> Huang-Tiller, Gillian C. "The Power of the Meta-Genre: Cultural,
>   Sexual, and Racial Politics of the American Modernist Sonnet."
>   Diss. U of Notre Dame, 2000. *DAI* 61 (2000): 1401. Print.

75. PUBLISHED INTERVIEW

List the person interviewed; the title of the interview (if any) or the label *Interview*; and the interviewer's name, if relevant. Then identify the source.

> Paretsky, Sarah. Interview. *Progressive*. Progressive Magazine, 14
>   Jan. 2008. Web. 12 Feb. 2010.

> Taylor, Max. "Max Taylor on Winning." *Time* 13 Nov. 2000: 66. Print.

76. UNPUBLISHED LETTER

Cite a published letter as a work in an anthology (see model 10). If the letter is unpublished, follow this form:

> Anzaldúa, Gloria. Letter to the author. 10 Sept. 2002. MS.

77. MANUSCRIPT OR OTHER UNPUBLISHED WORK

List the author's name; the title (if any) or a description of the material; the form of the material (such as *MS* for manuscript; *TS* for typescript) and any identifying numbers; and the name and location of the library or research institution housing the material, if applicable.

> Woolf, Virginia. "The Searchlight." N.d. TS. Ser. III, Box 4, Item 184.
>
> Papers of Virginia Woolf, 1902-1956. Smith Coll., Northampton.

78. LEGAL SOURCE

To cite a court case, give the names of the first plaintiff and defendant, the case number, the name of the court, and the date of the decision. To cite an act, give the name of the act followed by its Public Law (*Pub. L.*) number, the date the act was enacted, and its Statutes at Large (*Stat.*) cataloging number.

> Eldred v. Ashcroft. No. 01-618. Supreme Ct. of the US. 15 Jan. 2003.
>
> Print.

> Museum and Library Services Act of 2003. Pub. L. 108-81. 25 Sept.
>
> 2003. Stat. 117.991. Print.

Note: You do not need an entry on the list of works cited when you cite articles of the U.S. Constitution and laws in the U.S. Code.

A Student Research Essay, MLA Style

Student Writer

David Craig

On the following pages is an essay by David Craig that conforms to the MLA guidelines described in this chapter. Note that the essay has been reproduced in a narrow format to allow for annotation.

Craig 1

David Craig

Professor Turkman

English 219

8 December 2009

Texting and Messaging: The Language of Youth Literacy

The English language is under attack. At least, that is
what many people seem to believe. From concerned parents
to local librarians, everyone seems to have a negative
comment on the state of youth literacy today. They fear
that the current generation of grade school students will
graduate with an extremely low level of literacy, and they
point out that although language education hasn't changed,
kids are having more trouble reading and writing than in
the past. When asked about the cause of this situation,
many adults pin the blame on technologies such as texting
and instant messaging, arguing that electronic shortcuts
create and compound undesirable reading and writing
habits and discourage students from learning conventionally
correct ways to use language. But although the arguments
against messaging are passionate, evidence suggests that
they may not hold up.

The disagreements about messaging shortcuts are
profound, even among academics. John Briggs, an English
professor at the University of California, Riverside, says,

Name, instructor, course, date aligned at left

Title centered

Opens with attention-getting statement

Background on the problem of youth literacy

Thesis statement

Craig 2

"Americans have always been informal, but now the
informality of precollege culture is so ubiquitous that many
students have no practice in using language in any formal
setting at all" (qtd. in McCarroll). Such objections are
not new; Sven Birkerts of Mount Holyoke College argued
in 1999 that "[students] read more casually. They strip-
mine what they read" online and consequently produce
"quickly generated, casual prose" (qtd. in Leibowitz A67).
However, academics are also among the defenders of texting
and instant messaging (IM), with some suggesting that
messaging may be a beneficial force in the development
of youth literacy because it promotes regular contact
with words and the use of a written medium for
communication.

Instant messaging allows two individuals who are
separated by any distance to engage in real-time, written
communication. Although messaging relies on the
written word, many messagers disregard standard writing
conventions. For example, here is a snippet from an IM
conversation between two teenage girls:[1]

[1] This transcript of an IM conversation was collected
on 20 Nov. 2009. The teenagers' names are concealed to
protect privacy.

Quotation used as evidence

Definition and example of messaging

Explanatory note

Craig 3

Teen One: sorry im talkinto like 10 ppl at a time

Teen Two: u izzyful person

Teen Two: kwel

Teen One: hey i g2g

As this brief conversation shows, participants must use words to communicate via IMing, but their words do not have to be in standard English.

Writer considers argument that youth literacy is in decline

Figure explained in text and cited in parenthetical reference

Discussion of Figure 1

Regardless of one's views on messaging, the issue of youth literacy does demand attention because standardized test scores for language assessments, such as the verbal section of the College Board's SAT, have declined in recent years. This trend is illustrated in a chart distributed by the College Board as part of its 2002 analysis of aggregate SAT data (see Fig. 1).

The trend lines, which I added to the original chart, illustrate a significant pattern that may lead to the conclusion that youth literacy is on the decline. These lines display the seven-year paths (from 1995 to 2002) of math and verbal scores, respectively. Within this time period, the average SAT math score jumped more than ten points. The average verbal score, however, actually dropped a few points — and appears to be headed toward a further decline in the future. Corroborating this evidence is a report from the United States Department of Education's National Center for Education

Craig 4

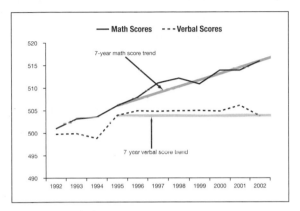

Fig. 1. Comparison of SAT math and verbal scores (1992–2002). Trend lines added. Source: Kristin Carnahan and Chiara Coletti, *Ten-Year Trend in SAT Scores Indicates Increased Emphasis on Math Is Yielding Results; Reading and Writing Are Causes for Concern* (New York: College Board, 2002; print; 9).

Figure labeled, titled, and credited to source; inserted at appropriate point in text

Statistics. According to this agency's study, the percentage of twelfth graders whose writing ability was "at or above the basic level" of performance dropped from 78 to 74 percent between 1998 and 2002 (Persky, Daane, and Jin 21).

Government source cited for statistical evidence

Based on the preceding statistics, parents and educators appear to be right about the decline in youth literacy. And this trend is occurring while electronic communication is

Writer acknowledges part of critics' argument; transition to next point

on the rise. According to the Pew Internet & American
Life Project, 81 percent of those aged 15-17 regularly
send text messages (Lenhart, Madden, Macgill, and Smith

Statistical evidence cited

21). In 2001, the most conservative estimate based on
Pew numbers showed that American youths spent, at a
minimum, nearly three million hours per day on instant
messaging services (Lenhart and Lewis 20). These numbers
hold steady today, and they may even be expanding thanks
to popular Web 2.0 sites — such as Facebook — that
incorporate chat functions. What's more, young messagers
seem to be using a new vocabulary.

Writer's field research introduced

In the interest of establishing the existence of a
messaging language, I analyzed 11,341 lines of text
from IM conversations between youths in my target
demographic: U.S. residents aged twelve to seventeen.
Young messagers voluntarily sent me chat logs, but they
were unaware of the exact nature of my research. Once
all of the logs had been gathered, I went through them,
recording the number of times messaging language was
used in place of conventional words and phrases. Then I
generated graphs to display how often these replacements
were used.

During the course of my study, I identified four types
of messaging language: phonetic replacements, acronyms,

abbreviations, and inanities. An example of phonetic replacement is using *ur* for *you are*. Another popular type of messaging language is the acronym; for a majority of the people in my study, the most common acronym was *lol*, a construction that means *laughing out loud*. Abbreviations are also common in messaging, but I discovered that typical IM abbreviations, such as *etc.*, are not new to the English language. Finally, I found a class of words that I call "inanities." These words include completely new words or expressions, combinations of several slang categories, or simply nonsensical variations of other words. My favorite from this category is *lolz*, an inanity that translates directly to *lol* yet includes a terminating *z* for no obvious reason.

In the chat transcripts that I analyzed, the best display of typical messaging lingo came from the conversations between two thirteen-year-old Texan girls, who are avid IM users. Figure 2 is a graph showing how often they used certain phonetic replacements and abbreviations. On the *y*-axis, frequency of replacement is plotted, a calculation that compares the number of times a word or phrase is used in messaging language with the total number of times that it is communicated in any form. On the *x*-axis, specific messaging words and phrases are listed.

Findings of field research presented

Figure introduced and explained

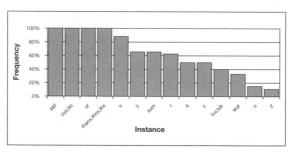

Figure labeled
and titled

Fig. 2. Usage of phonetic replacements and abbreviations in
messaging.

Discussion
of findings
presented
in Fig. 2

My research shows that the Texan girls use the first
ten phonetic replacements or abbreviations at least 50
percent of the time in their normal messaging writing.
For example, every time one of them writes *see*, there is
a parallel time when *c* is used in its place. In light of this
finding, it appears that the popular messaging culture
contains at least some elements of its own language. It
also seems that much of this language is new: no formal
dictionary yet identifies the most common messaging words
and phrases. Only in the heyday of the telegraph or on the
rolls of a stenographer would you find a similar situation,
but these "languages" were never a popular medium of
youth communication. Instant messaging, however, is very

Craig 8

popular among young people and continues to generate
attention and debate in academic circles.

My research shows that messaging is certainly wide-
spread, and it does seem to have its own particular vocabulary, **Writer returns to opposition argument**
yet these two factors alone do not mean it has a damaging
influence on youth literacy. As noted earlier, however, some
people claim that the new technology is a threat to the **Signal verb introduces quotation**
English language, as revealed in the following passage:

> Abbreviations commonly used in online instant
> messages are creeping into formal essays that
> students write for credit, said Debbie Frost, who **Block quotation for a quotation more than four lines long**
> teaches language arts and social studies to sixth-
> graders. . . . "You would be shocked at the writing I
> see. It's pretty scary. I don't get cohesive thoughts,
> I don't get sentences, they don't capitalize, and they
> have a lot of misspellings and bad grammar," she
> said. "With all those glaring mistakes, it's hard to see
> the content." ("Young Messagers") **Parenthetical reference uses brief title, author unknown**

Echoing Frost's concerns is Melanie Weaver, a professor at
Alvernia College, who taught a tenth-grade English class
as an intern. In an interview with the *New York Times*, she
said, "[When t]hey would be trying to make a point in a
paper, they would put a smiley face in the end [☺]. . . .
If they were presenting an argument and they needed to

Craig 9

present an opposite view, they would put a frown [☹]"
(qtd. in Lee).

Transition to
support of
thesis and
refutation of
critics

The critics of messaging are numerous. But if we
look to the field of linguistics, a central concept —
metalinguistics — challenges these criticisms and leads
to a more reasonable conclusion — that messaging has
no negative impact on a student's development of or
proficiency with traditional literacy.

Scholars of metalinguistics offer support for the claim
that messaging is not damaging to those who use it. As
noted earlier, one of the most prominent components of
messaging language is phonetic replacement, in which a
word such as *everyone* becomes *every1*. This type of wordplay
has a special importance in the development of an advanced
literacy, and for good reason. According to David Crystal,
an internationally recognized scholar of linguistics at the

Linguistic
authority cited
in support of
thesis

University of Wales, as young children develop and learn
how words string together to express ideas, they go through
many phases of language play. The singsong rhymes and
nonsensical chants of preschoolers are vital to their learning
language, and a healthy appetite for such wordplay leads to a
better command of language later in life (182).

As justification for his view of the connection between
language play and advanced literacy, Crystal presents an

Craig 10

argument for metalinguistic awareness. According to
Crystal, *metalinguistics* refers to the ability to "step back"
and use words to analyze how language works:

> If we are good at stepping back, at thinking in a more
> abstract way about what we hear and what we say,
> then we are more likely to be good at acquiring those
> skills which depend on just such a stepping back
> in order to be successful—and this means, chiefly,
> reading and writing. . . . [T]he greater our ability to
> play with language, . . . the more advanced will be
> our command of language as a whole. (Crystal 181)

If we accept the findings of linguists such as Crystal
that metalinguistic awareness leads to increased literacy,
then it seems reasonable to argue that the phonetic
language of messaging can also lead to increased metalinguistic awareness and, therefore, increases in overall
literacy. As instant messagers develop proficiency with a
variety of phonetic replacements and other types of IM
words, they should increase their subconscious knowledge
of metalinguistics.

Metalinguistics also involves our ability to write in a
variety of distinct styles and tones. Yet in the debate over
messaging and literacy, many critics assume that either
messaging or academic literacy will eventually win out

Ellipses and brackets indicate omissions and changes in quotation

Writer links Crystal's views to thesis

Another refutation of critics' assumptions

Craig 11

in a person and that the two modes cannot exist side by side. This assumption is, however, false. Human beings ordinarily develop a large range of language abilities, from the formal to the relaxed and from the mainstream to the subcultural. Mark Twain, for example, had an understanding of local speech that he employed when writing dialogue for *Huckleberry Finn*. Yet few people would argue that Twain's knowledge of this form of English had a negative impact on his ability to write in standard English.

However, just as Mark Twain used dialects carefully in dialogue, writers must pay careful attention to the kind of language they use in any setting. The owner of the language Web site *The Discouraging Word*, who is an anonymous English literature graduate student at the University of Chicago, backs up this idea in an e-mail to me:

> What is necessary, we feel, is that students learn how to shift between different styles of writing — that, in other words, the abbreviations and shortcuts of messaging should be used online . . . but that they should not be used in an essay submitted to a teacher. . . . Messaging might even be considered . . . a different way of reading and writing, one that requires specific and unique skills shared by certain communities.

Example from well-known work of literature used as support

Email correspondence cited in support of claim

Craig 12

The analytical ability that is necessary for writers to choose an appropriate tone and style in their writing is, of course, metalinguistic in nature because it involves the comparison of two or more language systems. Thus, youths who grasp multiple languages will have a greater natural understanding of metalinguistics. More specifically, young people who possess both messaging and traditional skills stand to be better off than their peers who have been trained only in traditional or conventional systems. Far from being hurt by their online pastime, instant messagers can be aided in standard writing by their experience with messaging language.

Writer synthe-
sizes evidence
for claim

The fact remains, however, that youth literacy seems to be declining. What, if not messaging, is the main cause of this phenomenon? According to the College Board, which collects data on several questions from its test takers, enrollment in English composition and grammar classes has decreased in the last decade by 14 percent (Carnahan and Coletti 11). The possibility of messaging causing a decline in literacy seems inadequate when statistics on English education for US youths provide other evidence of the possible causes. Simply put, schools in the United States are not teaching English as much as they used to. Rather than blaming texting and messaging language alone for the

Transition to
final point

Alternate
explanation
for decline
in literacy

Craig 13

decline in literacy and test scores, we must also look toward our schools' lack of focus on the teaching of standard English skills.

My findings indicate that the use of messaging poses virtually no threat to the development or maintenance of formal language skills among American youths aged twelve to seventeen. Diverse language skills tend to increase a person's metalinguistic awareness and, thereby, his or her ability to use language effectively to achieve a desired purpose in a particular situation. The current decline in youth literacy is not due to the rise of texting and messaging. Rather, fewer young students seem to be receiving an adequate education in the use of conventional English. Unfortunately, it may always be fashionable to blame new tools for old problems, but in the case of messaging, that blame is not warranted. Although messaging may expose literacy problems, it does not create them.

Transition to conclusion

Concluding paragraph sums up argument and reiterates thesis

Craig 14

Works Cited

Carnahan, Kristin, and Chiara Coletti. *Ten-Year Trend in
    SAT Scores Indicates Increased Emphasis on Math
    Is Yielding Results: Reading and Writing Are Causes
    for Concern*. New York: College Board, 2002.
    Print.

Crystal, David. *Language Play*. Chicago: U of Chicago P,
    1998. Print.

The Discouraging Word. "Re: Messaging and Literacy." E-mail
    to the author. 13 Nov. 2009. E-mail.

Lee, Jennifer 8. "I Think, Therefore IM." *New York Times*.
    New York Times, 19 Sept. 2002. Web. 14 Nov. 2009.

Leibowitz, Wendy R. "Technology Transforms Writing and
    the Teaching of Writing." *Chronicle of Higher Education*
    26 Nov. 1999: A67-68. Print.

Lenhart, Amanda, and Oliver Lewis. *Teenage Life Online:
    The Rise of the Instant-Message Generation and the
    Internet's Impact on Friendships and Family Relation-
    ships*. Washington: Pew Internet & Amer. Life Project,
    2001. Print.

Lenhart, Amanda, Mary Madden, Alexandra Rankin Macgill,
    and Aaron Smith. *Teens and Social Media*. Washington:
    Pew Internet & Amer. Life Project, 2007. Web. 8 Oct.
    2009.

Heading
centered

Report

Book

Email

Online news-
paper article

Article in a
newspaper

Works-cited
entries
double-spaced

First line of
each entry
flush with
left margin;
subsequent
lines indented

Craig 15

McCarroll, Christina. "Teens Ready to Prove Text-Messaging
      Skills Can Score SAT Points." *Christian Science Monitor*
      11 Mar. 2005. Web. 12 Nov. 2009.

Persky, Hilary R., Mary C. Daane, and Ying Jin. *The Nation's
      Report Card: Writing 2002*. NCES 2003-529. Washington:
      GPO, 2003. Print.

"Young Messagers Ask: Why Spell It Out?" *Columbus
      Dispatch* 10 Nov. 2002: C1. *LexisNexis Academic*. Web.
      14 Nov. 2009.

Government
document

Article from
an online
database

Chicago Style

The Sixteenth Edition of *The Chicago Manual of Style,* published in 2010, provides a complete guide to the system of documentation known as *Chicago* style, which has long been used in history and some other fields in the humanities, as well as in publishing.

For further reference, consult *The Chicago Manual* or a volume intended specifically for student writers, Kate L. Turabian's *A Manual for Writers of Research Papers, Theses, and Dissertations,* Seventh Edition (2007).

Formatting *Chicago* Manuscripts

Chicago offers general guidelines for formatting a paper, but it does not specifically discuss student-paper formats. Your instructor may have other requirements, so check before preparing your final draft.

- *Title page.* Center the full title of your paper, your name, the course name, the instructor's name, and the date submitted. Do not type a number on this page, but do count it; consequently, number the first page of text as page 2.

- *Margins and spacing.* Leave one-inch margins at the top, bottom, and sides of pages. Double-space the body of the text, including block quotations. Unless your instructor requests double-spacing throughout, single-space the notes and bibliographic entries, but double-space between entries.

- *Page numbers.* Number all pages (except the title page) in the upper right-hand corner. You may use a short title or your name before page numbers.

- *Long quotations.* Indent long quotations one-half inch from the left margin, and do not use quotation marks. In general, *Chicago* defines a long quotation as ten or more lines, though you may decide to set off shorter quotations for emphasis.

- *Headings.* *Chicago* style allows, but does not require, headings. Many students and instructors find them helpful.

• *Visuals.* Visuals (photographs, drawings, charts, graphs, and tables) should be placed as near as possible to the relevant text. Tables should be labeled *Table*, numbered, and captioned. All other visuals should be labeled *Figure* (abbreviated *Fig.*), numbered, and captioned. Remember to refer to each visual in your text, explaining how it contributes to the point(s) you are making.

Chicago Style for In-Text Citations, Notes, and Bibliography

In *Chicago* style, use superscript numbers ([1]) to mark citations in the text. Sequentially numbered citations throughout the text correspond to notes that contain either publication information about the source cited or explanatory or supplemental material not included in the main text. Place the superscript number for each note near the cited material—at the end of the relevant quotation, sentence, clause, or phrase. Type the number after any punctuation mark except the dash, and leave no space between the superscript and the preceding letter or punctuation mark. When you use signal phrases to introduce quotations or other source material, note that *Chicago* style requires you to use the present tense (*citing Bebout's studies, Meier points out*).

The notes themselves can be footnotes (each typed at the bottom of the page on which the superscript for it appears in the text) or endnotes (all typed on a separate page at the end of the text under the heading *Notes*). Be sure to check your instructor's preference. The first line of each note is indented like a paragraph (one-half inch) and begins with a number followed by a period, one space, and the first word. All remaining lines of the entry are typed flush with the left margin. Footnotes and endnotes should be single-spaced, with a double space between notes, unless your instructor prefers that the notes also be double-spaced.

IN THE TEXT

Sweig argues that Castro and Che Guevara were not the only key players in the Cuban Revolution of the late 1950s.[19]

IN THE FIRST NOTE

19. Julia Sweig, *Inside the Cuban Revolution* (Cambridge, MA: Harvard University Press, 2002), 9.

After giving complete information the first time you cite a work, shorten any additional references to that work: list only the author's last name followed by a comma, a shortened version of the title, a comma, and the page number. If the reference is to the same source cited in the previous note, you can use the Latin abbreviation *Ibid.* (for "in the same place") instead of the name and title.

IN FIRST AND SUBSEQUENT NOTES

19. Julia Sweig, *Inside the Cuban Revolution* (Cambridge, MA: Harvard University Press, 2002), 9.

20. Ibid., 13.

21. Ferguson, "Comfort of Being Sad," 63.

22. Sweig, *Cuban Revolution,* 21.

The alphabetical list of the sources in your paper is usually titled *Bibliography* in *Chicago* style. You may instead use the title *Sources Consulted, Works Cited,* or *Selected Bibliography* if it better describes your list.

In the bibliographic entry for a source, include the same information as in the first note for that source, but omit the specific page reference. However, give the *first* author's last name first, followed by a comma and the first name; separate the main elements of the entry with periods rather than commas; and do not enclose the publication information for books in parentheses. Type the first line flush with the left margin, and indent the subsequent lines of each one-half inch.

IN THE BIBLIOGRAPHY

Sweig, Julia. *Inside the Cuban Revolution.* Cambridge, MA: Harvard University Press, 2002.

Start the bibliography on a separate page after the main text and any endnotes. Continue the consecutive numbering of pages. Center the title *Bibliography* (without underlining, italics, or quotation marks) one inch below the top of the page. List sources alphabetically by authors' last names or, if an author is unknown, by the first major word in the title. The *Chicago Manual of Style* recommends single-spacing the entries and double-spacing between entries, but some instructors may prefer that you double-space the entire list.

DIRECTORY TO *CHICAGO* STYLE

PRINT AND ONLINE BOOKS

(Continued)

Chicago Style for Notes and Bibliographic Entries

The following examples demonstrate how to format both notes and bibliographic entries according to *Chicago* style. The note, which is numbered, appears first; the bibliographic entry, which is not numbered, appears below the note.

Print and Online Books

For the basic format for citing a book in *Chicago* style, see pp. 136–37. The note for a book typically includes four elements: the author's name, the title and subtitle, the publication information, and the page number(s) to which the note refers. The bibliographic entry for a book usually includes the first three of these elements, but they are styled somewhat differently: commas separate major elements of a note, but a bibliographic entry uses periods.

1. ONE AUTHOR

1. Nell Irvin Painter, *The History of White People* (New York: W. W. Norton, 2010), 119.

Painter, Nell Irvin. *The History of White People*. New York: W. W. Norton, 2010.

2. MULTIPLE AUTHORS

2. Margaret Macmillan and Richard Holbrooke, *Paris 1919: Six Months That Changed the World* (New York: Random House, 2003), 384.

Macmillan, Margaret, and Richard Holbrooke. *Paris 1919: Six Months That Changed the World*. New York: Random House, 2003.

When there are more than three authors, you may give the first-listed author followed by *et al.* in the note. In the bibliography, however, list all the authors' names.

2. Stephen J. Blank et al., *Conflict, Culture, and History: Regional Dimensions* (Miami: University Press of the Pacific, 2002), 276.

Blank, Stephen J., Lawrence E. Grinter, Karl P. Magyar, Lewis B. Ware, and Bynum E. Weathers. *Conflict, Culture, and History: Regional Dimensions*. Miami: University Press of the Pacific, 2002.

3. ORGANIZATION AS AUTHOR

3. World Intellectual Property Organization, *Intellectual Property Profile of the Least Developed Countries* (Geneva: World Intellectual Property Organization, 2002), 43.

World Intellectual Property Organization. *Intellectual Property Profile of the Least Developed Countries*. Geneva: World Intellectual Property Organization, 2002.

4. UNKNOWN AUTHOR

4. *Broad Stripes and Bright Stars* (Kansas City, MO: Andrews McMeel, 2002), 10.

Broad Stripes and Bright Stars. Kansas City, MO: Andrews McMeel, 2002.

5. ONLINE BOOK

5. Dorothy Richardson, *Long Day: The Story of a New York Working Girl, as Told by Herself* (1906; UMDL Texts, 2010),159, http://quod.lib.umich.edu/cgi/t/text/text-idx?c=moa;idno=AFS7156 .0001.001.

Richardson, Dorothy. *Long Day: The Story of a New York Working Girl, as Told by Herself*. 1906. UMDL Texts, 2010. http://quod. lib.umich.edu/cgi/t/text/text-idx?c=moa;idno=AFS7156.0001 .001.

6. ELECTRONIC BOOK (E-BOOK)

6. Manal M. Omar, *Barefoot in Baghdad* (Naperville, IL. Sourcebooks, 2010), Kindle edition, ch. 4.

Omar, Manal M. *Barefoot in Baghdad*. Naperville, IL: Sourcebooks, 2010. Kindle edition.

7. EDITED BOOK WITH NO AUTHOR

7. James H. Fetzer, ed., *The Great Zapruder Film Hoax: Deceit and Deception in the Death of JFK* (Chicago: Open Court, 2003), 56.

Fetzer, James H., ed. *The Great Zapruder Film Hoax: Deceit and Deception in the Death of JFK*. Chicago: Open Court, 2003.

CHICAGO **SOURCE MAP: Citing books**

Take information from the book's title page and copyright page (on the reverse side of the title page), not from the book's cover or a library catalog. Look carefully at the differences in punctuation between the note and the bibliographic entry.

① **Author.** In a note, list author first name first. In a bibliographic entry, list the first author last name first. List other authors first name first.

② **Title.** Italicize the title and subtitle and capitalize all major words.

③ **City of publication.** List the city (and country or state abbreviation for an unfamiliar city) followed by a colon. In a note only, city, publisher, and year appear in parentheses.

④ **Publisher.** Drop *Inc.*, *Co.*, *Publishing*, or *Publishers*. Follow with a comma.

⑤ **Publication year.** In a note, follow the year with the relevant page number. End with a period.

Citations for the book on p. 137 would look like this:

Endnote

    1. Louis Menand, *The Metaphysical Club* (New York: Farrar, Straus and Giroux, 2001), 178.

Bibliographic entry

Menand, Louis. *The Metaphysical Club*. New York: Farrar, Straus and Giroux, 2001.

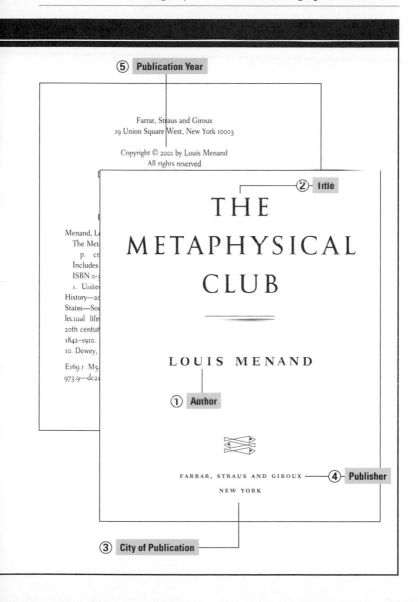

⑤ **Publication Year**

Farrar, Straus and Giroux
19 Union Square West, New York 10003

Copyright © 2001 by Louis Menand
All rights reserved

② **Title**

THE
METAPHYSICAL
CLUB

Menand, L
The Met
p. cr
Includes
ISBN 0-
1. Unite
History—2
States—Soc
lectual life
20th centur
1842–1910.
10. Dewey,

E169.1 .M5
973.9—dc21

LOUIS MENAND

① **Author**

FARRAR, STRAUS AND GIROUX ④ **Publisher**
NEW YORK

③ **City of Publication**

8. EDITED BOOK WITH AUTHOR

8. Leopold von Ranke, *The Theory and Practice of History*, ed. Georg G. Iggers (New York: Routledge, 2010), 135.

von Ranke, Leopold. *The Theory and Practice of History*. Edited by Georg G. Iggers. New York: Routledge, 2010.

9. SELECTION IN AN ANTHOLOGY OR CHAPTER IN A BOOK, WITH AN EDITOR

9. Denise Little, "Born in Blood," in *Alternate Gettysburgs*, ed. Brian Thomsen and Martin H. Greenberg (New York: Berkley Publishing Group, 2002), 245.

Give the inclusive page numbers of the selection or chapter in the bibliographic entry.

Little, Denise. "Born in Blood." In *Alternate Gettysburgs*, edited by Brian Thomsen and Martin H. Greenberg, 242–55. New York: Berkley Publishing Group, 2002.

10. INTRODUCTION, PREFACE, FOREWORD, OR AFTERWORD

10. Robert B. Reich, introduction to *Making Work Pay: America after Welfare*, ed. Robert Kuttner (New York: New Press, 2002), xvi.

Reich, Robert B. Introduction to *Making Work Pay: America after Welfare*, vii–xvii. Edited by Robert Kuttner. New York: New Press, 2002.

11. TRANSLATION

11. Suetonius, *The Twelve Caesars*, trans. Robert Graves (London: Penguin Classics, 1989), 202.

Suetonius. *The Twelve Caesars*. Translated by Robert Graves. London: Penguin Classics, 1989.

12. EDITION OTHER THAN THE FIRST

12. Dee Brown, *Bury My Heart at Wounded Knee: An Indian History of the American West,* 4th ed. (New York: Owl Books, 2007), 12.

Brown, Dee. *Bury My Heart at Wounded Knee: An Indian History of the American West,* 4th ed. New York: Owl Books, 2007.

13. MULTIVOLUME WORK

13. John Watson, *Annals of Philadelphia and Pennsylvania in the Olden Time,* vol. 2 (Washington, DC: Ross & Perry, 2003), 514.

Watson, John. *Annals of Philadelphia and Pennsylvania in the Olden Time*. Vol. 2. Washington, DC: Ross & Perry, 2003.

14. REFERENCE WORK

In a note, use *s.v.,* the abbreviation for the Latin *sub verbo* ("under the word") to help your reader find the entry

14. *Encyclopaedia Britannica,* s.v. "carpetbagger."

Do not list reference works such as encyclopedias or dictionaries in your bibliography.

15. WORK WITH A TITLE WITHIN THE TITLE

Use quotation marks around any title within a book title.

15. John A. Alford, *A Companion to "Piers Plowman"* (Berkeley: University of California Press, 1988), 195.

Alford, John A. *A Companion to "Piers Plowman."* Berkeley: University of California Press, 1988.

16. SACRED TEXT

16. Luke 18:24–25 (New International Version).

16. Qur'an 7:40–41.

Do not include a sacred text in the bibliography.

17. SOURCE QUOTED IN ANOTHER SOURCE

Identify both the original and the secondary source.

17. Frank D. Millet, "The Filipino Leaders," *Harper's Weekly*, March 11, 1899, quoted in Richard Slotkin, *Gunfighter Nation: The Myth of the Frontier in Twentieth-Century America* (New York: HarperCollins, 1992), 110.

Millet, Frank D. "The Filipino Leaders." *Harper's Weekly*, March 11, 1899. Quoted in Richard Slotkin, *Gunfighter Nation: The Myth of the Frontier in Twentieth-Century America* (New York: HarperCollins, 1992), 110.

Print and Online Periodicals

The note for an article in a periodical typically includes the author's name, the article title, and the periodical title. The format for other information, including the volume and issue numbers (if any), the date of publication, and the page number(s) to which the note refers, varies according to the type of periodical and whether you consulted it in print, on the Web, or in a database. In a bibliographic entry for a journal or magazine article from a database or print periodical, also give the inclusive page numbers.

18. ARTICLE IN A PRINT JOURNAL

18. Karin Lützen, "The Female World: Viewed from Denmark," *Journal of Women's History* 12, no. 3 (2000): 36.

Lützen, Karin. "The Female World: Viewed from Denmark." *Journal of Women's History* 12, no. 3 (2000): 34–38.

19. ARTICLE IN AN ONLINE JOURNAL

Give the DOI if there is one. If not, include the article URL. If page numbers are provided, include them as well.

19. Jeffrey J. Schott, "America, Europe, and the New Trade Order," *Business and Politics* 11, no. 3 (2009), doi:10.2202/1469-3569.1263.

Schott, Jeffrey J. "America, Europe, and the New Trade Order." *Business and Politics* 11, no. 3 (2009). doi:10.2202/1469-3569.1263.

20. JOURNAL ARTICLE FROM A DATABASE

For basic information on citing a periodical article from a database in *Chicago* style, see the source map on pp. 144–45.

20. W. Trent Foley and Nicholas J. Higham, "Bede on the Britons," *Early Medieval Europe* 17, no. 2 (2009), 157, doi:10.1111/j.1468-0254.2009.00258.x.

Foley, W. Trent, and Nicholas J. Higham. "Bede on the Britons." *Early Medieval Europe* 17, no. 2 (2009). 154–85. doi:10.1111/j.1468-0254.2009.00258.x.

21. ARTICLE IN A PRINT MAGAZINE

21. Terry McDermott, "The Mastermind: Khalid Sheikh Mohammed and the Making of 9/11," *New Yorker*, September 13, 2010, 42.

McDermott, Terry. "The Mastermind: Khalid Sheikh Mohammed and the Making of 9/11." *New Yorker*, September 13, 2010, 38–51.

22. ARTICLE IN AN ONLINE MAGAZINE

22. Tracy Clark-Flory, "Educating Women Saves Kids' Lives," *Salon*, September 17, 2010, http://www.salon.com/life /broadsheet/2010/09/17/education_women/index.html.

Clark-Flory, Tracy. "Educating Women Saves Kids' Lives." *Salon*, September 17, 2010. http://www.salon.com/life /broadsheet/2010/09/17/education_women/index.html.

23. MAGAZINE ARTICLE FROM A DATABASE

23. Sami Yousafzai and Ron Moreau, "Twisting Arms in Afghanistan," *Newsweek*, November 9, 2009, 8, Academic Search Premier (44962900).

Yousafzai, Sami, and Ron Moreau. "Twisting Arms in Afghanistan." *Newsweek*, November 9, 2009. 8. Academic Search Premier (44962900).

24. ARTICLE IN A PRINT NEWSPAPER

Do not include page numbers for a newspaper article, but you may include the section, if any.

24. Caroline E. Mayer, "Wireless Industry to Adopt Voluntary Standards," *Washington Post,* September 9, 2003, sec. E.

Mayer, Caroline E. "Wireless Industry to Adopt Voluntary Standards." *Washington Post*, September 9, 2003, sec. E.

If you provide complete documentation of a newspaper article in a note, you may not need to include it in the bibliography. Check your instructor's preference.

25. ARTICLE IN AN ONLINE NEWSPAPER

If the URL for the article is very long, use the URL for the newspaper's home page.

25. Andrew C. Revkin, "Arctic Melt Unnerves the Experts," New York Times, October 2, 2007, http://www.nytimes.com/2007/10/02/science/earth/02arct.html.

Revkin, Andrew C. "Arctic Melt Unnerves the Experts." *New York Times*, October 2, 2007. http://www.nytimes.com/2007/10/02/science/earth/02arct.html.

26. NEWSPAPER ARTICLE FROM A DATABASE

26. Demetria Irwin, "A Hatchet, Not a Scalpel, for NYC Budget Cuts," *New York Amsterdam News*, November 13, 2008, Academic Search Premier (35778153).

Irwin, Demetria. "A Hatchet, Not a Scalpel, for NYC Budget Cuts." *New York Amsterdam News*, November 13, 2008. Academic Search Premier (35778153).

27. BOOK REVIEW

After the information about the book under review, give publication information for the appropriate kind of source (see models 10–26).

27. Arnold Relman, "Health Care: The Disquieting Truth," review of *Tracking Medicine: A Researcher's Quest to Understand Health Care*, by John E. Wennberg, *New York Review of Books* 57, no. 14 (2010), 45.

Relman, Arnold. "Health Care: The Disquieting Truth." Review of *Tracking Medicine: A Researcher's Quest to Understand Health Care*, by John E. Wennberg. *New York Review of Books* 57, no. 14 (2010), 45–48.

Online Sources

In general, include the author (if given); the title of a work from a Web site (in quotation marks); the name of the site (in italics, if the site is an online publication, but otherwise neither italicized nor in

CHICAGO SOURCE MAP: Citing articles from databases

① **Author.** In a note, list author first name first. In the bibliographic entry, list the first author last name first, comma, first name; list other authors first name first.

② **Article title.** Enclose title and subtitle (if any) in quotation marks, and capitalize major words. In the notes section, put a comma before and after the title. In the bibliography, put a period before and after.

③ **Periodical title.** Italicize the title and subtitle, and capitalize all major words. For a magazine or newspaper, follow with a comma.

④ **Journal volume and issue numbers.** For journals, follow the title with the volume number, a comma, the abbreviation *no.*, and the issue number.

⑤ **Publication date.** For journals, enclose the publication year in parentheses and follow with a comma (in a note) or with a period (in a bibliography). For other periodicals, give the month and year or month, day, and year, followed by a comma.

⑥ **Retrieval information.** Provide the article's DOI, if one is given. If not, give the name of the database and an accession number, or a "stable or persistent" URL for the article in the database. Because you provide stable retrieval information, you do not need to identify the electronic format of the work (i.e., PDF, as in the example shown here). End with a period.

Citations for the journal article on p. 145 would look like this:

Endnote

1. Howard Schuman, Barry Schwartz, and Hannah D'Arcy, "Elite Revisionists and Popular Beliefs: Christopher Columbus, Hero or Villain?" *Public Opinion Quarterly* 69, no. 1 (2005), doi:10.1093/poq/nfi001.

Bibliographic entry

Schuman, Howard, Barry Schwartz, and Hannah D'Arcy. "Elite Revisionists and Popular Beliefs: Christopher Columbus, Hero or Villain?" *Public Opinion Quarterly* 69, no. 1 (2005). doi:10.1093/poq/nfi001.

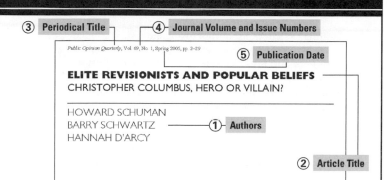

③ **Periodical Title**   ④ **Journal Volume and Issue Numbers**

Public Opinion Quarterly, Vol. 69, No. 1, Spring 2005, pp. 2–29

⑤ **Publication Date**

ELITE REVISIONISTS AND POPULAR BELIEFS
CHRISTOPHER COLUMBUS, HERO OR VILLAIN?

HOWARD SCHUMAN
BARRY SCHWARTZ
HANNAH D'ARCY

① **Authors**

② **Article Title**

Abstract   According to revisionist historians and American Indian activists, Christopher Columbus deserves condemnation for having brought slavery, disease, and death to America's indigenous peoples. We ask whether the general public's beliefs about Columbus show signs of reflecting these critical accounts, which increased markedly as the 1992 Quincentenary approached. Our national surveys, using several different question wordings, indicate that most Americans continue to admire Columbus because, as tradition puts it, "he discovered America," though only a small number of mainly older respondents speak of him in the heroic terms common in earlier years. At the same time, the percentage of Americans who reject traditional beliefs about Columbus is also small and is divided between those who simply acknowledge the priority of Indians as the "first Americans" and those who go further to view Columbus as a villain. The latter group of respondents, we find, show a critical stance toward modal American beliefs much more broadly.

We also analyze American history school textbooks for evidence of influence from revisionist writings, and we consider representations of Columbus in the mass media as well. Revisionist history can be seen as one consequence of the "minority rights revolution" that began after World War II and has achieved considerable success, but the endurance of Columbus's reputation—to a considerable extent even among the

⑥ **Retrieval Information**

HOWARD SCHUMAN is a research scientist and professor emeritus at the University of Michigan. BARRY SCHWARTZ is a professor emeritus at the University of Georgia. HANNAH D'ARCY is an independent statistical consultant who previously worked for the University of Michigan's Center for Statistical Consultation and Research. We thank Lawrence Bobo and Stanley Presser for stimulating us to do multiple validations, and we are grateful to the editor of *Public Opinion Quarterly* for recommendations that substantially improved our final presentation. In addition, we are much indebted for help during the course of the research to Virginia Hopcroft, Government Documents Librarian at Bowdoin College; Maria Krysan, University of Illinois at Chicago; Alyssa Miller, Evanston, Illinois; and Irina Poznansky, Departmental Librarian, Teachers College, Gottesman Libraries, Columbia University. Support for the research was drawn in part from a National Science Foundation grant (SES-0001844). Address correspondence to Howard Schuman; e-mail: hschuman@umich.edu.

doi:10.1093/poq/nfi001

CHICAGO SOURCE MAP: Citing works from Web sites

① **Author.** In a note, list author first name first. In a bibliographic entry, list the first author last name first, comma, first name; list additional authors first name first. Note that the host may serve as the author.

② **Document title.** Enclose the title in quotation marks, and capitalize all major words. In a note, put a comma before and after the title. In the bibliography, put a period before and after.

③ **Title of Web site.** Capitalize all major words. If the site's title is analogous to a book or periodical title, italicize it. In the notes section, put a comma after the title. In the bibliography, put a period after the title.

④ **Sponsor of site.** If the sponsor is the same as the author or site title, you may omit it. End with a comma (in the note) or a period (in the bibliography entry).

⑤ **Date of publication or last modification.** If no date is available, or if your instructor requests it, include your date of access (with the word *accessed*).

⑥ **Retrieval information.** Give the URL for the Web site. If you are required to include a date of access, put the word *accessed* and the date in parentheses after the URL. End with a period.

Citations for the Web site on p. 147 would look like this:

Endnote

1. Douglas Linder, "The Haymarket Riot Trial," *Famous Trials*, University of Missouri-Kansas City School of Law, 2006, http://www.law .umkc.edu/faculty/projects/FTrials/haymarket/haymarket.htm.

Bibliographic entry

Linder, Douglas.   "The Haymarket Riot Trial."   *Famous Trials*, University of

Missouri-Kansas City School of Law.   2006,   http://www.law.umkc.edu

/faculty/projects/FTrials/haymarket/haymarket.htm.

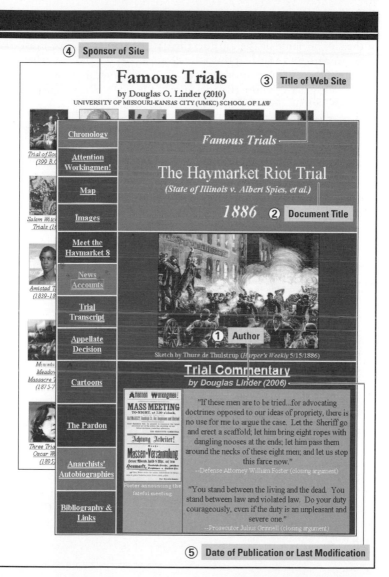

④ **Sponsor of Site**

Famous Trials
③ **Title of Web Site**

by Douglas O. Linder (2010)
UNIVERSITY OF MISSOURI-KANSAS CITY (UMKC) SCHOOL OF LAW

Famous Trials

Chronology

Attention
Workingmen!

Map

Images

Meet the
Haymarket 8

News
Accounts

Trial
Transcript

Appellate
Decision

Cartoons

The Pardon

Anarchists'
Autobiographies

Bibliography &
Links

The Haymarket Riot Trial
(State of Illinois v. Albert Spies, et al.)

1886 ② **Document Title**

① **Author**

Sketch by Thure de Thulstrup (*Harper's Weekly* 5/15/1886)

Trial Commentary
by Douglas Linder (2006)

Attention Workingmen!

MASS MEETING
TO-NIGHT, at 730 o'clock,
HAYMARKET, Randolph St., bet. Desplaines and Halsted

Achtung Arbeiter!

Massen-Versammlung
Heute Abend, halb 8 Uhr, auf dem

Foster announcing the fateful meeting

"If these men are to be tried...for advocating doctrines opposed to our ideas of propriety, there is no use for me to argue the case. Let the Sheriff go and erect a scaffold; let him bring eight ropes with dangling nooses at the ends; let him pass them around the necks of these eight men; and let us stop this farce now."
--Defense Attorney William Foster (closing argument)

"You stand between the living and the dead. You stand between law and violated law. Do your duty courageously, even if the duty is an unpleasant and severe one."
--Prosecutor Julius Grinnell (closing argument)

⑤ **Date of Publication or Last Modification**

quotation marks); the sponsor of the site, if different from the name of the site or name of the author; the date of publication or most recent update; and a URL. If the online source does not indicate when it was published or last modified, or if your instructor requests an access date, place it before the URL. For the basic format for citing a work from a Web site in *Chicago* style, see pp. 146–47.

28. WEB SITE

28. Rutgers School of Arts and Sciences, *The Rutgers Oral History Archive*, 2010, accessed September 17, 2010, http://oralhistory.rutgers.edu/.

Rutgers School of Arts and Sciences. *The Rutgers Oral History Archive*. 2010. Accessed September 17, 2010. http://oralhistory.rutgers.edu/.

29. WORK FROM A WEB SITE

29. Rose Cohen, "My First Job," *The Triangle Factory Fire*, Cornell University School of Industrial and Labor Relations, 2005, http://www.ilr.cornell.edu/trianglefire/texts/.

Cohen, Rose. "My First Job." *The Triangle Factory Fire*. Cornell University School of Industrial and Labor Relations. 2005. http://www.ilr.cornell.edu/trianglefire/texts/.

30. BLOG (WEB LOG) POST

Treat a blog post as a short work from a Web site (see model 29).

30. Jai Arjun Singh, "On the Road in the USSR," *Jabberwock* (blog), November 29, 2007, http://jaiarjun.blogspot.com/2007/11/on-road-in-ussr.html.

Chicago recommends that blog posts appear in the notes section only, not in the bibliography, unless the blog is cited frequently. Check your instructor's preference. A bibliography reference to an entire blog would look like this:

Singh, Jai Arjun. *Jabberwock* (blog). http://jaiarjun.blogspot.com/.

31. EMAIL AND OTHER PERSONAL COMMUNICATIONS

Cite email messages and other personal communications, such as letters and telephone calls, in the text or in a note only, not in the bibliography. (*Chicago* style recommends hyphenating *e-mail.*)

31. Kareem Adas, e-mail message to author, February 11, 2010.

32. PODCAST

Treat a podcast as a short work from a Web site (see model 29) and give as much of the following information as you can find: the author or speaker, the title or a description of the podcast, the title of the site, the site sponsor (if different from the author or site name), the type of podcast or file format, the date of posting or access, and the URL.

32. Barack Obama, "Weekly Address: A Solar Recovery," *The White House,* podcast video, July 3, 2010, http://www.whitehouse .gov/photos-and-video/video/weekly-address-a-solar-recovery.

Obama, Barack. "Weekly Address: A Solar Recovery." *The White House.* Podcast video. July 3, 2010. http://www.whitehouse .gov/photos-and-video/video/weekly-address-a-solar-recovery.

33. ONLINE AUDIO OR VIDEO

Treat an online audio or video source as a short work from a Web site (see model 29). If the source is downloadable, give the medium or file format before the URL (see model 32).

33. Alyssa Katz, "Did the Mortgage Crisis Kill the American Dream?" YouTube video, 4:32, posted by NYCRadio, June 24, 2009, http://www.youtube.com/watch?v=uivtwjwd_Qw.

Katz, Alyssa. "Did the Mortgage Crisis Kill the American Dream?" YouTube video, 4:32. Posted by NYCRadio. June 24, 2009. http://www.youtube.com/watch?v=uivtwjwd_Qw.

Other Sources

34. PUBLISHED OR BROADCAST INTERVIEW

34. Nina Totenberg, interview by Charlie Rose, *The Charlie Rose Show*, PBS, June 29, 2010.

Totenberg, Nina. Interview by Charlie Rose. *The Charlie Rose Show*. PBS, June 29, 2010.

Interviews you conduct are considered personal communications.

35. VIDEO OR DVD

35. Jim Carrey and Kate Winslet, *Eternal Sunshine of the Spotless Mind*, directed by Michel Gondry (2004; Los Angeles: Focus Features, 2004), DVD.

Carrey, Jim, and Kate Winslet. *Eternal Sunshine of the Spotless Mind*. Directed by Michel Gondry, 2004. Los Angeles: Focus Features, 2004. DVD.

36. SOUND RECORDING

36. Paul Robeson, *The Collector's Paul Robeson*, recorded 1959, Monitor MCD-61580, 1989, compact disc.

Robeson, Paul. *The Collector's Paul Robeson*. Recorded 1959. Monitor MCD-61580, 1989, compact disc.

37. WORK OF ART

Begin with the artist's name and the title of the work. If you viewed the work in person, give the medium, the date, and the name of the place where you saw it.

37. Mary Cassatt, *The Child's Bath*, oil on canvas, 1893, The Art Institute of Chicago, Chicago, IL.

Cassatt, Mary. *The Child's Bath,* oil on canvas, 1893. The Art Institute of Chicago, Chicago, IL.

If you refer to a reproduction, give the publication information.

37. Mary Cassatt, *The Child's Bath*, oil on canvas, 1893, on *Art Access*, The Art Institute of Chicago, last modified August 2004, http://www.artic.edu/artaccess/AA_Impressionist/pages/IMP_6.shtml#.

Cassatt, Mary. *The Child's Bath*. Oil on canvas, 1893. On *Art Access*, The Art Institute of Chicago. Last modified August 2004. http://www.artic.edu/artaccess/AA_Impressionist/pages/IMP_6.shtml#.

38. PAMPHLET, REPORT, OR BROCHURE

Information about the author or publisher may not be readily available, but give enough information to identify your source.

38. Jamie McCarthy, *Who Is David Irving?* (San Antonio, TX: Holocaust History Project, 1998).

McCarthy, Jamie. *Who Is David Irving?* San Antonio, TX: Holocaust History Project, 1998.

39. GOVERNMENT DOCUMENT

39. US House Committee on Ways and Means, *Report on Trade Mission to Sub-Saharan Africa*, 108th Cong., 1st sess. (Washington, DC: Government Printing Office, 2003), 28.

US House Committee on Ways and Means. *Report on Trade Mission to Sub-Saharan Africa*. 108th Cong., 1st sess. Washington, DC: Government Printing Office, 2003.

A Student Research Essay, *Chicago* Style

Student Writer

On the following pages is an essay by Amanda Rinder that conforms to the *Chicago* guidelines described in this chapter. Note that this essay has been reproduced in a narrow format to allow for annotation.

Amanda Rinder

Title announces
topic clearly
and succinctly

Sweet Home Chicago: Preserving the Past,

Protecting the Future of the Windy City

Title and
writer's name
centered

Amanda Rinder

Course title,
instructor's
name, and
date centered
at bottom of
title page

Twentieth-Century U.S. History

Professor Goldberg

November 27, 2006

Rinder 2

Only one city has the "Big Shoulders" described by Carl
Sandburg: Chicago (fig. 1). So renowned are its skyscrapers
and celebrated building style that an entire school of
architecture is named for Chicago. Presently, however,
the place that Frank Sinatra called "my kind of town" is
beginning to lose sight of exactly what kind of town it
is. Many of the buildings that give Chicago its distinctive
character are being torn down in order to make room for
new growth. Both preserving the classics and encouraging
new creation are important; the combination of these
elements gives Chicago architecture its unique flavor.

Paper refers to each figure by number

Double-spaced text

Fig. 1. Chicago skyline, circa 1940s. (Postcard courtesy of
Minnie Dangberg.)

Figure caption includes number, short title, and source

Rinder 3

Witold Rybczynski, a professor of urbanism at the University
of Pennsylvania, told the *New York Times*, "Of all the cities
we can think of . . . we associate Chicago with new things,
with building new. Combining that with preservation is a
difficult task, a tricky thing. It's hard to find the middle
ground in Chicago."[1] Yet finding a middle ground is essential
if the city is to retain the original character that sets it apart
from the rest. In order to maintain Chicago's distinctive
identity and its delicate balance between the old and the
new, the city government must provide a comprehensive
urban plan that not only directs growth, but calls for the
preservation of landmarks and historic districts as well.

Chicago's inclination toward unadorned, sturdy
buildings began in the late nineteenth century with the
aptly named Chicago School, a movement led by Louis
Sullivan, John Wellborn Root, and Daniel Burnham and
based on Sullivan's adage, "Form follows function."[2]
Burnham and Root's Reliance Building (fig. 2) epitomizes
this vision: simple, yet possessing a unique angular
beauty.[3] The early skyscraper, the very symbol of the
Chicago style, represents the triumph of function and utility
over sentiment, America over Europe, and perhaps even
the frontier over the civilization of the East Coast.[4] These
ideals of the original Chicago School were expanded upon

Margin notes:

Source cited using super-script numeral

Opening paragraph concludes with thesis statement

Second para-graph provides background

Rinder 4

by architects of the Second Chicago School. Frank Lloyd Wright's legendary organic style and the famed glass and steel constructions of Mies van der Rohe are often the first images that spring to mind when one thinks of Chicago.

Yet the architecture that is the city's defining attribute is being threatened by the increasing tendency toward development. The root of Chicago's preservation problem lies in the enormous drive toward economic expansion and the potential in Chicago for such growth.

Clear transition from previous paragraph

Fig. 2. The Reliance Building. (Photo courtesy of The Art Institute of Chicago.)

Rinder 5

The highly competitive market for land in the city means
that properties sell for the highest price if the buildings
on them can be obliterated to make room for newer, larger
developments. Because of this preference on the part of
potential buyers, the label "landmark" has become a stigma
for property owners. "In other cities, landmark status is
sought after — in Chicago, it's avoided at all costs," notes
Alan J. Shannon of the *Chicago Tribune*.[5] Even if owners
wish to keep their property's original structure, designation
as a landmark is still undesirable as it limits the renovations
that can be made to a building and thus decreases its value.
Essentially, no building that has even been recommended
for landmark status may be touched without the approval
of the Commission on Chicago Historical and Architectural
Landmarks, a restriction that considerably diminishes the
appeal of the real estate. "We live in a world where the
owners say, 'If you judge my property a landmark you are
taking money away from me.' And in Chicago the process
is stacked in favor of the economics," says former city
Planning Commissioner David Mosena.[6]

Nowhere is this clash more apparent than on North
Michigan Avenue — Chicago's Magnificent Mile. The historic
buildings along this block are unquestionably some of
the city's finest works. In addition, the Mile is one of

Signal verb "notes" frames quotation

"Magnificent Mile" illustrates conflict between development and preservation

Rinder 6

Chicago's most prosperous districts. The small-scale, charming buildings envisioned by Arthur Rubloff, the real estate developer who first conceived of the Magnificent Mile in the late 1940s, could not accommodate the crowds. Numerous high-rises, constructed to accommodate the masses that flock to Michigan Avenue, interrupt the cohesion and unity envisioned by the original planners of the Magnificent Mile. In *Chicago's North Michigan Avenue*, John W. Stamper says that with the standard height for new buildings on the avenue currently at about sixty-five stories, the "pleasant shopping promenade" has become a "canyon-like corridor."[7]

Evidence supports claim made in paragraph's topic sentences

Many agree that the individual style of Michigan Avenue is being lost. In 1995, the same year that the Landmarks Preservation Council of Illinois declared the section of Michigan Avenue from Oak Street to Roosevelt Road one of the state's ten most endangered historic sites, the annual sales of the Magnificent Mile ran around $1 billion and were increasing at an annual rate of about five to seven percent.[8] Clearly, the property's potential as part of a commercial hub is taking priority over its architectural and historic value. The future of this district rests on a precarious balance between Chicago's responsibility for its own heritage and Chicagoans' desire for economic gain.

Additional
example
introduced

Perhaps the best single example of the conflict between preservation and development in Chicago is the case of the McCarthy Building (fig. 3). Built in 1872, the McCarthy was designed by John M. Van Osdel, Chicago's first professional architect. Paul Gapp, a *Chicago Tribune* architecture critic, described it as "a stunningly appealing relic from Chicago's 19th century Renaissance era."[9] The McCarthy was made a landmark in 1984, but it wasn't long before developers recognized the potential of the property, situated on Block

Source of
image quoted
in figure
caption

Fig. 3. The McCarthy Building. (From the University of Illinois at Chicago, *Chicago Imagebase*, http://www.uic.edu/depts/ahaa /imagebase.)

37 of State Street, directly across from Marshall Field's.
With plans for a $300 million retail and office complex
already outlined, developers made a $12.3 million bid
for the property, promising to preserve the McCarthy and
integrate it into the complex. The city readily agreed.
However, a series of modifications over the next two years
completely transformed the original plan. With the old
structure now useless to the project, developers made
subsequent proposals to preserve just the facade, or even
to move the entire McCarthy Building to another location.
When these propositions didn't work out, the developers
began offering to preserve other buildings in exchange
for permission to demolish the McCarthy. Gapp admitted
that the city was caught in a difficult situation: if it
protected the McCarthy, it would be impeding development
in an important urban renewal area, and if it allowed
demolition, Chicago's landmark protection ordinance would
be completely devalued. He nonetheless urged city officials
to choose the "long view" and preserve the McCarthy.[10]
However, the developers' offer to buy and restore the
Reliance Building, at a cost of between $7 million and $11
million, and to contribute $4 million to other preservation
efforts, prevailed. In September 1987, the Chicago City
Council voted to revoke the McCarthy's landmark status.

Introduction of counter-evidence that large number of significant buildings diminishes value of each

Ironically, Chicago's rich architectural heritage may work against its own preservation. With so many significant buildings, losing one does not seem as critical as perhaps it should. The fact that Chicago boasts some forty-five Mies buildings, seventy-five Frank Lloyd Wright buildings, and numerous other buildings from the first and second Chicago Schools may inspire a nonchalant attitude toward preservation.[11]

The razing of the McCarthy Building in 1987 exposes the problems inherent in Chicago's landmark policy. But the real tragedy is that none of the plans for development of the property were ever carried out. Block 37 remains vacant to this day. Clearly, the city needs creative and vigilant urban planning.

Call for planning to address economic costs of preservation

To uphold Chicago's reputation as an architectural jewel, the city must manage development by easing the economic burdens that preservation entails. Some methods that have been suggested for this are property tax breaks for landmark owners and transferable development rights, which would give landmark owners bonuses for developing elsewhere. Overall, however, the city's planning and landmarks commissions simply need to become more involved, working closely with developers throughout the entire design process.

Rinder 10

The effectiveness of an earnest but open-minded approach to urban planning has already been proven in Chicago. Union Station (fig. 4) is one project that worked to the satisfaction of both developers and preservationists. Developers U.S. Equities Realty Inc. and Amtrak proposed replacing the four floors of outdated office space above the station with more practical high-rise towers. This offer allowed for the preservation of the Great Hall and other public spaces within the station itself. "We are preserving the best of the historical landmark . . . and at the same time creating an adaptive reuse that will bring

Example of successful planning introduced

NEW UNION STATION, CHICAGO.

Fig. 4. Union Station, circa 1925. (Postcard courtesy of Minnie Dangberg.)

back some of the old glory of the station," Cheryl Stein of U.S. Equities told the *Tribune*.[12] The city responded to this magnanimous offer in kind, upgrading zoning on the site to permit additional office space and working with developers to identify exactly which portions of the original structure needed to be preserved. Today, the sight of Union Station, revitalized and bustling, is proof of the sincere endeavors of developers and city planners alike.

Conclusion offers hope of a solution

In the midst of abandonment and demolition, buildings such as Union Station and the Reliance Building offer Chicago some hope for a future that is as architecturally rich as its past. The key to achieving this balance of preserving historic treasures and encouraging new development is to view the city not so much as a product, but as a process. Robert Bruegmann, author of *The Architects and the City*, defines a city as "the ultimate human artifact, our most complex and prodigious social creation, and the most tangible result of the actions over time of all its citizens."[13] Nowhere is this sentiment more relevant than in Chicago. Comprehensive urban planning will ensure that the city's character, so closely tied to its architecture, is preserved.

Rinder 12

Notes

1. Tracie Rozhon, "Chicago Girds for Big Battle over Its Skyline," *New York Times*, November 12, 2000, Academic Search Premier (28896783).

Newspaper article in database

2. *Columbia Encyclopedia*, Sixth Ed., s.v. "Louis Sullivan."

3. David Garrard Lowe, *Lost Chicago* (New York: Watson-Guptill Publications, 2000), 123.

4. Daniel Bluestone, *Constructing Chicago* (New Haven: Yale University Press, 1991), 105.

5. Alan J. Shannon, "When Will It End?" *Chicago Tribune*, September 11, 1987, quoted in Karen J. Dilibert, *From Landmark to Landfill* (Chicago: Chicago Architectural Foundation, 2000), 11.

Indirect source

6. Steve Kerch, "Landmark Decisions," *Chicago Tribune*, March 18, 1990, sec. 16.

7. John W. Stamper, *Chicago's North Michigan Avenue* (Chicago: University of Chicago Press, 1991), 215.

8. Alf Siewers, "Success Spoiling the Magnificent Mile?" *Chicago Sun-Times*, April 9, 1995, http://www.sun-times.com/.

Newspaper article online

9. Paul Gapp, "McCarthy Building Puts Landmark Law on a Collision Course with Developers," *Chicago Tribune*, April 20, 1986, quoted in Karen J. Dilibert, *From Landmark to Landfill* (Chicago: Chicago Architectural Foundation, 2000), 4.

Rinder 13

Reference to
previous source

10. Ibid.

11. Rozhon, "Chicago Girds for Big Battle."

Second refer-
ence to source

12. Kerch, "Landmark Decisions."

13. Robert Bruegmann, *The Architects and the City*

(Chicago: University of Chicago Press, 1997), 443.

Rinder 14

Bibliography

Bluestone, Daniel. *Constructing Chicago*. New Haven: Yale
    University Press, 1991.

Bruegmann, Robert. *The Architects and the City*. Chicago:
    University of Chicago Press, 1997.

Dilibert, Karen J. *From Landmark to Landfill*. Chicago:
    Chicago Architectural Foundation, 2000.

Kerch, Steve. "Landmark Decisions." *Chicago Tribune*, March
    18, 1990, sec. 16.

Lowe, David Garrard. *Lost Chicago*. New York: Watson-Guptill
    Publications, 2000.

Rozhon, Tracie. "Chicago Girds for Big Battle over Its
    Skyline." *New York Times*, November 12, 2000.
    Academic Search Premier (28896783).

Siewers, Alf. "Success Spoiling the Magnificent Mile?"
    Chicago Sun-Times, April 9, 1995. http://www.sun
    -times.com/.

Stamper, John W. *Chicago's North Michigan Avenue*. Chicago:
    University of Chicago Press, 1991.

Bibliography
starts on
new page

Book

Pamphlet

Newspaper
article

Article from
database

Bibliography
entries use
hanging indent
and are not
numbered

6

Research in the Social Sciences

Resources in the Social Sciences

GENERAL REFERENCE SOURCES FOR THE SOCIAL SCIENCES

International Encyclopedia of the Social and Behavioral Sciences. Ed. Neil J. Smelser and Paul B. Baltes. 26 vols. Amsterdam: Elsevier, 2001. Supplies four thousand articles about topics and terms from the major areas in the social and behavioral sciences.

INDEXES AND DATABASES FOR THE SOCIAL SCIENCES

ABI/INFORM. Ann Arbor: ProQuest, 1971–. Indexes and abstracts offer full-text business journals, news, reports, business cases, and more.

PAIS International. New York: Public Affairs Information Service, 1972–. Formerly *PAIS Bulletin*, 1977–1990; *PAIS Foreign Language Index*, 1972–1990; and *Public Affairs Information Service Bulletin*, 1915–1976. Indexes over twelve hundred social science periodicals plus pamphlets, agency reports, government documents, and books on politics, economics, business administration, international relations, and social topics.

Social Sciences Citation Index. Philadelphia: Institute for Scientific Information, 1956–. Indexes citations made in over a thousand social science

journals; entries allow tracing influence through the frequency of later citations of books and periodicals. (online via Web of Science)

Social Sciences Full Text. New York: Wilson, 1983–. Indexes and abstracts articles from over six hundred major periodicals on disciplines including anthroplogy, psychology, sociology, social work, health, law, criminology, public administration, urban studies, political science, geography, and many other social science areas.

WEB RESOURCES FOR THE SOCIAL SCIENCES

FedStats: One Stop Shopping for Federal Statistics
www.fedstats.gov
> Consolidates access to statistics and data from over seventy federal agencies.

Infomine: Scholarly Internet Resource Collections
infomine.ucr.edu
> Supplies indexed and annotated links to databases, government resources, maps, teaching resources, and other materials of academic interest for business, law, geography, and other social sciences.

Internet Crossroads in Social Science Data
disc.wisc.edu/newcrossroads/index.asp
> Offers hundreds of annotated links to data sources; maintained by the Data and Information Services Center at the University of Wisconsin, Madison.

Intute: Social Sciences
www.intute.ac.uk/socialsciences/
> Facilitates access to thousands of selected resources organized by subject areas or geography.

Quick Reference
www.lib.utexas.edu/refsites/index.html
> Provides access to business and reference resources.

U.S. Census Bureau
www.census.gov
> Supplies demographic, economic, and social data about the U.S. population.

Voice of the Shuttle: Web Site for Humanities Research
vos.ucsb.edu
> Specializes in highlights, top sites, and links to extensive resources
> in the humanities but also includes anthropology, archaeology, law,
> and political science as well as regional, cultural, media, minority,
> and gender studies.

Anthropology

GENERAL REFERENCE SOURCES FOR ANTHROPOLOGY

Encyclopedia of Anthropology. Ed. H. James Birx. 5 vols. Thousand Oaks:
> Sage, 2005. Supplies articles, many illustrated, defining and explain-
> ing anthropological terms and topics and including biographical
> entries.

INDEXES AND DATABASES FOR ANTHROPOLOGY

Abstracts in Anthropology. Amityville: Baywood, 1970–. Indexes and ab-
> stracts articles from periodicals about physical, linguistic, and
> cultural anthropology and about archaeological sites and artifacts.

Anthropological Literature. Cambridge: Harvard, 1979–. Indexes articles and
> essays on anthropology and archaeology, including art history,
> demography, economics, and religious studies.

WEB RESOURCES FOR ANTHROPOLOGY

Anthro.net
anthro.net
> Allows searches and provides extensive links to reviewed sites and
> bibliographic references in anthropology and archaeology.

Anthropology in the News
anthropology.tamu.edu/news/
> Lists links to current anthropology-related news stories.

Anthropology Resources on the Internet
www.anthropology-resources.net
> Links to an extensive array of resources on anthropology and

archaeology, including academic institutions, museums, and electronic discussion groups.

AnthroSource. Arlington: American Anthropological Association, 2005–. Complete full-text archive of the association's journals and other periodicals.

ArchNet — WWW Virtual Library — Archaeology
archnet.asu.edu
Links to resources and field sites in archaeology, grouped by region, subject, museum, academic institution, and so forth.

Fieldwork: The Anthropologist in the Field
www.theanthropologistinthefield.com
Creates a "fieldwork experience" including definitions of terms, graphics, and information about the procedures of anthropologists in the field.

Business and Economics

GENERAL REFERENCE SOURCES FOR BUSINESS AND ECONOMICS

Blackwell Encyclopedia of Management. Ed. Cary L. Cooper. 12 vols. Malden: Blackwell, 2005. Offers articles by experts on central areas of management along with bibliographies organized into volumes on topics such as business ethics, entrepreneurship, marketing, and organizational behavior.

Encyclopedia of Business and Finance. Ed. Burton S. Kaliski. 2nd ed. 2 vols. Detroit: Macmillan Reference, 2007. Over three hundred articles on areas including accounting, economics, finance, information systems, law, management, and marketing.

International Encyclopedia of Business and Management. 7 vols. 2002. Includes over seven hundred entries covering biographies of important figures and general and country-specific business and management topics.

The New Palgrave Dictionary of Economics. Ed. Steven N. Durlaf and Lawrence E. Blume. 8 vols. New York: Palgrave, 2008. Supplies thousands of entries, including bibliographies on economic history, methods, philosophy, theories, controversies, and major figures.

Occupational Outlook Handbook. 1949–; biennial. Offers information about more than two hundred occupations, including requirements, conditions, earnings, locations, and projections.

INDEXES AND DATABASES FOR
BUSINESS AND ECONOMICS

Business Index. New York: Wilson, 1979–. Covers more than eight hundred business periodicals and newspapers as well as hundreds of other sources.

Business Periodicals Index. New York: Wilson, 1958–. Formerly *Industrial Arts Index*, 1913–1957. Indexes and abstracts articles from over 250 business periodicals and newspapers.

EconLit. Nashville: American Economic Association, 1969–. Covers worldwide literature on economics with citations and abstracts, with full text of some articles.

Encyclopedia of Business Information Sources. Detroit: Gale Group, 2011. Lists indexes of periodicals, databases, sources of statistical information, organizations, and other resources available on hundreds of business topics.

Gale Group F&S Index United States Annual. Detroit: Gale Group, 2009. Indexes by industry, product, and company name, supplying full text and abstracts from over 2,500 periodicals on business and financial topics.

International Bibliography of Economics. 1952–. Lists articles, books, and other resources about economics, including history and policy, as well as topics such as money, income, production, and markets.

WEB RESOURCES FOR
BUSINESS AND ECONOMICS

The BizTech Network
www.brint.com
  Allows searches and provides links to articles, papers, magazines, tools, and many other resources for business, finance, management, and information technology issues.

Bloomberg Businessweek
www.businessweek.com
> Offers online versions of some *Bloomberg Businessweek* stories, quick news updates, stock and mutual-fund tracking data, and advertisements — some of which may, in fact, be useful.

Economic Report of the President
www.gpoaccess.gov/eop/index.html
> Annual report prepared by the chair of the Council of Economic Advisors that gives an overview of the nation's economy with data that cover income, employment, and production.

Galaxy Business General Resources
www.galaxy.com/dir44/Business_and_Commerce
> Links to a variety of resources for business; includes prices, statistics, trends, and general reading sources.

globalEDGE
globaledge.msu.edu
> Specializes in links to international business resources, data, and materials for business students.

IPL — Business and Economics
www.ipl.org/IPLBrowse/GetSubject?vid=13&tid=6607&parent=0
> Alphabetically lists links to many different resources, including sites on careers in the business world.

Resources for Economists
rfe.org/
> A well-organized guide to resources and data sponsored by the American Economic Association.

Rutgers Accounting Web
raw.rutgers.edu
> Contains information on and links to all areas of accounting, including searches and resources on finance, taxation, government agencies, and publications.

SEC EDGAR Database
www.sec.gov/edgar.shtml
> The Electronic Data Gathering, Analysis, and Retrieval (EDGAR) system is the U.S. Securities and Exchange Commission's archive of

business filings. Includes various search capabilities and a wide range of information.

Communications, Journalism, and Linguistics

GENERAL REFERENCE SOURCES FOR COMMUNICATIONS, JOURNALISM, AND LINGUISTICS

Communication Yearbook. Ed. Charles T. Salmon. New York: Routledge, 2010. Includes essays reviewing current topics each year from various viewpoints.

Encyclopedic Dictionary of Semiotics, Media, and Communications. Ed. Marcel Danesi. Toronto: U of Toronto P, 2000. Includes entries that define and describe terms, concepts, people, schools of thought, and movements in various disciplines, including semiotics, media and communication studies, anthropology, psychology, and computer science.

International Encyclopedia of Communication. Ed. Wolfgang Donsbach. 12 vols. Malden: Blackwell, 2010. Supplies extended entries on communications — ancient and modern, verbal and nonverbal — as well as historical and current influences and processes.

International Encyclopedia of Linguistics. Ed. William J. Frawley. 4 vols. Oxford: Oxford UP, 2003. Provides entries, generally with bibliographies, on linguistic terms and topics, languages, language families, and related topics.

Webster's New World Dictionary of Media and Communications. Ed. Richard Weiner. New York: Macmillan Reference, 1996. Supplies brief entries defining terms used in publishing, broadcasting, journalism, film, public relations, and related areas.

INDEXES AND DATABASES FOR COMMUNICATIONS, JOURNALISM, AND LINGUISTICS

Communication Abstracts. Beverly Hills: Sage, 1978-. Indexes and abstracts articles from communication and speech periodicals.

Communication and Mass Media Complete. Ipswich: EBSCO, 2004. Indexes and abstracts for over five hundred journals and full-text coverage of four hundred others, with some offering materials back to 1915.

Language and Language Behavior Abstracts (LLBA). San Diego: ProQuest, 1967–. Provides the definitive index to materials on the nature and use of language. Covers research in linguistics (the nature and structure of human speech), in language (speech sounds, sentence and word structure, meaning in language forms, spelling, phonetics), and in pathologies of speech, language, and hearing.

WEB RESOURCES FOR COMMUNICATIONS, JOURNALISM, AND LINGUISTICS

American Amateur Press Association
www.aapainfo.org
> Provides examples of amateur journalism, tips from professional journalists, and links to resources for writers.

American Communication Association
www.americancomm.org
> The American Communication Association sponsors this full-coverage site, with links to the subfields in communications organized by field and by interest.

Communication Studies Resources
www.uiowa.edu/~commstud/resources
> From the University of Iowa, this site offers a wide range of links to listservs, journals, Web research guides, and electronic style guides in fields from advertising to rhetoric.

Investigative Reporters and Editors
www.ire.org
> An organization dedicated to teaching the skills and issues of investigative journalism; the site's resource center includes a database of more than eleven thousand abstracts of investigative articles.

Linguistic Society of America
www.lsadc.org
> Provides information on many aspects of linguistics and links to related resources.

Links to Friendly Communications Homepages
www.csufresno.edu/comm/wscalink.htm
> From the Western States Communication Association, this site provides easy access to many organizational home pages in communications.

SIL International: Partners in Language Development
www.sil.org
> Offers information about language communities worldwide. Supports research in all areas of linguistics.

The WWW Virtual Library — Communications and Media
vlib.org/Communication
> Provides search capability and numerous links to resources on media, broadcasting, communications, and news.

Education

GENERAL REFERENCE SOURCES FOR EDUCATION

Encyclopedia of Education. Ed. James W. Guthrie. 2nd ed. 8 vols. New York: Macmillan Reference, 2003. Supplies full articles, especially on historical topics.

Encyclopedia of Educational Research. Ed. Robert L. Ebel. 4th ed. 4 vols. New York: Macmillan, 1992. Summarizes research studies and includes bibliographies.

Encyclopedia of Physical Education, Fitness, and Sports. 4 vols. 1977–1985, 1991. Includes articles on historical topics, fitness, training, nutrition, exercise, and specific activities and sports.

The International Encyclopedia of Education. Ed. Penelope Peterson et al. 3rd ed. 8 vols. Amsterdam: Elsevier, 2010. Contains over twelve hundred entries organized alphabetically within twenty-two major categories, including adult education, girls and women in education, policy and planning, and vocational education and training.

International Encyclopedia of Education: Research and Studies. Ed. Torsten Husen and T. Neville Postlethwaite. 10 vols. Oxford: Pergamon, 1985–1992. Supplies full entries on many general and specialized areas of education.

INDEXES AND DATABASES FOR EDUCATION

CSA Physical Education Index. Bethesda: CSA, 1970–. Indexes articles on physical education and sports from several hundred periodicals.

Current Index to Journals in Education (CIJE). Phoenix: Oryx Press, 1969. Indexes and abstracts articles from education periodicals; *Resources*

in Education (1966–) abstracts unpublished materials such as reports and curriculum guides.

Education: A Guide to Reference and Information Sources. Ed. Nancy Patricia O'Brien. 2nd ed. Englewood: Libraries Unlimited, 2000. Guide to books, periodicals, and databases about education.

Education Index. New York: Wilson, 1929–. Indexes articles from over 350 education periodicals.

ERIC (Educational Resources Information Center). Washington: Institute of Education Sciences, 1966–. Lists more than 1.2 million articles, papers, and reports on education from more than 650 journals.

WEB RESOURCES FOR EDUCATION

EdWeb: Exploring Technology and School Reform
edwebproject.org/
> Supplies information and access to resources on education, educational policy, current reform efforts, and the impact of technological innovation on education.

National Center for Education Statistics (NCES)
nces.ed.gov
> Provides access to information about U.S. education, including publications, surveys, and other data on student achievement, current issues, and related topics.

U.S. Department of Education (ED.gov)
www.ed.gov
> Includes information on federal education priorities, financial aid, federal programs and funding, publications, research and statistics.

Ethnic Studies

GENERAL REFERENCE SOURCES FOR ETHNIC STUDIES

The African American Almanac. Ed. Brigham Narins. 10th ed. Detroit: Gale Group, 2007. Discusses African American history and present-day issues, and includes a bibliography, illustrations, lists, and other data.

Asian American Almanac. Ed. Irene Natividad and Susan B. Gail. 2nd ed. Detroit: Gale Group, 2004. Explores the culture and history of American descendents of Asian and Pacific Island immigrants.

The Asian American Encyclopedia. Ed. Franklin Ng. 6 vols. North Belmore: Marshall Cavendish, 1995. Discusses the history, language, and culture of both large and small groups of Asian Americans — Chinese, Filipinos, Japanese, Indians, Koreans, Vietnamese, Hmong, and Pacific Islanders — and their influences on and experiences in American culture.

Atlas of the North American Indian. By Carl Waldman. Rev. ed. New York: Facts on File, 2000. Includes maps, illustrations, and explanatory text on Native American history, culture, migrations, lands, wars, and other topics from ancient to recent times.

Blackwell Companion to Jewish Culture: From the Eighteenth Century to the Present. Ed. Glenda Abramson, 1989. Supplies articles on Jewish culture, notable figures, and contributions in the humanities, sciences, and social sciences.

Dictionary of Asian American History. Ed. Hyung-chan Kim. New York: Greenwood Press, 1986. Provides essays and brief definitions on the history of Asians and Pacific Islanders in the United States, including cultural and social background, major events, and legal history.

Dictionary of Mexican American History. By Matt S. Meier and Feliciano Rivera. New York: Greenwood Press, 1981. Includes entries on history, politics, and social topics, including a chronology, a glossary, statistical tables, and maps.

Encyclopedia of Native American Tribes. By Carl Waldman. 3rd ed. New York: Checkmark Books, 2006. Supplies articles, including illustrations, about 150 tribes and general topics.

Encyclopedia of World Cultures. 10 vols. Detroit: Gale Group, 1991–1996. Supplies entries and bibliographies on cultural groups.

Handbook of North American Indians. 15 vols. Washington: Smithsonian Institution, 1978–. Provides essays, including bibliographies and illustrations, on many cultural and historical topics.

Harvard Encyclopedia of American Ethnic Groups. Ed. Stephan Thernstrom et al. Cambridge: Belknap, 1980–. Contains articles, maps, and tables on 106 ethnic groups, regional groups, and related topics.

The Hispanic-American Almanac. By Sonia Benson. Detroit: Gale Group, 2003. Discusses Hispanic American history and present-day issues, and includes bibliographies, illustrations, lists, and other materials.

A Native American Encyclopedia: History, Culture, and Peoples. By Barry M. Pritzker. New York: Oxford, 2000. Provides information on contemporary and historical customs, dress, habitat, weapons, government, and religions of over two hundred North American Indian groups; organized by geographical area and alphabetically within each area.

Sourcebook of Hispanic Culture in the United States. Ed. David William Oster. Chicago: American Library Association, 1982. Supplies annotated entries on books, periodicals, and other materials about major Hispanic groups.

The State of Black America. Ed. Stephanie Jones. New York: National Urban League, 2010. Includes articles on various social, economic, political, legal, and educational topics of current concern, analyzed by the National Urban League.

We the People: An Atlas of America's Ethnic Diversity. By James Paul Allen and Eugene James Turner. New York: Macmillan, 1988. Supplies maps, explanatory text, and bibliographies on the origins and migrations of sixty-six ethnic groups.

INDEXES AND DATABASES FOR ETHNIC STUDIES

Afro-American Reference: An Annotated Bibliography of Selected Sources. Ed. Nathaniel Davis. Westport: Greenwood, 1985. Supplies annotated entries about reference books and research collections on African Americans.

American Indian History Online. New York: Facts on File, 2006. Database that includes articles, biographies, and primary sources representing more than six hundred Native American groups.

Asian American Studies: An Annotated Bibliography and Research Guide. Ed. Hyung-chan Kim. Westport: Greenwood, 1989. Lists books and articles on a range of topics.

Chicano Database. 1967–. Includes the *Chicano Periodical Index,* 1967–1988 and *Chicano Index* (1989–). Indexes resources on Mexican Americans and has recently added other Spanish-speaking groups.

A Comprehensive Bibliography for the Study of American Minorities. 2 vols. New York: New York University Press, 1976. Early guide to resources on thirty-seven minority groups.

Ethnic NewsWatch. Ann Arbor: ProQuest, 1985–. Indexes and supplies full articles from periodicals representing a wide range of ethnic viewpoints.

Handbook of Latin American Studies. Austin: University of Texas Press, 1935–. A selective, annotated bibliography of scholarly works on Latin America. This is an excellent source of citations for any topic in Latin American studies, including Hispanic populations in the United States. Now prepared by the Hispanic Division of the Library of Congress, an electronic version of this work, *HLAS Online,* is available at lcweb2.loc.gov/hlas. The site can searched by keyword or subject heading in English, Spanish, or Portuguese.

Hispanic American Periodicals Index (HAPI). Los Angeles: UCLA Latin American Center, 1970–. Indexes articles from over four hundred periodicals treating Hispanic topics in Latin America and the United States.

International Index to Black Periodicals. 1984–. Formerly *Index to Periodical Articles by and about Blacks,* 1971–1983, and *Index to Periodical Articles by and about Negroes,* 1960–1972. Indexes and abstracts articles from 150 periodicals.

Native Americans: An Annotated Bibliography. Ed. Frederick E. Hoxie and Harvey Markowitz. Pasadena: Salem Press, 1991. Lists articles and books, including those focused on a single tribe.

Native Americans: Current Issues. Ed. Larry V. Parks. New York: Nova Science, 2002. Provides resources on current issues facing Native Americans, such as Indian law, Indian heritage, and gaming.

Native Americans: Social, Economic, and Political Aspects: A Bibliography. By Joan Nordquist. Santa Cruz: Reference and Research Services, 1998. Popular bibliography of articles and books concerning Native Americans.

Women of Color in the United States: A Guide to the Literature. By Bernice Redfern. New York: Garland, 1989. Supplies annotated entries on major resources.

WEB RESOURCES FOR ETHNIC STUDIES

Africa Web Links: An Annotated Resource List
www.africa.upenn.edu/Home_Page/WWW_Links.html
Annotated links and other resources on African and black culture,

history, and issues, from the African Studies Center at the University of Pennsylvania.

The African-American Mosaic: A Library of Congress Resource Guide for the Study of Black History and Culture
lcweb.loc.gov/exhibits/african/intro.html
> Samples of information and images from the collections of the Library of Congress on colonization, abolition, migration, and the WPA.

Ancestors in the Americas
www.cetel.org
> Companion site to the PBS series with resources and documents on Asian and Asian American history.

CLNet (Chicano-Latino Network)
clnet.ucla.edu
> Includes links to Chicano and Latino research, curricula, regional information, data, and other information.

LANIC (Latin American Network Information Center)
lanic.utexas.edu
> Provides access by country or topic to a great range of cultural, political, historical, economic, statistical, and other information for over twenty-five Latin American countries.

NativeWeb: Resources for Indigenous Cultures Around the World
www.nativeweb.org
> Consolidates hundreds of links to resources, data, news, and information about events concerning native and indigenous peoples, organized by subject, country, and region.

The WWW Virtual Library—Asian Studies
vlib.org/AsianStudies
> Contains a broad range of information and resources, including links to subject-oriented bibliographies on many individual countries.

Gender and Women's Studies

GENERAL REFERENCE SOURCES FOR GENDER AND WOMEN'S STUDIES

The Dictionary of Feminist Theory. By Maggie Humm. 2nd ed. Columbus: Ohio State University Press, 1995. Covers theoretical issues in feminism and is particularly useful for placing these issues in historical

context. The work is also helpful for pinpointing primary documents related to feminist theory.

Encyclopedia of Lesbian, Gay, Bisexual, and Transgender History in America. Ed. Marc Stein. 3 vols. New York: Scribner, 2004. Offers over five hundred articles on individuals, professions, legal issues, events, and communities that are significant in GLBT history.

Encyclopedia of Women and Gender: Sex Similarities and Differences and the Impact of Society on Gender. Ed. Judith Worell. 2 vols. San Diego: Academic Press, 2001. Provides lengthy technical articles on the psychology of women and gender, covering such topics as gender and achievement, aging, child care, and body image concerns.

Routledge International Encyclopedia of Women: Global Women's Issues and Knowledge. Ed. Cheris Kramarae and Dale Spender. 4 vols. New York: Routledge, 2000. A record of women's knowledge and experience, offering essays on international approaches to the arts, economic development, education, health and reproduction, sexuality, households, families, politics, and peace and violence.

Women in the Third World: An Encyclopedia of Contemporary Issues. Ed. Edith H. Altbach and Nelly P. Stromquist. New York: Garland, 1998. Offers substantial overviews of topics related to women in the developing world, including theoretical issues, political and legal contexts, sex-role ideologies, demographics, economics, and the environment. It also provides regional surveys.

Women's Studies Encyclopedia. Ed. Helen Tierney. 3 vols. Westport: Greenwood, 1999. Supplies articles on studies of women from the viewpoints of the natural sciences, the humanities, and the social sciences, including both historical background and recent research.

INDEXES AND DATABASES FOR GENDER AND WOMEN'S STUDIES

Contemporary Women's Issues. Farmington Hills: Gale Group, 1992–. Indexes and offers some full-text articles on women's health and human rights, drawing from journals, books, and the publications of government and other agencies.

Introduction to Library Research in Women's Studies. 1998. Supplies annotated source lists and guidance about research in this area.

Women's Studies International. Baltimore: NISC, 1972–. Indexes and abstracts
   articles on topics such as education, employment, family, history, and
   sex roles.

WEB RESOURCES FOR GENDER AND WOMEN'S STUDIES

The American Studies Web
lamp.georgetown.edu/asw
   Includes links to research sources for gender studies, among other
   topics in American studies.

International Gay and Lesbian Review
gaybookreviews.info
   Provides abstracts and reviews of many books related to lesbian, gay,
   bisexual, and transgender studies.

Literary Resources — Feminism and Women's Literature
ethnicity.rutgers.edu/~jlynch/Lit/women.html
   Devoted entirely to women writers and feminist criticism.

Women's Studies Database
www.mith.umd.edu/WomensStudies
   Includes images, government documents, bibliographies, and other
   resources, as well as links to other sites and library collections.

WSSLinks: Women and Gender Studies
libr.org/wss/WSSLinks/index.html
   Annotated links for women's studies covering art, education, film,
   health, history, music, philosophy, politics, science and technology,
   sexuality, and theology. Links are chosen by an editorial team from
   the Women's Studies Section of the Association of College and
   Research Libraries.

Geography

GENERAL REFERENCE SOURCES FOR GEOGRAPHY

Dictionary of Human Geography. Ed. Ron Johnson et al. 5th ed. New York:
   Blackwell, 2009. Entries on over three hundred key terms and central
   debates in human geography.

Geo-Data: The World Geographical Encyclopedia. Farmington Hills: Gale, 2003. Includes relief maps and descriptions of the physical geography of every country in the world.

World Geographical Encyclopedia. 5 vols. New York: McGraw-Hill, 1995. Contains information on the environments, populations, economies, histories, and cultures of over 190 countries and a general study of geography and world statistics; arranged in volumes by continent and organized thematically within each volume.

INDEXES AND DATABASES FOR GEOGRAPHY

Geographical Abstracts: Physical Geography. Amsterdam: Elsevier, 1989–. Formerly part of *Geological Abstracts: Paleontology and Stratigraphy.* Indexes and abstracts articles from over one thousand periodicals as well as books, papers, and reports on physical geography and cartography, including topics such as landforms, climatology, hydrology, and meteorology.

WEB RESOURCES FOR GEOGRAPHY

CU Boulder Internet Resources for Geographers
www.colorado.edu/geography/virtdept/resources/contents.htm
   Links to references, lists, journals, organizations, libraries, map collections, databases, and other resources in geography.

Manual of Federal Geographic Data Products: USGS Index
www.brown.edu/Departments/Taubman_Center/databank/fedgis.html
   Provides maps, photographs, and reports on topics such as mineral and energy resources, water and flood conditions, and earthquake information, plus links to resources from other federal agencies.

U.S. Gazetteer
www.census.gov/cgi-bin/gazetteer
   Searches for locations in the United States, identifying them for viewing and for finding corresponding census data.

The WWW Virtual Library — Geography
www.icomos.org/WWW_VL_Geography.html
   Organizes linked resources, maps, databases of names, data, and other materials by subject, including countries and academic institutions.

Law and Criminal Justice

GENERAL REFERENCE SOURCES FOR LAW AND CRIMINAL JUSTICE

Encyclopedia of the American Constitution. Ed. Leonard Williams Levy et al. 6
vols. New York: Macmillan Library Reference, 2000. Contains long
articles on laws, acts, decisions, notable figures, and historical periods, combining legal, historical, and political science viewpoints.

*Encyclopedia of the American Judicial System: Studies of the Principal Institutions
and Processes of Law.* Ed. Robert J. Janosik. 3 vols. New York: Macmillan
Library Reference, 1987. Supplies essays on legal history, processes,
and issues.

Encyclopedia of Crime and Justice. Ed. Joshua Dressler. 2nd ed. 4 vols. 2002.
Supplies articles, including reference lists, on major topics, including differing points of view.

Guide to American Law: Everyone's Legal Encyclopedia. 12 vols. St. Paul:
West, 1985, 1990–1995. Supplies definitions and articles for non-
lawyers on legal terms, topics, history, theory, and institutions.
Includes an extensive appendix with sample forms, documents, and
a time line.

The Oxford Companion to American Law. Ed. Kermit L. Hall. New York:
Oxford, 2002. Contains nearly five hundred alphabetically arranged
entries comprising biographies, concepts, current legal issues, definitions, descriptions of law enforcement agents and institutions
(such as detectives and the FBI), and summaries of cases.

INDEXES AND DATABASES FOR LAW AND CRIMINAL JUSTICE

Current Law Index. Farmington Hills: Gale, 1980–. Indexes hundreds of
law periodicals.

Index to Legal Periodicals and Books. New York: Wilson, 1994–. Indexes articles from over four hundred law sources, including an archive of
periodicals dating from 1908.

LexisNexis: Legal. Bethesda: LexisNexis, 1998–. The *LexisNexis* databases
include cases, codes, and research under the Legal tab. Of particular
note is the ability to search for the full text of state and federal court
decisions (also known as *case law*) by keyword, party name, or citation,

and the Law Reviews section, which offers the full text of scholarly articles that analyze legal issues in depth.

WestLaw Campus Research. Eagan: West, 2002–. Database and legal research service providing access to legal resources, news articles, and business information.

WEB RESOURCES FOR LAW AND CRIMINAL JUSTICE

ASIL Guide to Electronic Resources for International Law
www.asil.org/erghome.cfm
> Sponsored by the American Society of International Law, this site provides advice on research and extensive links to all major areas of international law.

Cornell Law School Legal Information Institute
www.law.cornell.edu
> The Legal Information Institute is a research and electronic publishing activity of the Cornell Law School. Popular collections include the U.S. Code, Supreme Court opinions, and Wex, a free legal dictionary and encyclopedia.

FindLaw
www.findlaw.com
> Legal resources organized by subject: accidents and injuries, bankruptcy and debt, and so on. A database on Supreme Court decisions covers 1893 to the present.

HeinOnline
heinonline.org
> Fully searchable legal database with images and content going back over four centuries.

Hieros Gamos Worldwide Legal Directories
www.hg.org
> Link library specializing in foreign and international law.

Internet Legal Resource Guide
www.ilrg.com
> An extensive index, by category, of selected Web sites and files; designed for laypersons as well as legal scholars.

Law Library Research Exchange (LLRX)
www.llrx.com/sources.html
> Blog and links provide up-to-date information on a range of legal research and issues with a particular focus on technology.

National Criminal Justice Reference Service
www.ncjrs.org
> Provides extensive information, statistics, and reports about criminal justice, crime prevention, courts, law enforcement, and related topics, with links to federal agencies, offices, and databases.

U.S. Department of Justice
www.justice.gov
> Supplies links to Department of Justice divisions, offices, and programs, as well as links to other federal and criminal justice sites.

The WWW Virtual Library — Law
vlib.org/Law
> Presents an extensive array of sites and resources, organized by legal specialty and topic, as well as by law school, legal firm, journal, government agency, and so on.

Political Science

GENERAL REFERENCE SOURCES FOR POLITICAL SCIENCE

Almanac of American Politics: The President, the Senators, the Representatives, the Governors: Their Records and Election Results, Their States and Districts. Ed. Michael Barone and Richard E. Cohen. Washington: National Journal, 1972–. Biennial. Analyzes state and national politics, including data and maps.

Congressional Quarterly. Washington: CQ Roll Call, 1945–. Analyzes national politics, including congressional legislation and voting records, presidential speeches, and Supreme Court decisions.

Political Handbook of the World. Ed. Arthur S. Banks and Thomas C. Muller. Binghamton: CSA Publications, 1927–. Supplies current political information about individual countries and their connections through intergovernmental bodies.

State Legislative Sourcebook: A Resource Guide to Legislative Information in the 50 States. Topeka: Government Research Service, 1986–; annual. Lists publications and telephone numbers for state legislatures.

INDEXES AND DATABASES FOR POLITICAL SCIENCE

PAIS International. New York: Public Affairs Information Service, 1972–. Indexes and abstracts journals, select books, and government documents in areas such as public administration, economics, and international relations.

Political Science: A Guide to Reference and Information Sources. By Henry E. York. Englewood: Libraries Unlimited, 1990. Supplies annotated entries on political science sources, including databases, research collections, and organizations.

Population Index. 1935–. Ceased in print 1999. Supplies abstracts of periodical articles and other resources dealing with population theories, studies, research methods, statistics, and changes in patterns of birth, migration, and death. (Available online at jstor.org/journals, or for 1986–2000 at popindex.princeton.edu.)

United States Political Science Documents. Pittsburgh: University Center for International Studies, 1975–. Ceased in print 1991. Indexes scholarly periodicals in political science.

Worldwide Political Science Abstracts. Ann Arbor: ProQuest, 1975. Formerly *Political Science Abstracts* (1975–2000) and *ABC Pol Sci: A Bibliography of Current Contents: Political Science and Government* (1984–2000). Supplies tables of contents from several hundred periodicals in political science, government, economics, law, and sociology.

WEB RESOURCES FOR POLITICAL SCIENCE

Country Studies
memory.loc.gov/frd/cs/
    Online editions of book-length country profiles produced for U.S. diplomats by the Federal Research Division of the Library of Congress. The site includes substantial information on each nation's culture, history, economy, and political system; it is searchable by topic and country. Be sure to check publication dates; some country studies may provide outdated information.

Fedworld
www.fedworld.gov
> Links to government services and databases. Provides good search facil-
> ities and explanations, with information on how to order materials.

The Gallup Organization
www.gallup.com
> Allows searches and includes up-to-date information and links to a
> variety of polling-related news items.

Political Resources on the Net
www.politicalresources.net
> Contains political sites, organized by country, with links to parties, gov-
> ernments, organizations, and other political resources; allows searches.

Political Science Resources on the Web
www.lib.umich.edu/govdocs/polisci.html
> Provides extensive annotated links and searches to many political
> sites and publications.

THOMAS: Legislative Information on the Internet
thomas.loc.gov
> A site for current and historical federal legislation resources from
> the Library of Congress, with searches and links to current legisla-
> tion, *Congressional Record* archives, historical documents, and other
> government resources.

United Nations
www.un.org
> A good general site, with links to many UN offices, policies, and
> activities. Also available in French and Spanish.

The White House
www.whitehouse.gov
> The presidential site, with links to the president and vice president,
> commonly requested federal services, news, a virtual library, and
> other executive-branch links.

Psychology

GENERAL REFERENCE SOURCES FOR PSYCHOLOGY

Corsini Encyclopedia of Psychology and Behavioral Science. Ed. W. Edward
Craighead and Charles B. Nemeroff. 4 vols. New York: Wiley, 2002.

Provides over twelve hundred entries covering biographical information on important figures, the history of psychology, psychological
theory, and concepts and techniques in areas such as applied, cognitive, educational, physiological, and social psychology.

Diagnostic and Statistical Manual of Mental Disorders (DSM-IV). 4th ed. rev.
Washington: American Psychological Association, 2000. The main
tool for classifying and describing mental health disorders. Published in 1994 with a text revision in 2000; a new edition is expected
in 2012.

Encyclopedia of Psychology. Ed. Alan E. Kazdin. 8 vols. Washington: American Psychological Association, 2000. Supplies articles, along with
reference lists, on many topics in psychology, including biographies
of notable figures.

Oxford Companion to the Mind. Ed. Richard Gregory. New York: Oxford,
2004. Provides definitions and articles on topics and major figures
in psychology, and includes other approaches to the mind as varied
as the computer sciences, the fine arts, medicine, and traditional
myths.

INDEXES AND DATABASES FOR PSYCHOLOGY

Bibliographic Guide to Psychology. New York Public Library. Boston: G. K.
Hall, 1974–2003. Comprehensively lists materials in all areas of
psychology.

PsycARTICLES. Washington: American Psychological Association, 1894–.
Offers full-text access to over seventy journals. Included when you
search PsycINFO.

PsycINFO. Washington: American Psychological Association, 1927–. Formerly *Psychological Abstracts*, indexes and abstracts articles from
over fourteen hundred psychology periodicals on many topics such
as developmental, educational, experimental, and social psychology.

WEB RESOURCES FOR PSYCHOLOGY

American Psychological Association
www.apa.org
The APA home page, with access to an online documents search tool
and information for students in psychology.

Association for Psychological Science
www.psychologicalscience.org
> Formerly the American Psychological Society, offers links to journals, departments, discussion groups, and research information.

Behavior Analysis Resources
www.coedu.usf.edu/behavior/bares.htm
> Links to resources in behavioral psychology.

National Institute of Mental Health
nimh.nih.gov
> Mental health information along with research and statistics from the federal agency.

Neuropsychology Central
www.neuropsychologycentral.com
> Links to almost any aspect of neuropsychology.

Psychology Virtual Library
www.vl-site.org/psychology
> Good general links to major international psychology sites.

PsychWeb
www.psywww.com
> Contains helpful information and numerous links to psychology resources; geared to students and teachers.

Social Psychology Network
www.socialpsychology.org
> The largest social-psychology database on the Internet; has search capability and links to more than five thousand resources.

Sociology and Social Work

GENERAL REFERENCE SOURCES FOR SOCIOLOGY AND SOCIAL WORK

Blackwell Dictionary of Sociology: A User's Guide to Sociological Language. By Allan G. Johnson. 2nd ed. Malden: Blackwell, 2000. Entries cover key topics and biographical subjects in sociology.

Blackwell Encyclopedia of Sociology Online. Ed. George Ritzer. Malden: Blackwell, 2007–. Extensive coverage of major current and historical topics and definitions of key terms, also published in print in eleven volumes.

Encyclopedia of Social Work. 20th ed. 4 vols. Washington: NASW Press, 2008. Supplies articles on social work, covering current issues such as adolescent behavior, divorce, homelessness, immigration, and welfare.

Encyclopedia of Sociology. Ed. Edgar F. Borgatta, Rhonda J. V. Montgomery. 2nd ed. 5 vols. New York: Macmillan Reference, 2000. An essential reference that contains articles on key topics from race and class to pregnancy and abortion and more current topics such as privacy and the Internet.

International Encyclopedia of Sociology. Ed. Frank McGill and Hector L. Delgado. 2 vols. Chicago: Fitzroy Dearborn, 1996. Contains 335 entries that illustrate the main topics and concerns in the field of sociology.

INDEXES AND DATABASES FOR SOCIOLOGY AND SOCIAL WORK

Social Work Abstracts. Washington: NASW Press, 1965–. Produced by the National Association of Social Workers. Indexes and abstracts resources related to social work.

Sociological Abstracts. San Diego: Sociological Abstracts, 1952–. Indexes and abstracts articles, books, papers, and other resources on diverse topics, including the history, methods, and perspectives of the major fields in sociology.

WEB RESOURCES FOR SOCIOLOGY AND SOCIAL WORK

American Sociological Association
asanet.org
    Resources for sociology include a style guide.

Annual Reviews of Sociology Online
www.annurev.org/journal/soc
    Allows searches of databases for downloadable abstracts.

Social Work and Social Services Web Sites
gwbweb.wustl.edu/resources/pages/socialservicesresourcesintro.aspx
    Provides information on abuse and violence, addiction, alternative medicine, emotional support, gender issues, and welfare.

A Sociological Tour through Cyberspace
www.trinity.edu/~mkearl/index.html
    Provides links within sociology, including theory, data, methods, paper-writing guides, and inquiry help.

SocioSite
www.sociosite.net/
> A social science information system; allows searches and research in any sociological subject.

The SocioWeb
www.socioweb.com
> A general site of links and resources, including searches by topic.

The WWW Virtual Library — Sociology
socserv.mcmaster.ca/w3virtsoclib
> Links to sites covering research centers, discussion groups, e journals, organizations, and university departments.

APA Style

Many fields in the social sciences ask students to follow the basic guidelines prescribed by the American Psychological Association (APA) for formatting manuscripts and documenting various kinds of sources.

For further reference on APA style, consult the *Publication Manual of the American Psychological Association*, Sixth Edition (2010).

DIRECTORY TO APA STYLE FOR IN-TEXT CITATIONS

1. Basic format for a quotation, *192*
2. Basic format for a paraphrase or summary, *193*
3. Two authors, *193*
4. Three to five authors, *193*
5. Six or more authors, *194*
6. Corporate or group author, *194*
7. Unknown author, *194*
8. Two or more authors with the same last name, *194*
9. Two or more works by an author in a single year, *195*
10. Two or more sources in one parenthetical reference, *195*
11. Indirect source, *195*
12. Email and other personal communication, *195*
13. Electronic document, *196*
14. Table or figure reproduced in the text, *197*

APA Style for In-Text Citations

APA style requires parenthetical references in the text to document quotations, paraphrases, summaries, and other material from a source. These citations correspond to full bibliographic entries in the list of references at the end of the text.

Note that APA style generally calls for using the past tense or present perfect tense for signal verbs: *Baker (2003) showed* or *Baker (2003) has shown*. Use the present tense only to discuss results (*the experiment demonstrates*) or widely accepted information (*researchers agree*).

An in-text citation in APA style always indicates *which source* on the references page the writer is referring to, and it explains *in what year* the material was published; for quoted material, the in-text citation also indicates *where* in the source the quotation can be found.

1. BASIC FORMAT FOR A QUOTATION

Generally, use the author's name in a signal phrase to introduce the cited material, and place the date, in parentheses, immediately after the author's name. The page number, preceded by *p.*, appears in parentheses after the quotation.

> Gitlin (2001) pointed out that "political critics, convinced that the media are rigged against them, are often blind to other substantial reasons why their causes are unpersuasive" (p. 141).

If the author is not named in a signal phrase, place the author's name, the year, and the page number in parentheses after the quotation: (*Gitlin, 2001, p. 141*). For a long, set-off quotation (more than forty words), place the page reference in parentheses one space after the final quotation.

For electronic texts or other works without page numbers, you may use paragraph numbers, if the source includes them, preceded by the abbreviation *para.*

Driver (2007) has noticed "an increasing focus on the role of land" in policy debates over the past decade (para. 1).

2. BASIC FORMAT FOR A PARAPHRASE OR SUMMARY

Include the author's last name and the year as in model 1, but omit the page or paragraph number unless the reader will need it to find the material in a long work.

Gitlin (2001) has argued that critics sometimes overestimate the influence of the media on modern life.

3. TWO AUTHORS

Use both names in all citations. Use *and* in a signal phrase, but use an ampersand (&) instead in a parenthetical reference.

Babcock and Laschever (2003) have suggested that many women do not negotiate their salaries and pay raises as vigorously as their male counterparts do.

A recent study has suggested that many women do not negotiate their salaries and pay raises as vigorously as their male counterparts do (Babcock & Laschever, 2003).

4. THREE TO FIVE AUTHORS

List all the authors' names for the first reference.

Safer, Voccola, Hurd, and Goodwin (2003) reached somewhat different conclusions by designing a study that was less dependent on subjective judgment than were previous studies.

In subsequent references, use just the first author's name plus *et al.* ("and others").

Based on the results, Safer et al. (2003) determined that the apes took significant steps toward self-expression.

5. SIX OR MORE AUTHORS

Use only the first author's name and *et al.* in every citation.

As Soleim et al. (2002) demonstrated, advertising holds the potential for manipulating "free-willed" consumers.

6. CORPORATE OR GROUP AUTHOR

If the name of the organization or corporation is long, spell it out the first time you use it, followed by an abbreviation in brackets. In later references, use the abbreviation only.

FIRST CITATION   (Centers for Disease Control and Prevention [CDC], 2006)
LATER CITATIONS (CDC, 2006)

7. UNKNOWN AUTHOR

Use the title or its first few words in a signal phrase or in parentheses. Italicize a book or report title; place an article title in quotation marks.

The school profiles for the county substantiate this trend (*Guide to secondary schools,* 2003).

8. TWO OR MORE AUTHORS WITH THE SAME LAST NAME

If your list of references includes works by different authors with the same last name, include the authors' initials in each citation.

G. Jones (2001) conducted the groundbreaking study on teenage childbearing.

9. TWO OR MORE WORKS BY AN AUTHOR IN A SINGLE YEAR

Assign lowercase letters (*a, b,* and so on) alphabetically by title, and include the letters after the year.

Gordon (2004b) examined this trend in more detail.

10. TWO OR MORE SOURCES IN ONE PARENTHETICAL REFERENCE

List sources by different authors in alphabetical order by authors' last names, separated by semicolons. List works by the same author in chronological order, separated by commas.

(Cardone, 2004; Lai, 2002)

(Lai, 2000, 2002)

11. INDIRECT SOURCE

Use the phrase *as cited in* to indicate that you are reporting information from a secondary source. Name the original source in a signal phrase, but list the secondary source in your list of references.

Amartya Sen developed the influential concept that land reform was necessary for "promoting opportunity" among the poor (as cited in Driver, 2007, para. 2).

12. EMAIL AND OTHER PERSONAL COMMUNICATION

Cite any personal letters, email messages, electronic postings, telephone conversations, or interviews with the person's initial(s) and last name, the identification *personal communication,* and the date. Do not include personal communications in the reference list.

R. Tobin (personal communication, November 4, 2009) supported his claims about music therapy with new evidence.

13. ELECTRONIC DOCUMENT

Cite a Web or electronic document as you would a print source, using the author's name and date.

Link and Phelan (2005) argued for broader interventions in public health that would be accessible to anyone, regardless of individual wealth.

The APA recommends the following for electronic sources without names, dates, or page numbers:

AUTHOR UNKNOWN

Use a shortened form of the title in a signal phrase or in parentheses (see model 7). If an organization is the author, see model 6.

DATE UNKNOWN

Use the abbreviation *n.d.* (for "no date") in place of the year: (*Hopkins, n.d.*).

NO PAGE NUMBERS

Many works found online or in electronic databases lack stable page numbers. (Use the page numbers for an electronic work in a format, such as PDF, that has stable pagination.) If paragraph numbers are included in such a source, use the abbreviation *para.* (*Giambetti, 2006, para. 7*). If no paragraph numbers are included but the source includes headings, give the heading and identify the paragraph in the section:

Jacobs and Johnson (2007) have argued that "the South African media is still highly concentrated and not very diverse in terms of race and class" (South African Media after Apartheid, para. 3).

14. TABLE OR FIGURE REPRODUCED IN THE TEXT

Number figures (graphs, charts, illustrations, and photographs) and tables separately.

For a table, place the label (*Table 1*) and an informative heading (*Hartman's Key Personality Traits*) above the table; below, provide information about its source.

Table 1
Hartman's Key Personality Traits

Trait category	Color			
	Red	Blue	White	Yellow
Motive	Power	Intimacy	Peace	Fun
Strengths	Loyal to tasks	Loyal to people	Tolerant	Positive
Limitations	Arrogant	Self-righteous	Timid	Uncommitted

Note. Table is adapted from information found at *The Hartman Personality Profile,* by N. Hayden. Retrieved February 24, 2009, from students.cs.byu.edu/~nhayden/Code/index.php

For a figure, place the label (*Figure 3*) and a caption indicating the source below the image. If you do not cite the source of the table or figure elsewhere in your text, you do not need to include the source on your list of references.

APA Style for Content Notes

APA style allows you to use content notes to expand or supplement your text. Indicate such notes in the text by superscript numerals ([1]). Type the notes themselves on a separate page after the last page of

the text, under the heading *Footnotes,* which should be centered at the top of the page. Double-space all entries. Indent the first line of each note five spaces, but begin subsequent lines at the left margin.

SUPERSCRIPT NUMBER IN TEXT

The age of the children involved in the study was an important factor in the selection of items for the questionnaire.[1]

FOOTNOTE

[1]Marjorie Youngston Forman and William Cole of the Child Study Team provided great assistance in identifying appropriate items for the questionnaire.

APA Style for a List of References

The alphabetical list of the sources cited in your document is called *References.* If your instructor asks that you list everything you have read — not just the sources you cite — call the list *Bibliography.*

All the entries in this section of the book use hanging indent format, in which the first line aligns on the left and subsequent lines indent one-half inch or five spaces. This is the customary APA format both for final copy and for manuscripts. Here are guidelines for preparing a list of references:

- Start your list on a separate page after the text of your document but before any appendices or notes. Continue to number pages consecutively.

- Type the heading *References,* neither italicized nor in quotation marks, centered one inch from the top of the page.

- Begin each entry flush left with the left margin, but indent subsequent lines one-half inch or five spaces. Double-space the entire list.

- List sources alphabetically by authors' (or editors') last names. If no author is given, alphabetize the source by the first major word of the

title, disregarding *A, An,* or *The.* If the list includes two or more works by the same author, list them in chronological order. (For two or more works by the same author in the same year, see model 5.)

• Italicize titles and subtitles of books and periodicals. Do not italicize titles of articles, and do not enclose them in quotation marks.

• For titles of books and articles, capitalize only the first word of the title and the subtitle and any proper nouns or proper adjectives.

• For titles of periodicals, capitalize all major words.

Guidelines for Author Listings

List authors' last names first, and use only initials for first and middle names. The in-text citations point readers toward particular sources in your list of references.

NAME CITED IN SIGNAL PHRASE IN TEXT

Driver (2007) has noted . . .

NAME IN PARENTHETICAL CITATION IN TEXT

. . . (Driver, 2007).

BEGINNING OF ENTRY IN LIST OF REFERENCES

Driver, T. (2007).

Models 1–5 below explain how to arrange author names. The information that follows the name of the author depends on the type of work you are citing—a book (models 6–15); a print periodical (models 16–23); an electronic source (models 24–35); or another kind of source (models 36–46). Consult the model that most closely resembles the kind of source you are using.

1. ONE AUTHOR

Give the last name, a comma, the initial(s), and the date in parentheses.

Lightman, A. P. (2002).

2. MULTIPLE AUTHORS

List up to seven authors, last name first, with commas separating authors' names and an ampersand (&) before the last author's name.

Walsh, M. E., & Murphy, J. A. (2003).

Note: For a work with more than seven authors, list the first six, then an ellipses (. . .), then the final author's name.

3. CORPORATE OR GROUP AUTHOR

Resources for Rehabilitation. (2003).

4. UNKNOWN AUTHOR

Begin with the work's title. Italicize book titles, but do not italicize article titles or enclose them in quotation marks. Capitalize only the first word of the title and subtitle (if any) and proper nouns and proper adjectives.

National Geographic atlas of the Middle East. (2003).

5. TWO OR MORE WORKS BY THE SAME AUTHOR

List two or more works by the same author in chronological order. Repeat the author's name in each entry.

Goodall, J. (1999).

Goodall, J. (2002).

If the works appeared in the same year, list them alphabetically by title, and assign lowercase letters (*a*, *b*, etc.) after the dates.

Shermer, M. (2002a). On estimating the lifetime of civilizations. *Scientific American*, *287*(2), 33.

Shermer, M. (2002b). Readers who question evolution. *Scientific American*, *287*(1), 37.

Books

6. BASIC FORMAT FOR A BOOK

Begin with the author name(s). (See models 1–5.) Then include the publication year, the title and subtitle, the city and state (or country) of publication, and the publisher. The source map on pp. 204–05 shows where to find this information in a typical book.

Levick, S. E. (2003). *Clone being: Exploring the psychological and social dimensions*. Lanham, MD: Rowman & Littlefield.

7. EDITOR

Dickens, J. (Ed.). (1995). *Family outing: A guide for parents of gays, lesbians, and bisexuals.* London, England: Peter Owen.

To cite a book with an author and an editor, place the editor's name, followed by a comma and the abbreviation *Ed.*, in parentheses after the title.

Austin, J. (1995). *The province of jurisprudence determined* (W. E. Rumble, Ed.). Cambridge, England: Cambridge University Press.

8. SELECTION IN A BOOK WITH AN EDITOR

Burke, W. W., & Nourmair, D. A. (2001). The role of personality assessment in organization development. In J. Waclawski & A. H. Church (Eds.), *Organization development: A data-driven approach to organizational change* (pp. 55–77). San Francisco, CA: Jossey-Bass.

9. TRANSLATION

Al-Farabi, A. N. (1998). *On the perfect state* (R. Walzer, Trans.). Chicago, IL: Kazi.

10. EDITION OTHER THAN THE FIRST

Moore, G. S. (2002). *Living with the earth: Concepts in environmental health science* (2nd ed.). New York, NY: Lewis.

11. MULTIVOLUME WORK

Barnes, J. (Ed.). (1995). *Complete works of Aristotle* (Vols. 1–2). Princeton, NJ: Princeton University Press.

Note: If you cite one volume of a multivolume work, list the volume used, instead of the complete span of volumes, in parentheses after the title.

APA SOURCE MAP: Citing books

Take information from the book's title page and copyright page (on the reverse side of the title page), not from the book's cover or a library catalog.

① **Author.** List all authors' last names first, and use only initials for first and middle names. For more about citing authors, see models 1–5.

② **Publication year.** Enclose the year of publication in parentheses.

③ **Title.** Italicize the title and any subtitle. Capitalize only the first word of the title and the subtitle and any proper nouns or proper adjectives.

④ **City and state of publication.** List the city of publication and the country or state abbreviation followed by a colon.

⑤ **Publisher.** Give the publisher's name, dropping any *Inc.*, *Co.*, or *Publishers*.

A citation for the work on p. 205 would look like this:

  ①   ②   ③

Tsutsui, W. (2004). *Godzilla on my mind: Fifty years of the king of monsters*. New York, NY: Palgrave Macmillan.

       ④   ⑤

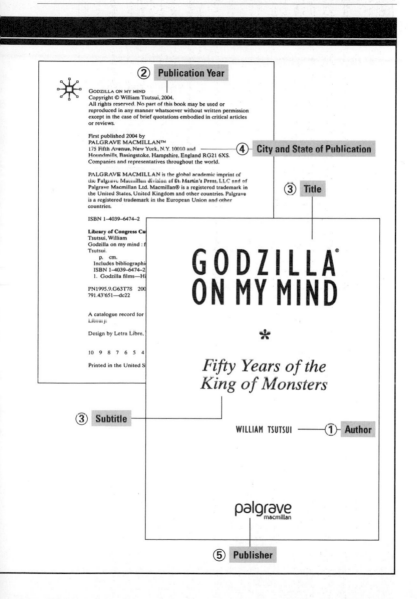

② **Publication Year**

GODZILLA ON MY MIND
Copyright © William Tsutsui, 2004.
All rights reserved. No part of this book may be used or
reproduced in any manner whatsoever without written permission
except in the case of brief quotations embodied in critical articles
or reviews.

First published 2004 by
PALGRAVE MACMILLAN™
175 Fifth Avenue, New York, N.Y. 10010 and
Houndmills, Basingstoke, Hampshire, England RG21 6XS.
Companies and representatives throughout the world.

④ **City and State of Publication**

PALGRAVE MACMILLAN is the global academic imprint of
the Palgrave Macmillan division of St. Martin's Press, LLC and of
Palgrave Macmillan Ltd. Macmillan® is a registered trademark in
the United States, United Kingdom and other countries. Palgrave
is a registered trademark in the European Union and other
countries.

③ **Title**

ISBN 1-4039-6474-2

Library of Congress Ca
Tsutsui, William
Godzilla on my mind : f
Tsutsui.
    p. cm.
    Includes bibliographi
    ISBN 1-4039-6474-2
    1. Godzilla films—Hi

PN1995.9.G63T78   200
791.43'651—dc22

A catalogue record for
Library.

Design by Letra Libre.

10 9 8 7 6 5 4

Printed in the United S

GODZILLA®
ON MY MIND

✳

*Fifty Years of the
King of Monsters*

③ **Subtitle**

WILLIAM TSUTSUI ——① **Author**

palgrave
macmillan

⑤ **Publisher**

12. ARTICLE IN A REFERENCE WORK

If no author is listed, begin with the title.

Dean, C. (1994). Jaws and teeth. In *The Cambridge encyclopedia of human evolution* (pp. 56–59). Cambridge, England: Cambridge University Press.

13. REPUBLISHED BOOK

Piaget, J. (1952). *The language and thought of the child.* London, England: Routledge & Kegan Paul. (Original work published 1932.)

14. INTRODUCTION, PREFACE, FOREWORD, OR AFTERWORD

Klosterman, C. (2007). Introduction. In P. Shirley, *Can I keep my jersey?: 11 teams, 5 countries, and 4 years in my life as a basketball vagabond* (pp. v–vii). New York, NY: Villard-Random House.

15. BOOK WITH A TITLE WITHIN THE TITLE

Klarman, M. J. (2007). Brown v. Board of Education *and the civil rights movement.* New York, NY: Oxford University Press.

Print Periodicals

Begin with the author name(s). (See models 1–5.) Then include the publication date (year only for journals, and year, month, and day for other periodicals); the article title; the periodical title; the volume and issue numbers, if any; and the page numbers. The basic format for a reference-list entry for an article in a periodical is outlined on pp. 208–9.

16. ARTICLE IN A JOURNAL PAGINATED BY VOLUME

O'Connell, D. C., & Kowal, S. (2003). Psycholinguistics: A half
century of monologism. *The American Journal of Psychology,
116*, 191–212.

17. ARTICLE IN A JOURNAL PAGINATED BY ISSUE

If each issue begins with page 1, include the issue number after
the volume number.

Hall, R. E. (2000). Marriage as vehicle of racism among women of
color. *Psychology: A Journal of Human Behavior, 37*(2), 29–40.

18. ARTICLE IN A MAGAZINE

Ricciardi, S. (2003, August 5). Enabling the mobile work force. *PC
Magazine, 22,* 46.

19. ARTICLE IN A NEWSPAPER

Faler, B. (2003, August 29). Primary colors. Race and fundraising.
The Washington Post, p. A5.

20. EDITORIAL OR LETTER TO THE EDITOR

Zelneck, B. (2003, July 18). Serving the public at public universities
[Letter to the editor]. *The Chronicle Review,* p. B18.

21. UNSIGNED ARTICLE

Annual meeting announcement. (2003, March). *Cognitive Psychology,
46,* 227.

22. REVIEW

Ringel, S. (2003). [Review of the book *Multiculturalism and the ther-
apeutic process*]. *Clinical Social Work Journal, 31,* 212–213.

APA SOURCE MAP: Citing articles from print periodicals

① **Author.** List all authors' last names first, and use only initials for first and middle names. For more about citing authors, see models 1–5.

② **Publication date.** Enclose the date in parentheses. For journals, use only the year. For magazines and newspapers, use the year, a comma, the month (spelled out), and the day, if given.

③ **Article title.** Do not italicize or enclose article titles in quotation marks. Capitalize only the first word of the article title and subtitle and any proper nouns or proper adjectives.

④ **Periodical title.** Italicize the periodical title (and subtitle, if any), and capitalize all major words.

⑤ **Volume and issue numbers.** Follow the periodical title with a comma, and then give the volume number (italicized) and, without a space in between, the issue number (if given) in parentheses.

⑥ **Page numbers.** Give the inclusive page numbers of the article. For newspapers only, include the abbreviation p. ("page") or pp. ("pages") before the page numbers. End the citation with a period.

A citation for the periodical article on p. 209 would look like this:

①   ②   ③

Etzioni, A. (2006). Leaving race behind: Our growing Hispanic population

creates a golden opportunity. *The American Scholar,* *75*(2), 20–30.

④   ⑤   ⑥

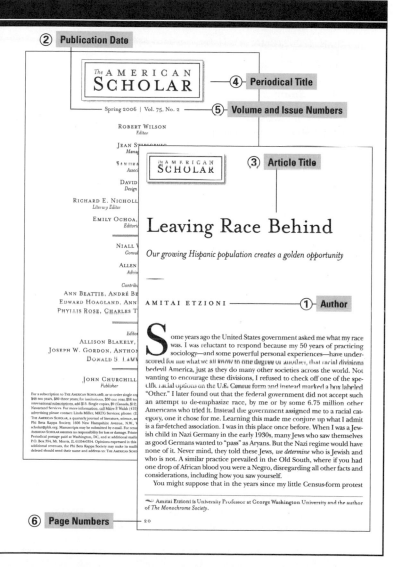

② **Publication Date**

The AMERICAN SCHOLAR

④— **Periodical Title**

Spring 2006 | Vol. 75. No. 2 —⑤— **Volume and Issue Numbers**

ROBERT WILSON
Editor

JEAN STIPICEVIC
Mana

SANDRA
Associ

DAVID
Design

RICHARD E. NICHOLL
Literary Editor

EMILY OCHOA,
Editori

NIALL
Consu

ALLEN
Advis

Contribu
ANN BEATTIE, ANDRÉ BE
EDWARD HOAGLAND, ANN
PHYLLIS ROSE, CHARLES T

Edito
ALLISON BLAKELY,
JOSEPH W. GORDON, ANTHON
DONALD S. LAMM

JOHN CHURCHILL
Publisher

For a subscription to THE AMERICAN SCHOLAR, or to order single co
$48 two years, $69 three years; for institutions, $50 one year, $98 two
international subscriptions, add $15. Single copies, $9 (Canada, $12);
Newsstand Services. For more information, call Máire P. Walsh (415)
advertising please contact: Linda Miller, MKTG Services; phone: (2
THE AMERICAN SCHOLAR, a quarterly journal of literature, science, an
Phi Beta Kappa Society, 1606 New Hampshire Avenue, N.W., W
AMERICAN SCHOLAR assumes no responsibility for loss or damage. Printe
Periodical postage paid at Washington, DC, and at additional mailin
P.O. Box 354, Mt. Morris, IL 61054-0354. Opinions expressed in this
additional revenues, the Phi Beta Kappa Society may make its maili
deleted should send their name and address to: THE AMERICAN SCHO

The AMERICAN SCHOLAR

③ **Article Title**

Leaving Race Behind

Our growing Hispanic population creates a golden opportunity

AMITAI ETZIONI ——————①— **Author**

Some years ago the United States government asked me what my race was. I was reluctant to respond because my 50 years of practicing sociology—and some powerful personal experiences—have under-scored for me what we all know to one degree or another, that racial divisions bedevil America, just as they do many other societies across the world. Not wanting to encourage these divisions, I refused to check off one of the spe-cific racial options on the U.S. Census form and instead marked a box labeled "Other." I later found out that the federal government did not accept such an attempt to de-emphasize race, by me or by some 6.75 million other Americans who tried it. Instead the government assigned me to a racial cat-egory, one it chose for me. Learning this made me conjure up what I admit is a far-fetched association. I was in this place once before. When I was a Jew-ish child in Nazi Germany in the early 1930s, many Jews who saw themselves as good Germans wanted to "pass" as Aryans. But the Nazi regime would have none of it. Never mind, they told these Jews, *we determine* who is Jewish and who is not. A similar practice prevailed in the Old South, where if you had one drop of African blood you were a Negro, disregarding all other facts and considerations, including how you saw yourself.

You might suppose that in the years since my little Census-form protest

～ Amitai Etzioni is University Professor at George Washington University and the author of *The Monochrome Society.*

⑥ **Page Numbers** —— 20

23. PUBLISHED INTERVIEW

Smith, H. (2002, October). [Interview with A. Thompson]. *The Sun*, pp. 4–7.

Electronic Sources

Updated guidelines for citing electronic resources are maintained at the APA's Web site (www.apa.org).

When citing sources accessed online or from an electronic database, include as many of the following elements as you can find:

- *Author.* Give the author's name, if available.

- *Publication date.* Include the date of electronic publication or of the latest update, if available. Use *n.d.* ("no date") when the publication date is unavailable.

- *Title.* List the title of the document, neither italicized nor in quotation marks.

- *Print publication information.* For articles from online journals, newspapers, or reference databases, give the publication title and other publishing information as you would for a print periodical. (See models 16–23.)

- *Retrieval information.* For a work from a database, do the following: if the article has a DOI (digital object identifier), include that number after the publication's information; do not include the name of the database. If there is no DOI, write *Retrieved from* followed by the URL for the journal's home page (not the database URL). For a work found on a Web site, write *Retrieved from* and include the URL. If the work seems likely to be updated or has no date of publication, include the retrieval date. If the URL will not fit on one line, break it only before a punctuation mark; do not break *http://*.

24. ARTICLE FROM AN ONLINE PERIODICAL

Give the author, date, title, and publication information as you would for a print document. Include both the volume and issue numbers for all journal articles. If the article has a digital object identifier

(DOI), include it. If there is no DOI, include the URL for the periodical's home page or for the article (if the article is difficult to find from the home page). For newspaper articles accessible from a searchable Web site, give the site URL only.

> Barringer, F. (2008, February 7). In many communities, it's not easy going green. *The New York Times*. Retrieved from http://www. nytimes.com

> Cleary, J. M., & Crafti, N. (2007). Basic need satisfaction, emotional eating, and dietary restraint as risk factors for recurrent overeating in a community sample. *E-Journal of Applied Psychology, 2*(3), 27–39. Retrieved from http://ojs.lib.swin .edu.au/index.php/ejap/article/view/90/118

25. ARTICLE FROM A DATABASE

Give the author, date, title, and publication information as you would for a print document. Include both the volume and issue numbers for all journal articles. If the article has a DOI, include it. If there is no DOI, write *Retrieved from* and the URL of the journal's home page (not the URL of the database). The source map on pp. 212–13 shows where to find this information for a typical article from a database.

> Hazleden, R. (2003, December). Love yourself: The relationship of the self with itself in popular self-help texts. *Journal of Sociology, 39*(4), 413–428. Retrieved from http://jos.sagepub .com

> Morley, N. J., Ball, L. J., & Ormerod, T. C. (2006). How the detection of insurance fraud succeeds and fails. *Psychology, Crime, & Law, 12*(2), 163–180. doi:10.1080/10683160512331316325

APA SOURCE MAP: Citing articles from databases

(1) **Authors.** Include the author's name as you would for a print source. List all authors' last names first, and use initials for first and middle names. For more about citing authors, see models 1–5.

(2) **Publication date.** Enclose the date in parentheses. For journals, use only the year. For magazines and newspapers, use the year, a comma, the month, and the day if given.

(3) **Article title.** Capitalize only the first word of the article title and the subtitle and any proper nouns or proper adjectives.

(4) **Periodical title.** Italicize the periodical title and capitalize the first letter of all non-prepositions.

(5) **Print publication information.** For journals and magazines, give the volume number (italicized) and the issue number (in parentheses). For journals only, give the inclusive page numbers.

(6) **Retrieval information.** If the article has a DOI (digital object identifier), include that number after the publication information; do not include the name of the database. If there is no DOI, write *Retrieved from* followed by the URL of the journal's home page (not the database URL).

A citation for the article on p. 213 would look like this:

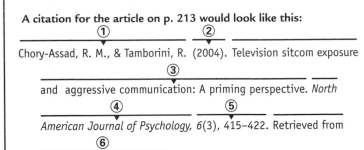

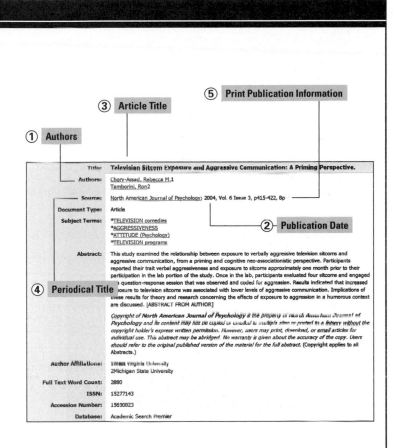

③ Article Title

⑤ Print Publication Information

① Authors

Title:	Television Sitcom Exposure and Aggressive Communication: A Priming Perspective.
Authors:	Chory-Assad, Rebecca M.1 Tamborini, Ron2
Source:	North American Journal of Psychology; 2004, Vol. 6 Issue 3, p415-422, 8p
Document Type:	Article
Subject Terms:	*TELEVISION comedies *AGGRESSIVENESS *ATTITUDE (Psychology) *TELEVISION programs
Abstract:	This study examined the relationship between exposure to verbally aggressive television sitcoms and aggressive communication, from a priming and cognitive neo-associationistic perspective. Participants reported their trait verbal aggressiveness and exposure to sitcoms approximately one month prior to their participation in the lab portion of the study. Once in the lab, participants evaluated four sitcoms and engaged in a question-response session that was observed and coded for aggression. Results indicated that increased exposure to television sitcoms was associated with lower levels of aggressive communication. Implications of these results for theory and research concerning the effects of exposure to aggression in a humorous context are discussed. [ABSTRACT FROM AUTHOR] *Copyright of North American Journal of Psychology is the property of North American Journal of Psychology and its content may not be copied or emailed to multiple sites or posted to a listserv without the copyright holder's express written permission. However, users may print, download, or email articles for individual use. This abstract may be abridged. No warranty is given about the accuracy of the copy. Users should refer to the original published version of the material for the full abstract. (Copyright applies to all Abstracts.)*
Author Affiliations:	1West Virginia University 2Michigan State University
Full Text Word Count:	2890
ISSN:	15277143
Accession Number:	15630823
Database:	Academic Search Premier

② Publication Date

④ Periodical Title

26. ABSTRACT FOR AN ONLINE ARTICLE

Gudjonsson, G. H., & Young, S. (2010). Does confabulation in
memory predict suggestibility beyond IQ and memory?
[Abstract]. *Personality & Individual Differences, 49*, 65–67.
doi:10.1016/j.paid.2010.03.014

27. DOCUMENT FROM A WEB SITE

The APA refers to works that are not peer reviewed, such as
reports, press releases, brochures, and presentation slides, as "gray
literature." Include all of the following information that you can find:
the author's name; the publication date (or *n.d.* if no date is available);
the title of the document; the title of the site or larger work, if any;
any publication information available in addition to the date;
Retrieved from and the URL. Provide your date of access only if no
publication date is given. The source map on pp. 216–217 shows
where to find this information for an article from a Web site.

Behnke, P. C. (2006, February 22). The homeless are everyone's
problem. *Authors' Den*. Retrieved from http://www.authorsden
.com/visit/viewArticle.asp?id=21017

Hacker, J. S. (2006). The privatization of risk and the growing economic
insecurity of Americans. *Items and Issues, 5*(4), 16–23. Retrieved
from http://publications.ssrc.org/items/items5.4/Hacker.pdf

What parents should know about treatment of behavioral and
emotional disorders in preschool children. (2006). *APA Online*.
Retrieved from http://www.apa.org/releases/kidsmed.html

28. CHAPTER OR SECTION OF A WEB DOCUMENT

Follow model 24. After the chapter or section title, type *In* and
give the document title, with identifying information, if any, in
parentheses. End with the date of access and the URL.

Salamon, Andrew. (n.d.). War in Europe. In *Childhood in times of war* (chap. 2). Retrieved April 11, 2005, from http://remember.org/jean

29. EMAIL MESSAGE OR REAL-TIME COMMUNICATION

Because the APA stresses that any sources cited in your list of references be retrievable by your readers, you should not include entries for email messages, real-time communications (such as IMs), or any other postings that are not archived in the list of references. Instead, cite these sources in your text as forms of personal communication (see p. 195).

30. ONLINE POSTING

List an online posting in the references list only if the message is retrievable from a mailing list's archive. Give the author's name and the posting's date and subject line. Include other identifying information in square brackets. End with the retrieval statement and the URL of the archived message.

Troike, R. C. (2001, June 21). Buttercups and primroses [Electronic mailing list message]. Retrieved from http://listserv.linguistlist.org/archives/ads-l.html

Wittenberg, E. (2001, July 11). Gender and the Internet [Newsgroup message]. Retrieved from news://comp.edu.composition

31. WEB LOG (BLOG) POST

Spaulding, P. (2008, April 16). I did laundry rather than watch tonight's debate [Web log post]. Retrieved from http://pandagon.blogsome.com/

APA SOURCE MAP: Citing works from Web sites

(1) **Author.** If one is given, include the author's name (see models 1–5). List last names first, and use only initials for first names. The site's sponsor may be the author. If no author is identified, begin the citation with the title of the document.

(2) **Publication date.** Enclose the date of publication or latest update in parentheses. Use *n.d.* ("no date") when no publication date is available.

(3) **Title of work.** Capitalize only the first word of the title and subtitle and any proper nouns or proper adjectives.

(4) **Title of Web site.** Italicize the title. Capitalize all major words.

(5) **Retrieval information.** Write *Retrieved from* and include the URL. If the work seems likely to be updated, include the retrieval date.

A citation for the Web document on p. 217 would look like this:

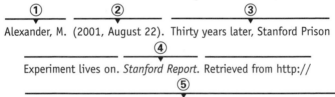

Alexander, M. (2001, August 22). Thirty years later, Stanford Prison

Experiment lives on. *Stanford Report*. Retrieved from http://

news-service.stanford.edu/news/2001/august22/prison2-822.html

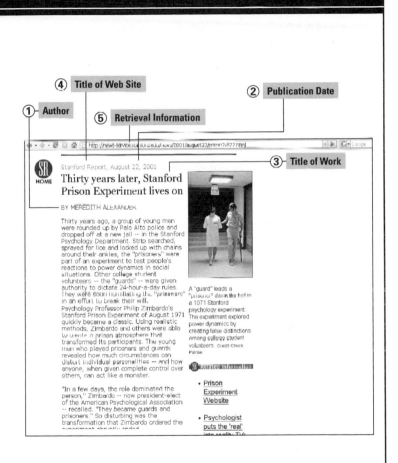

④ **Title of Web Site**

② **Publication Date**

① **Author**

⑤ **Retrieval Information**

http://news-service.stanford.edu/news/2001/august22/prison?vR22.html

③ **Title of Work**

Stanford Report, August 22, 2001

Thirty years later, Stanford Prison Experiment lives on

BY MEREDITH ALEXANDER

Thirty years ago, a group of young men were rounded up by Palo Alto police and dropped off at a new jail -- in the Stanford Psychology Department. Strip searched, sprayed for lice and locked up with chains around their ankles, the "prisoners" were part of an experiment to test people's reactions to power dynamics in social situations. Other college student volunteers -- the "guards" -- were given authority to dictate 24-hour-a-day rules. They were soon humiliating the "prisoners" in an effort to break their will. Psychology Professor Philip Zimbardo's Stanford Prison Experiment of August 1971 quickly became a classic. Using realistic methods, Zimbardo and others were able to create a prison atmosphere that transformed its participants. The young men who played prisoners and guards revealed how much circumstances can distort individual personalities -- and how anyone, when given complete control over others, can act like a monster.

"In a few days, the role dominated the person," Zimbardo -- now president-elect of the American Psychological Association -- recalled. "They became guards and prisoners." So disturbing was the transformation that Zimbardo ordered the experiment abruptly ended.

A "guard" leads a "prisoner" down the hall in a 1971 Stanford psychology experiment. The experiment explored power dynamics by creating false distinctions among college student volunteers. Credit: Chuck Painter

Related information

- Prison Experiment Website

- Psychologist puts the 'real' into reality TV

32. WIKI ENTRY

Use the date of posting, if there is one, or *n.d.* for "no date" if there is none. Include the retrieval date because wiki content can change frequently.

Happiness. (2007, June 14). Retrieved March 24, 2008, from
    PsychWiki: http://www.psychwiki.com/wiki/Happiness

33. ONLINE AUDIO OR VIDEO FILE

Klusman, P. (2008, February 13). An engineer's guide to cats
    [Video file]. Video posted to http://www.youtube.com
    /watch?v=mHXBL6bzAR4

O'Brien, K. (2008, January 31). Developing countries. *KUSP's life
    in the fast lane* [Audio file]. Retrieved from http://kusp.org
    /shows/fast.html

34. DATA SET

U.S. Department of Education, Institute of Education Sciences.
    (2009). *NAEP state comparisons* [Data set]. Retrieved from
    http://nces.ed.gov/nationsreportcard/statecomparisons/

35. COMPUTER SOFTWARE

PsychMate [Computer software]. (2003). Available from Psychology
    Software Tools: http://pstnet.com/products/psychmate

Other Sources (Including Online Versions)

36. GOVERNMENT PUBLICATION

Office of the Federal Register. (2003). *The United States government
    manual 2003/2004*. Washington, DC: U.S. Government Printing
    Office.

Cite an online government document as you would a printed government work, adding the date of access and the URL. If there is no date, use *n.d.*

> U.S. Public Health Service. (1999). *The surgeon general's call to*
>   *action to prevent suicide.* Retrieved November 5, 2003, from
>   http://www.mentalhealth.org/suicideprevention/calltoaction
>   .asp

37. DISSERTATION

If you retrieved the dissertation from a database, give the database name and the accession number, if one is assigned.

> Lengel, L. L. (1968). *The righteous cause: Some religious aspects of*
>   *Kansas populism.* Retrieved from ProQuest Digital Dissertations.
>   (6900033)

If you retrieve a dissertation from a Web site, give the type of dissertation, the institution, and year after the title, and provide a retrieval statement.

> Meeks, M. G. (2006). *Between abolition and reform: First-year*
>   *writing programs, e-literacies, and institutional change* (Doctoral
>   dissertation, University of North Carolina). Retrieved from
>   http://dc.lib.unc.edu/etd/

38. TECHNICAL OR RESEARCH REPORT

Give the report number, if available, in parentheses after the title.

> McCool, R., Fikes, R., & McGuinness, D. (2003). *Semantic Web tools*
>   *for enhanced authoring* (Report No. KSL-03-07). Stanford, CA:
>   Knowledge Systems Laboratory.

39. CONFERENCE PROCEEDINGS

Mama, A. (2001). Challenging subjects: Gender and power in African contexts. In *Proceedings of Nordic African Institute Conference: Rethinking power in Africa*. Uppsala, Sweden, 9–18.

40. PAPER PRESENTED AT A MEETING OR SYMPOSIUM, UNPUBLISHED

Cite the month of the meeting if it is available.

Jones, J. G. (1999, February). *Mental health intervention in mass casualty disasters*. Paper presented at the Rocky Mountain Region Disaster Mental Health Conference, Laramie, WY.

41. POSTER SESSION

Barnes Young, L. L. (2003, August). *Cognition, aging, and dementia*. Poster session presented at the 2003 Division 40 APA Convention, Toronto, Ontario, Canada.

42. FILM, VIDEO, OR DVD

Mottola, G. (Director). (2007). *Superbad* [Motion picture]. United States: Sony.

43. TELEVISION PROGRAM, SINGLE EPISODE

Imperioli, M. (Writer), & Buscemi, S. (Director). (2002). Everybody hurts [Television series episode]. In D. Chase (Executive Producer), *The Sopranos*. New York, NY: HBO.

44. TELEVISION SERIES

Abrams, J. J., Lieber, J., & Lindelof, D. (2004). *Lost* [Television series]. New York, NY: WABC.

45. AUDIO PODCAST

Noguchi, Yugi. (2010, 24 May). BP hard to pin down on oil spill claims. [Audio podcast]. *NPR morning edition*. Retrieved from http://www.npr.org/templates/story/story.php?storyld =127038021

46. RECORDING

The Avalanches. (2001). Frontier psychiatrist. On *Since I left you* [CD]. Los Angeles: Elektra/Asylum Records.

A Student Research Essay, APA Style

Student Writer

Tawnya Redding

On the following pages is a paper by Tawnya Redding that conforms to the APA guidelines described in this chapter. Note that this essay has been reproduced in a narrow format to allow for annotation.

Running head
(fifty charac-
ters or fewer)
appears flush
left on first line
of title page

Page number
appears flush
right on first
line of every
page

Title, name,
and affiliation
centered and
double-spaced

Running Head: MOOD MUSIC   1

Mood Music: Music Preference and the Risk for Depression

and Suicide in Adolescents

Tawnya Redding

Psychology 480

Professor Ede

February 23, 2009

MOOD MUSIC   2

Abstract

There has long been concern for the effects that certain
genres of music (such as heavy metal and country) have on
youth. While a correlational link between these genres and
increased risk for depression and suicide in adolescents has
been established, researchers have been unable to pinpoint
what is responsible for this link, and a causal relationship
has not been determined. This paper will begin by
discussing correlational literature concerning music
preference and increased risk for depression and suicide, as
well as the possible reasons for this link. Finally, studies
concerning the effects of music on mood will be discussed.
This examination of the literature on music and increased
risk for depression and suicide points out the limitations of
previous research and suggests the need for new research
establishing a causal relationship for this link as well as
research into the specific factors that may contribute to an
increased risk for depression and suicide in adolescents.

Heading
centered

No indentation

Use of passive
voice appropri-
ate for social
sciences

Clear, straight-
forward
description
of literature
under review

Conclusions
indicated

Double-spaced
text

Full title
centered

Paragraphs
indented

Background
information
about review
supplied

Questions
focus reader's
attention

Mood Music: Music Preference and the Risk for Depression
and Suicide in Adolescents

Music is a significant part of American culture. Since
the explosion of rock and roll in the 1950s there has been
a concern for the effects that music may have on listeners,
and especially on young people. The genres most likely
to come under suspicion in recent decades have included
heavy metal, country, and blues. These genres have been
suspected of having adverse effects on the mood and
behavior of young listeners. But can music really alter
the disposition and create self-destructive behaviors in
listeners? And if so, which genres and aspects of those
genres are responsible? The following review of the
literature will establish the correlation between potentially
problematic genres of music such as heavy metal and
country and depression and suicide risk. First, correlational
studies concerning music preference and suicide risk will
be discussed, followed by a discussion of the literature
concerning the possible reasons for this link. Finally,
studies concerning the effects of music on mood will be
discussed. Despite the link between genres such as heavy
metal and country and suicide risk, previous research has
been unable to establish the causal nature of this link.

The Correlation Between Music and Depression and Suicide Risk

Studies over the past two decades have set out to answer this question by examining the correlation between youth music preference and risk for depression and suicide. A large portion of these studies have focused on heavy metal and country music as the main genre culprits associated with youth suicidality and depression (Lacourse, Claes, & Villeneuve, 2001; Scheel & Westefeld, 1999; Stack & Gundlach, 1992). Stack and Gundlach (1992) examined the radio airtime devoted to country music in 49 metropolitan areas and found that the higher the percentages of country music airtime, the higher the incidence of suicides among whites. The researchers hypothesized that themes in country music (such as alcohol abuse) promoted audience identification and reinforced a preexisting suicidal mood, and that the themes associated with country music were responsible for elevated suicide rates. Similarly, Scheel and Westefeld (1999) found a correlation between heavy metal music listeners and an increased risk for suicide, as did Lacourse et al. (2001).

Reasons for the Link: Characteristics of Those Who Listen to Problematic Music

Unfortunately, previous studies concerning music preference and suicide risk have been unable to determine a

Boldface headings help organize review

Parenthetical references follow APA style

MOOD MUSIC   5

Discussion of correlation vs. causation points out limitations of previous studies

causal relationship and have focused mainly on establishing a correlation between suicide risk and music preference. This leaves the question open as to whether an individual at risk for depression and suicide is attracted to certain genres of music or whether the music helps induce the mood — or both. Some studies have suggested that music preference may simply be a reflection of other underlying problems associated with increased risk for suicide (Lacourse et al., 2001; Scheel & Westefeld, 1999). For example, in research done by Scheel and Westefeld (1999), adolescents who listened to heavy metal were found to have lower scores on the Reason for Living Inventory and several of its subscales, a self-report measure designed to assess potential reasons for not committing suicide. These adolescents were also found to have lower scores on several subscales of the Reason for Living Inventory,

Alternative explanations considered

including responsibility to family along with survival and coping beliefs. Other risk factors associated with suicide and suicidal behaviors include poor family relationships, depression, alienation, anomie, and drug and alcohol abuse (Lacourse et al., 2001). Lacourse et al. (2001) examined 275 adolescents in the Montreal region with a preference for heavy metal and found that this preference was not significantly related to suicide risk when other risk factors were controlled for. This was also the conclusion of Scheel and Westefeld (1999), in which music preference for heavy metal was

MOOD MUSIC   6

thought to be a red flag for suicide vulnerability, suggesting that the source of the problem may lie more in personal and familial characteristics.

George, Stickle, Rachid, and Wopnford (2007) further explored the correlation between suicide risk and music preference by attempting to identify the personality characteristics of those with a preference for different genres of music. A sample of 358 individuals was assessed for preference of 30 different styles of music along with a number of personality characteristics, including self-esteem, intelligence, spirituality, social skills, locus of control, openness, conscientiousness, extraversion, agreeableness, emotional stability, hostility, and depression (George et al., 2007). The thirty styles of music were then categorized into eight factors: rebellious (for example, punk and heavy metal), classical, rhythmic and intense (including hip-hop, rap, and pop), easy listening, fringe (for example, techno), contemporary Christian, jazz and blues, and traditional Christian. The results revealed an almost comprehensively negative personality profile for those who preferred to listen to the rebellious and rhythmic and intense categories, while those who preferred classical music tended to have a comprehensively positive profile. Like Scheel and Westefeld (1999) and Lacourse et al. (2001), this study also supports the theory that youth are drawn to certain genres of music

based on already existing factors, whether they be related to personality or situational variables.

Reasons for the Link: Characteristics of Problematic Music

Transition links paragraphs

Another possible explanation is that the lyrics and themes of the music have an effect on listeners. In this scenario, music is thought to exacerbate an already depressed mood and hence contribute to an increased risk for suicide. This was the proposed reasoning behind higher suicide rates in whites in Stack and Gundlach's (1992) study linking country music to suicide risk. In this case, the themes associated with country music were thought to promote audience identification and reinforce preexisting self-destructive behaviors (such as excessive alcohol consumption). Stack (2000) also studied individuals with a musical preference for blues to determine whether the genre's themes could increase the level of suicide acceptability. The results demonstrated that blues fans were no more accepting of suicide than nonfans, but that blues listeners were found to have low religiosity levels,

Need for more research indicated

an important factor for suicide acceptability (Stack, 2000). Despite this link between possible suicidal behavior and a preference for blues music, the actual suicide behavior of blues fans has not been explored, and thus no concrete associations can be made.

The Effect of Music on Mood

While studies examining the relationship between music genres such as heavy metal, country, and blues have been able to establish a correlation between music preference and suicide risk, it is still unclear from these studies what effect music has on the mood of the listener. Previous research has suggested that some forms of music can both improve and depress mood (Lai, 1999; Siedliecki & Good, 2006; Smith & Noon, 1998). Lai (1999) found that changes in mood were more likely to be found in an experimental group of depressed women versus a control group. It was also found that both the experimental and control groups showed significant increases in the tranquil mood state, but the amount of change was not significant between the groups (Lai, 1999). This study suggests that music can have a positive effect on depressed individuals when they are allowed to choose the music they are listening to. In a similar study, Siedliecki and Good (2006) found that music can increase a listener's sense of power and decrease depression, pain, and disability. Researchers randomly assigned 60 African American and Caucasian participants with chronic nonmalignant pain to a standard music group (offering them a choice of instrumental music types — piano, jazz, orchestra, harp, and synthesizer), a patterning music group (asking them to choose music to

Discussion of previous research

ease muscle tension, to facilitate sleep, or to decrease anxiety), or a control group. There were no statistically significant differences between the two music groups. However, the music groups had significantly less pain, depression, and disability than the control group (Siedliecki & Good, 2006). On the other hand, Martin, Clark, and Pearce (1993) identified a subgroup of heavy metal fans who reported feeling worse after listening to their music of choice. Although this subgroup did exist, there was also evidence that listening to heavy metal results in more positive affect, and it was hypothesized that those who experience negative effects after listening to their preferred genre of heavy metal may be most at risk for suicidal behaviors (Martin et al., 1993).

Smith and Noon (1998) also determined that music can have a negative effect on mood. Six songs were selected for the particular theme they embodied: (1) vigorous, (2) fatigued, (3) angry, (4) depressed, (5) tense, and (6) all moods. The results indicated that selections 3–6 had significant effects on the mood of participants, with selection 6 (all moods) resulting in the greatest positive change in the mood and selection 5 (tense) resulting in the greatest negative change in mood. Selection 4 (depressed) was found to sap the vigor and increase anger/hostility in participants, while

selection 5 (tense) significantly depressed participants
and made them more anxious. Although this study did not
specifically comment on the effects of different genres
on mood, the results do indicate that certain themes can
indeed depress mood. The participants for this study were
undergraduate students who were not depressed, and thus
it seems that certain types of music can have a negative
effect on the mood of healthy individuals.

Is There Evidence for a Causal Relationship?

Despite the correlation between certain music genres
(especially heavy metal) and increased risk for depression
and suicidal behaviors in adolescents, it remains unclear
whether these types of music can alter the mood of at-
risk youth in a negative way. This view of the correlation
between music and suicide risk is supported by a meta-
analysis done by Baker and Bor (2008), in which the
authors assert that most studies reject the notion that
music is a causal factor and suggest that music preference
is more indicative of emotional vulnerability. However, it
is still unknown whether these genres can negatively alter
mood at all, and if they can, whether the themes and lyrics
associated with the music are responsible. Clearly, more
research is needed to further examine this correlation, as a
causal link between these genres of music and adolescent
suicide risk has yet to be shown. However, even if the

Conclusion
indicates need
for further
research

MOOD MUSIC   11

theory put forth by Baker and Bor and other researchers
is true, it is still important to investigate the effects that
music can have on those who may be at risk for suicide and
depression. Even if music genres are not the ultimate cause
of suicidal behavior, they may act as a catalyst that further
pushes adolescents into a state of depression and increased
risk for suicidal behavior.

MOOD MUSIC   12

References

Baker, F., & Bor, W. (2008). Can music preference indicate
    mental health status in young people? *Australasian*
    Psychiatry, 16(4), 284–288. Retrieved from http://
    www3.interscience.wiley.com/journal/118565538
    /home

George, D., Stickle, K., Rachid, F., & Wopnford, A. (2007). The
    association between types of music enjoyed and cognitive,
    behavioral, and personality factors of those who listen.
    Psychomusicology, 19(2), 32–56.

Lacourse, E., Claes, M., & Villeneuve, M. (2001). Heavy
    metal music and adolescent suicidal risk. *Journal of*
    Youth and Adolescence, 30(3), 321–332.

Lai, Y. (1999). Effects of music listening on depressed
    women in Taiwan. *Issues in Mental Health Nursing, 20,*
    229–246. doi: 10.1080/016128499248637

Martin, G., Clark, M., & Pearce, C. (1993). Adolescent
    suicide: Music preference as an indicator of vulner-
    ability. *Journal of the American Academy of Child and*
    Adolescent Psychiatry, 32, 530–535.

Scheel, K., & Westefeld, J. (1999). Heavy metal music and
    adolescent suicidality: An empirical investigation. *Adoles-*
    cence, 34(134), 253–273.

Siedliecki, S., & Good, M. (2006). Effect of music on power,
    pain, depression and disability. *Journal of Advanced*

*References
begin on new
page*

*Journal article
from a data-
base, no DOI*

*Print journal
article*

*Journal article
from a data-
base with DOI*

MOOD MUSIC   13

Nursing, 54(5), 553 – 562. doi: 10.1111/j.1365-2648
.2006.03860.x

Smith, J. L., & Noon, J. (1998). Objective measurement of
mood change induced by contemporary music. *Journal
of Psychiatric & Mental Health Nursing, 5,* 403 – 408.

Stack, S. (2000). Blues fans and suicide acceptability. *Death
Studies, 24,* 223 – 231.

Stack, S., & Gundlach, J. (1992). The effect of country
music on suicide. *Social Forces, 71*(1), 211 – 218.
Retrieved from http://socialforces.unc.edu/

7

Research in the Natural and Physical Sciences and in Mathematics

Resources in the Natural and Physical Sciences and in Mathematics

GENERAL REFERENCE SOURCES FOR THE NATURAL AND PHYSICAL SCIENCES AND FOR MATHEMATICS

CRC Handbook of Chemistry and Physics. Ed. William M. Haynes. 91st ed. Boca Raton: CRC, 1913–2010. Supplies frequently used formulas, constants, properties of elements and compounds, atomic weights, and numerous illustrative charts and tables for reference.

Encyclopedia of Physical Science and Technology. Ed. Robert A. Meyers. 3rd ed. 18 vols. Burlington: Academic Press, 2001. Supplies extensive articles on topics in the physical sciences and technology, including bibliographies, glossaries, and illustrations.

McGraw-Hill Dictionary of Scientific and Technical Terms. 6th ed. New York: McGraw-Hill, 2003. Supplies pronunciations and definitions for thousands of terms used in the pure and applied sciences.

McGraw-Hill Encyclopedia of Science and Technology. 10th ed. 20 vols. New York: McGraw-Hill, 2007. Supplies articles with bibliographies and illustrations for extensive coverage of topics in all scientific fields, with

updated coverage of the earth sciences, environmental studies, engineering, medicine, chemistry, and other rapidly developing fields; many smaller specialized McGraw-Hill scientific encyclopedias derive from this major work.

Van Nostrand's Scientific Encyclopedia. Ed. Glenn D. Considine. 9th ed. 2 vols. New York: Wiley-Interscience, 2002. Supplies articles explaining and defining a wide variety of terms and topics in the sciences, medicine, and mathematics.

INDEXES AND DATABASES FOR THE NATURAL AND PHYSICAL SCIENCES AND FOR MATHEMATICS

Abstracts and Indexes in Science and Technology: A Descriptive Guide. By Delores B. Owen. 2nd ed. Metuchen: Scarecrow Press, 1985. Supplies detailed information on specialized abstracts and indexes available for the various scientific disciplines.

General Science Index. New York: Wilson, 1978–. Indexes and abstracts about 190 periodicals covering the sciences, mathematics, medicine, and environmental studies; some versions offer full-text articles.

Information Sources in Science and Technology. By C. D. Hurt. Englewood: Libraries Unlimited, 1998. Annotated guide to general and specialized resources for twenty-one scientific, medical, and technological disciplines.

Science Citation Index. Philadelphia: Institute for Scientific Information, 1955–. Indexes and abstracts citations in articles from over six thousand scientific periodicals; entries allow tracing influence through the frequency of later citations by other researchers.

WEB RESOURCES FOR THE NATURAL AND PHYSICAL SCIENCES AND FOR MATHEMATICS

EurekAlert
www.eurekalert.org
Under the sponsorship of the American Association for the Advancement of Science, posts news of scientific, medical, and technological research advances; also includes glossaries, dictionaries, and other reference materials for major scientific fields.

Infomine: Scholarly Internet Resource Collections
infomine.ucr.edu

> Supplies indexed and annotated links to databases and other resources of academic interest in biology, medicine, mathematics, and the physical sciences.

New Scientist
www.newscientist.com

> Supplies engaging news, articles, and blogs in many scientific fields, including specialized topics.

NIST (National Institute of Standards and Technology) Virtual Library
nvl.nist.gov

> Includes extensive links to sites, databases, and journals in many fields, including biotechnology, chemistry, mathematics, computer science, engineering, and physics.

Science
www.sciencemag.org

> The online version of *Science,* published weekly by the American Association for the Advancement of Science. Provides free access to news about scientific advances and career information.

Science.gov
Science.gov

> Offers search tools and access to databases and the research results and content from the Web sites of fourteen federal agencies.

> (See also the resources listed for the applied sciences in Chapter 8.)

Astronomy

GENERAL REFERENCE SOURCES FOR ASTRONOMY

Encyclopedia of Astronomy and Astrophysics. Ed. Paul Murdin. 4 vols. Bristol: Institute of Physics, 2001. Supplies extensive articles, including glossaries and bibliographies, on major topics in these fields.

INDEXES AND DATABASES FOR ASTRONOMY

ARIBIB — ARI Bibliographic Database for Astronomical Reference. 1969–2000. Formerly *Astronomisches Jahresbericht,* 1900–1968. Indexes and abstracts

articles from periodicals, books, papers, and other materials, extensively covering astronomy, space research, astrophysics, planets, stars, and related topics.

WEB RESOURCES
FOR ASTRONOMY

AstroWeb: Astronomy/Astrophysics on the Internet
www.cv.nrao.edu/fits/www/astronomy.html

> Provides a collaborative database of items, links, and data sorted by such categories as images, observations, data, publications, organizations, people, and research specialties.

NASA

www.nasa.gov

> Covers the aerospace program, space and earth sciences, technology applications, and topics such as shuttles and space stations; also provides links to other NASA resources and images.

SAO/NASA Astrophysics Data System
adswww.harvard.edu

> A searchable library of over eight million records, abstracts, and links, operated by the Smithsonian Astrophysical Observatory at the Harvard-Smithsonian Center for Astrophysics.

WebStars—Astrophysics in Cyberspace
heasarc.nasa.gov/docs/outreach/webstars.html

> Supplies engaging annotations and images for links to astronomy, the solar system, and space exploration.

Chemistry

GENERAL REFERENCE
SOURCES FOR CHEMISTRY

Kirk-Othmer Encyclopedia of Chemical Technology. 5th ed. 27 vols. New York: Wiley, 2007–. Supplies hundreds of articles on the properties and uses of chemical substances as well as on other topics related to chemical processes, methods, and technology.

Merck Index: An Encyclopedia of Chemicals, Drugs, and Biologicals. 14th ed. Whitehouse Station: Merck, 2006. Available in print and online, this encyclopedia offers information and entries on over ten thousand chemicals and drugs.

Van Nostrand's Encyclopedia of Chemistry. Ed. Glenn E. Considine. 5th ed. New York: Wiley-Interscience, 2005. Available in print and online. Supplies articles on chemistry-related topics as diverse as food chemistry, plant chemistry, pollution, and energy sources.

INDEXES AND DATABASES FOR CHEMISTRY

Chemical Abstracts. Columbus: American Chemical Society, 1907 . Indexes and abstracts articles from over fourteen thousand periodicals, as well as books, reports, and other materials covering all major chemical fields.

Chemical Reviews. Washington: American Chemical Society, 1924–. 8/yr. Covers all areas of chemistry; includes comprehensive bibliographies.

How to Find Chemical Information: A Guide for Practicing Chemists, Educators, and Students. By Robert E. Maizell. 3rd ed. New York: Wiley-Interscience, 1998. Explains the contents of and ways to use major print and electronic resources in chemistry.

WEB RESOURCES FOR CHEMISTRY

American Chemical Society
acs.org
> Provides searches of American Chemical Society resources as well as information on news, events, and publications.

Chemical Information Sources Wikibook
en.wikibooks.org/wiki/Chemical_Information_Sources
> Chemical Information Sources from Indiana University is a wikibook guide to Internet and Web resources in chemistry; offers both alphabetical and keyword searches in a useful format.

Molecular Visualization Tools and Sites
www.indiana.edu/~cheminfo/ca_mvts.html
> Links to all the major Chime and RasMol sites as well as to various other free and commercial visualization sites.

The WWW Virtual Library — Chemistry
www.liv.ac.uk/Chemistry/Links/
> Links to universities and organizations as well as to chemistry resources and other virtual libraries.

Earth Sciences

GENERAL REFERENCE SOURCES FOR EARTH SCIENCES

A Dictionary of Earth Sciences. Ed. Michael Allaby. 3rd ed. New York: Oxford, 2003. Includes over six thousand entries covering fields such as climatology, exonomic geology, geochemistry, oceanography, petrology, and volcanology.

Encyclopedia of Earth Sciences. Ed. Rhodes W. Fairbridge et al. 20 vols. to date. Springer, 1966–. Supplies articles in volumes focused on specific topics, including oceanography, mineralogy, paleontology, geology, climatology, and other specialized areas.

Encyclopedia of Earth System Science. Ed. William A. Nierenberg. 4 vols. Burlington: Academic Press, 1992. Provides thorough coverage of topics in this specialized field.

Encyclopedia of Minerals. Ed. William L. Roberts et al. 2nd ed. New York: Van Nostrand-Reinhold, 1990–. Supplies descriptions and some color photographs of more than twenty-five hundred minerals.

The Facts on File Dictionary of Earth Science. By Jacqueline Smith. Rev. ed. New York: Facts on File, 2006. Lists general definitions of over thirty-seven hundred terms; includes cross-references.

McGraw-Hill Dictionary of Earth Science. 2nd ed. New York: McGraw-Hill, 2003. Defines thousands of terms used in the various engineering fields, geology, mineralogy, crystallography, and paleontology.

McGraw-Hill Dictionary of Geology and Mineralogy. 2nd ed. New York: McGraw-Hill, 2003. Contains over seven thousand terms and expressions, each arranged under the field of geology and mineralogy in which it is used, including physical and historical geology, plate tectonics, and petrology.

INDEXES AND DATABASES FOR EARTH SCIENCES

GeoRef. 1969–. Formerly *Bibliography and Index of Geology* and *Bibliography of North American Geology*, 1931–1972, and *Bibliography and Index of Geology Exclusive of North America*, 1933–1968. Indexes articles on many geological topics, supplying a comprehensive database for the field.

WEB RESOURCES FOR EARTH SCIENCES

Center for International Earth Science Information Network
www.ciesin.org
>Consolidates scientific data, interactive services, and access to resources on the global environment, under the auspices of the Earth Institute at Columbia University.

The Encyclopedia of Earth
www.eoearth.org
>A digital archive of material, including reports on "hot topics," Congressional Research Service reports, and abstracts and links to over fourteen thousand reports on population and the environment. This site is a project of the National Council for Science and the Environment.

Hawaii Center for Volcanology
www.soest.hawaii.edu/GG/hcv.html
>Provides links to numerous volcano sites, including the Hawaiian Volcano Observatory.

Internet Resources in the Earth Sciences
www.lib.berkeley.edu/EART/EarthLinks.html
>An annotated list of sites in the earth sciences and more specialized fields such as seismology, weather, and oceanography.

NASA's Global Change Master Directory (GCMD)
gcmd.nasa.gov
>Offers over twenty-five thousand data set and service descriptions. Allows searches and includes links to other sources.

National Geophysical Data Center
www.ngdc.noaa.gov
>Supplies information—including satellite data—for environmental

studies and specialized fields such as marine geology, glaciology, and paleoclimatology.

USGS (United States Geological Survey)
www.usgs.gov

Provides highlights, fact sheets, information on federal programs and initiatives, and access to extensive resources and databases on geology, biology, water resources, mapping, and related topics.

The WWW Virtual Library — Earth Sciences
vlib.org/EarthScience

Categorizes its numerous links by subject; includes many subdisciplines such as oceanography and meteorology.

Life Sciences

GENERAL REFERENCE SOURCES FOR LIFE SCIENCES

Encyclopedia of Bioethics. Ed. Stephen Gerrard Post. 3rd ed. 5 vols. New York: Macmillan Reference, 2004. Includes articles on life science ethics, policies, legal issues, religious perspectives, and related issues.

Encyclopedia of Human Biology. Ed. Renato Dulbecco. 2nd ed. 9 vols. San Diego: Academic Press, 1997. Provides hundreds of extensive articles on biological topics as diverse as anthropology, biochemistry, ecology, genetics, and physiology.

The Encyclopedia of Mammals. Ed. David Macdonald. 2nd ed. 3 vols. New York: Facts on File, 2006. Entries cover every living species of mammal; emphasize animal behavior, conservation, and ecology; and are accompanied by over eight hundred full-color illustrations.

Encyclopedia of Microbiology. Ed. Joshua Lederberg. 2nd ed. 4 vols. San Diego: Academic Press, 2000. Supplies thorough coverage of topics in this specialized field.

Grzimek's Animal Life Encyclopedia. Ed. Bernhard Grzimek. 2nd ed. 17 vols. Detroit: Gale Group, 2003–2004. Provides articles and illustrations on the various kinds of animal life.

Grzimek's Encyclopedia of Mammals. 2nd ed. 5 vols. New York: McGraw-Hill, 1989. Supplies photographs and articles with bibliographies on mammal groups, including detailed coverage of many species.

Oxford Dictionary of Natural History. Ed. Michael Allaby. New York: Oxford, 1985. Provides thousands of definitions and explanations about the various types of plants and animals, plus genetics, biochemistry, and earth sciences.

Walker's Mammals of the World. By Ronald M. Nowak. 6th ed. 2 vols. Baltimore: Johns Hopkins University Press, 1999. Supplies entries, many illustrated, on mammal types, and includes a bibliography of sources cited.

INDEXES AND DATABASES FOR LIFE SCIENCES

Biological and Agricultural Index Plus. New York: Wilson, 1964–. Formerly *Agricultural Index,* 1916–1964. Indexes and abstracts over 380 periodicals covering a wide range of agricultural and biological topics such as animal husbandry, zoology, genetics, botany, food production, and environmental studies.

BIOSIS. New York: Thomson Reuters, 1926–. Includes access to *Biological Abstracts* and *Zoological Record.* Indexes and abstracts articles from roughly ninety-five hundred periodicals, comprehensively covering biology and biomedicine.

Cumulative Index to Nursing and Allied Health Literature (CINAHL). Glendale: CINAHL Information Systems, 1961–. Indexes and abstracts hundreds of periodicals on nursing and related health areas.

PubMed. Bethesda: National Library of Medicine, 1948–. Comprehensive, free database maintained by the National Library of Medicine. Includes access to the MEDLINE database and *Index Medicus,* 1879–1926; 1960–2004. Formerly *Quarterly Cumulative Index Medicus,* 1927–1959. Includes more than twenty million citations, including full-text articles from thousands of major medical and health care periodicals, excluding popular magazines.

WEB RESOURCES FOR LIFE SCIENCES

Biology Links
mcb.harvard.edu/biolinks.html
        An extensive list of resources and links for specialties within the biosciences from Harvard University.

Centers for Disease Control and Prevention
www.cdc.gov

The home page of the famous virus hunters, with links to what they do, research facilities, other sites, and a wide range of useful government data.

Links to the Genetic World
www.ornl.gov/sci/techresources/Human_Genome/links.shtml
Human Genome Project information as well as keyword searches and links to numerous genetics-related sites.

National Human Genome Research Institute
www.genome.gov
The home page for this important research project; situated at the National Institutes of Health.

National Institutes of Health
www.nih.gov
The central government organization dealing with health issues; site includes news, health information, grant descriptions, and links to scientific resources and to NIH suborganizations.

National Science Foundation: Biological Sciences
www.nsf.gov/dir/index.jsp?org=BIO
The site of the primary government agency funding scientific research. Allows a search of its Biology Directorate's sources and includes links to online documents, grants, and specific fields within biology.

NetVet Veterinary Resources and the Electronic Zoo
netvet.wustl.edu
From the Washington University Division of Comparative Medicine, NetVet includes links to special fields in veterinary medicine, numerous sites for particular animals, and an electronic zoo.

Pasteur Institute
www.pasteur.fr/english.html
Allows keyword searches of the Pasteur Institute's server and many other English language–based bioscience servers.

Scott's Botanical Links
www.ou.edu/cas/botany-micro/bot-linx
Includes annotated lists of databases and detailed descriptions of links to other botanical sites.

The WWW Virtual Library — Biosciences
vlib.org/Biosciences
> Categorizes information by provider and subject. Includes many links to journals, subdisciplines, and related sites.

(See also the resources listed for agriculture in Chapter 8 on the applied sciences.)

Mathematics

GENERAL REFERENCE SOURCES FOR MATHEMATICS

CRC Concise Encyclopedia of Mathematics. Ed. Eric W. Weisstein. 2nd ed. Boca Raton: CRC, 2003. Supplies frequently used mathematical functions, equations, factors, formulas, measurements, statistics, and abbreviations.

Encyclopedic Dictionary of Mathematics. By Mathematical Society of Japan and Kiyoshi Ito. 4 vols. Cambridge: MIT Press, 1987. Includes articles defining many mathematical terms and topics.

INDEXES AND DATABASES FOR MATHEMATICS

Mathematical Reviews. Providence: American Mathematical Society, 1940-. Online as MathSciNet, indexes and abstracts extensive resources in all areas of mathematics, including theory, history, probability, games, circuits, and related topics.

WEB RESOURCES FOR MATHEMATICS

Math Archives: Topics in Mathematics
archives.math.utk.edu/topics
> Devoted to math issues of special interest to undergraduate students. Includes societies, projects, research, competitions, and career issues.

Mathematics on the Web
www.ams.org/mathweb
> Offers literature guides and links, references, topical guides, and links to individuals from the American Mathematical Society.

Math Forum Internet Mathematics Library
mathforum.org/library
> Provides extensive links to all areas of mathematics, including math education from elementary through college levels.

The Most Common Errors in Undergraduate Mathematics
www.math.vanderbilt.edu/~schectex/commerrs
> From Eric Schecter at Vanderbilt University.

Wolfram MathWorld
mathworld.wolfram.com
> An alphabetical search list of important terms and concepts.

(See also the resources listed for engineering in Chapter 8 on the applied sciences.)

Physics

GENERAL REFERENCE SOURCES FOR PHYSICS

American Institute of Physics Handbook. 3rd ed. New York: McGraw-Hill, 1972. Supplies formulas and other reference materials, specifically selected for the physicist.

Encyclopedia of Physics. By Joseph Rosen. New York: Facts on File, 2004. Includes extensive articles written for a general audience on major topics in the field.

Handbook of Physics. Ed. Walter Benenson et al. New York: Springer, 2006. Contains fundamental concepts, formulas, rules, theorems, and tables of standard values and material properties; topics discussed include classical mathematics, elementary particles, electric circuits, and error analysis.

McGraw-Hill Dictionary of Physics. 3rd ed. New York: McGraw-Hill, 2003. Defines thousands of key terms from eighteen areas of physics and other closely connected fields.

INDEXES AND DATABASES FOR PHYSICS

Information Sources in Physics. Ed. Dennis F. Shaw. 3rd ed. New York: Butterworths, 1994. Supplies entries on print and electronic resources in physics.

Inspec. London: Institute of Electrical Engineers, 1898–. Indexes and abstracts periodicals and other resources in major areas of physics and in related scientific fields.

WEB RESOURCES FOR PHYSICS

AIP American Institute of Physics
www.aip.org
> Links to societies, publications, career services, and databases from the American Institute of Physics.

American Physical Society
www.aps.org
> Allows quick access to professional activities and databases.

Contemporary Physics Education Project
www.cpepweb.org
> Provides links to several interactive explanations of fields in physics and lists of other sites.

NASA
www.nasa.gov
> The home page contains useful links to current NASA projects.

The Net Advance of Physics
web.mit.edu/~redingtn/www/netadv
> Includes the *Physics Encyclopedia* and a collection of review articles in physics arranged by subject.

Physics Astronomy Online
www.physlink.com
> Contains articles on current news items, links to journals and physics departments, and a question-and-answer feature.

PhysicsWorld
physicsworld.org
   Allows access to physics societies, databases, projects, news, and events.

U.S. Department of Energy
www.energy.gov
   Contains data on current research and developments in physics.

The WWW Virtual Library — Physics
vlib.org/Physics
   Categorizes links by subject.

CSE Style

   Writers in the physical sciences, the life sciences, and mathematics use the documentation and format style of the Council of Science Editors (CSE). Guidelines for citing print and electronic sources can be found in *Scientific Style and Format: The CSE Manual for Authors, Editors, and Publishers*, Seventh Edition (2006).

CSE Style for In-Text Citations

   In CSE style, citations within an essay follow one of three formats.

- The *citation-sequence format* calls for a superscript number or a number in parentheses after any mention of a source. The sources are numbered in the order they appear. Each number refers to the same source every time it is used. The first source mentioned in the paper is numbered *1,* the second source is numbered *2,* and so on.

- The *citation-name format* also calls for a superscript number or a number in parentheses after any mention of a source. The numbers are added after the list of references is completed and alphabetized, so that the source numbered *1* is alphabetically first in the list of references, *2* is alphabetically second, and so on.

- The *name-year format* calls for the last name of the author and the year of publication in parentheses after any mention of a source. If

the last name appears in a signal phrase, the name-year format allows for giving only the year of publication in parentheses.

Before deciding which system to use, check a current journal in the field or ask an instructor about the preferred style in a particular course or discipline.

1. IN-TEXT CITATION USING CITATION-SEQUENCE OR CITATION-NAME FORMAT

VonBergen[12] provides a complete discussion of this phenomenon.

For the citation-sequence and citation-name formats, you would use the same superscript[12] for each subsequent citation of this work by VonBergen.

2. IN-TEXT CITATION USING NAME-YEAR FORMAT

VonBergen (2003) provides a complete discussion of this phenomenon.

Hussar's two earlier studies of juvenile obesity (1995, 1999) examined only children with diabetes.

The classic examples of such investigations (Morrow 1968; Bridger et al. 1971; Franklin and Wayson 1972) still shape the assumptions of current studies.

CSE Formats for a List of References

The citations in the text of an essay correspond to items on a list titled *References*, which starts on a new page at the end of the essay. Continue to number the pages consecutively, center the title *References*

one inch from the top of the page, and double-space before beginning the first entry.

The order of the entries depends on which CSE format you follow:

- *Citation-sequence format*: number and list the references in the order the references are first cited in the text.

- *Citation-name format*: list and number the references in alphabetical order.

- *Name-year format*: list the references, unnumbered, in alphabetical order.

In the following examples, you will see that the citation-sequence and citation-name formats call for listing the date after the publisher's name in references for books and after the periodical name in references for articles. The name-year format calls for listing the date immediately after the author's name in any kind of reference.

CSE style also specifies the treatment and placement of the following basic elements in the list of references:

- *Author*. List all authors last name first, and use only initials for first and middle names. Do not place a comma after the author's last name, and do not place periods after or spaces between the initials. Use a period after the last initial of the last author listed.

- *Title*. Do not italicize or underline titles and subtitles of books and titles of periodicals. Do not enclose titles of articles in quotation marks. For books and articles, capitalize only the first word of the title and any proper nouns or proper adjectives. Abbreviate and capitalize all major words in a periodical title.

As you refer to these examples, pay attention to how publication information (publishers for books, details about periodicals for articles) and other specific elements are styled and punctuated.

DIRECTORY TO CSE STYLE FOR REFERENCES

Books

For the basic format for citing a book, see pp. 252–53.

1. ONE AUTHOR

CITATION-SEQUENCE AND CITATION-NAME

1. Buchanan M. Nexus: small worlds and the groundbreaking theory of networks. New York: Norton; 2003.

NAME-YEAR

Buchanan M. 2003. Nexus: small worlds and the groundbreaking theory of networks. New York: Norton.

CSE SOURCE MAP: Citing books

Note that, depending on whether you are using the citation-sequence or citation-name format or the name-year format, the date placement will vary.

① **Author.** List authors' last names first, and use initials for first and middle names, with no periods or spaces. Use a period only after the last initial of the last author.

②, ⑥ **Publication year.** In name-year format, put the year of publication immediately after the author name(s). In citation-sequence or citation-name format, put the year of publication after the publisher's name.

③ **Title.** Do not italicize or put quotation marks around titles and subtitles of books. Capitalize only the first word of the title and any proper nouns or proper adjectives.

④ **City of publication.** List the city of publication (and the country or state abbreviation for unfamiliar cities) followed by a colon.

⑤ **Publisher.** Give the publisher's name. In citation-sequence or citation-name format, follow with a semicolon. In name-year format, follow with a period.

A citation for the book on p. 253 would look like this:

Citation-sequence or citation-name format

    ①   **③**   **④**   **⑤**

1. Wilson EO. The diversity of life. Cambridge: Belknap Press of Harvard University Press; 1992.

                ⑥

Name-year format

    ①   **②**   **③**   **④**   **⑤**

Wilson EO. 1992. The diversity of life. Cambridge: Belknap Press of Harvard University Press.

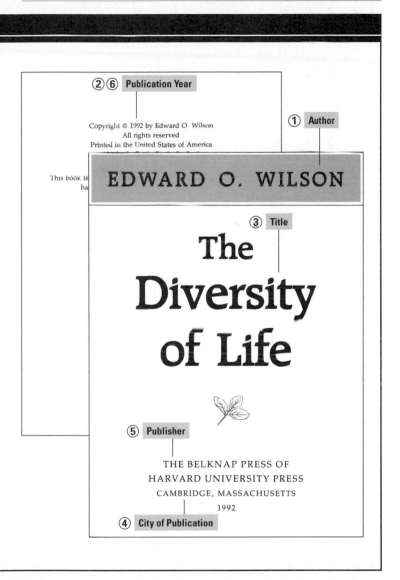

(2)(6) **Publication Year**

Copyright © 1992 by Edward O. Wilson
All rights reserved
Printed in the United States of America

(1) **Author**

This book is
ha

EDWARD O. WILSON

(3) **Title**

The
Diversity
of Life

(5) **Publisher**

THE BELKNAP PRESS OF
HARVARD UNIVERSITY PRESS
CAMBRIDGE, MASSACHUSETTS
1992

(4) **City of Publication**

2. TWO OR MORE AUTHORS

CITATION-SEQUENCE AND CITATION-NAME

2. Wojciechowski BW, Rice NM. Experimental methods in kinetic studies. 2nd ed. St. Louis (MO): Elsevier Science; 2003.

NAME-YEAR

Wojciechowski BW, Rice NM. 2003. Experimental methods in kinetic studies. 2nd ed. St. Louis (MO): Elsevier Science.

3. ORGANIZATION AS AUTHOR

CITATION-SEQUENCE AND CITATION-NAME

3. World Health Organization. The world health report 2002: reducing risks, promoting healthy life. Geneva (Switzerland): The Organization; 2002.

Place the organization's abbreviation at the beginning of the name-year entry, and use the abbreviation in the corresponding in-text citation. Alphabetize the entry by the first word of the full name, not by the abbreviation.

NAME-YEAR

[WHO] World Health Organization. 2002. The world health report 2002: reducing risks, promoting healthy life. Geneva (Switzerland): The Organization.

4. BOOK PREPARED BY EDITOR(S)

CITATION-SEQUENCE AND CITATION-NAME

4. Torrence ME, Isaacson RE, editors. Microbial food safety in animal agriculture: current topics. Ames: Iowa State University Press; 2003.

NAME-YEAR

Torrence ME, Isaacson RE, editors. 2003. Microbial safety in animal agriculture: current topics. Ames: Iowa State University Press.

5. SECTION OF A BOOK WITH AN EDITOR

CITATION-SEQUENCE AND CITATION-NAME

5. Kawamura A. Plankton. In: Perrin MF, Wursig B, Thewissen JGM, editors. Encyclopedia of marine mammals. San Diego: Academic Press; 2002. p. 939–942.

NAME-YEAR

Kawamura A. 2002. Plankton. In: Perrin MF, Wursig B, Thewissen JGM, editors. Encyclopedia of marine mammals. San Diego: Academic Press. p. 939–942.

6. CHAPTER OF A BOOK

CITATION-SEQUENCE AND CITATION-NAME

6. Honigsbaum M. The fever trail: in search of the cure for malaria. New York: Picador; 2003. Chapter 2, The cure; p. 19–38.

NAME-YEAR

Honigsbaum M. 2003. The fever trail: in search of the cure for malaria. New York: Picador. Chapter 2, The cure; p. 19–38.

7. PAPER OR ABSTRACT IN CONFERENCE PROCEEDINGS

CITATION-SEQUENCE AND CITATION-NAME

7. Gutierrez AP. Integrating biological and environmental factors in crop system models [abstract]. In: Integrated Biological Systems Conference; 2003 Apr 14–16; San Antonio, TX. Beaumont (TX): Agroeconomics Research Group; 2003. p. 14–15.

NAME-YEAR

Gutierrez AP. 2003. Integrating biological and environmental factors in crop system models [abstract]. In: Integrated Biological Systems Conference; 2003 Apr 14–16; San Antonio, TX. Beaumont (TX): Agroeconomics Research Group. p. 14–15.

CSE SOURCE MAP: Citing articles from periodicals

Note that date placement will vary, depending on whether you are using the citation-sequence or citation-name format or the name-year format.

① **Author.** List all authors' last names first, and use only initials for first and middle names. Do not place periods after or spaces between the initials. Use a period after the last initial of the last author.

②,⑤ **Publication date.** In name-year format, put publication date after author name(s). In citation-sequence or citation-name format, put publication date after periodical title. For journals, use only the year; use the year and month (and day) for publications without volume numbers.

③ **Title and subtitle of article.** Capitalize only the first word of the title and any proper nouns or proper adjectives.

④ **Title of periodical.** Capitalize all major words and end with a period. Follow the guidelines in the CSE manual for abbreviating journal titles.

⑥ **Publication information.** For articles from scholarly journals, give the volume number, the issue number if available (in parentheses), and then a colon.

⑦ **Page numbers.** Give the inclusive page numbers, and end with a period.

Citations for the article on p. 257 would look like this:

Citation-sequence or citation-name format

         ①   **③**

1. Narechania A. Hearing is believing: ivory-billed sightings leave field biologists wanting to hear more. Am Scholar. 2005;74(3):84–97.

                                  ④   **⑤**   **⑥**   **⑦**

Name-year format

    ①   **②**   **③**

Narechania A. 2005. Hearing is believing: ivory-billed sightings leave field biologists wanting to hear more. Am Scholar. 74(3):84–97.

                               ④   **⑥**   **⑦**

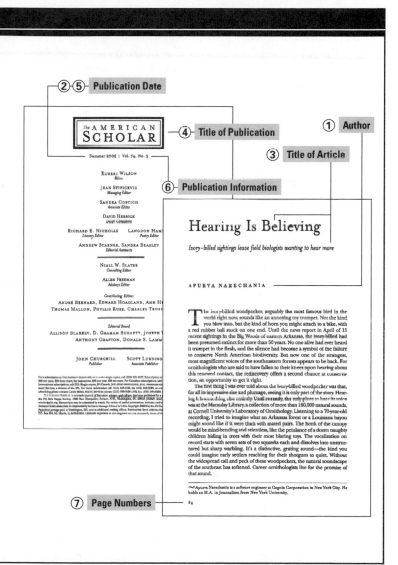

Publication Date ② ⑤

the AMERICAN
SCHOLAR

Summer 2005 | Vol. 74, No. 3

④ **Title of Publication**

① **Author**

③ **Title of Article**

⑥ **Publication Information**

Hearing Is Believing

Ivory-billed sightings leave field biologists wanting to hear more

APURVA NARECHANIA

The ivory-billed woodpecker, arguably the most famous bird in the world right now, sounds like an annoying toy trumpet. Not the kind you blow into, but the kind of horn you might attach to a bike, with a red rubber ball stuck on one end. Until the news report in April of 15 recent sightings in the Big Woods of eastern Arkansas, the ivory-billed had been presumed extinct for more than 50 years. No one alive had ever heard it trumpet in the flesh, and the silence had become a symbol of the failure to conserve North American biodiversity. But now one of the strangest, most magnificent voices of the southeastern forests appears to be back. For ornithologists who are said to have fallen to their knees upon hearing about this renewed contact, the rediscovery offers a second chance at conservation, an opportunity to get it right.

The first thing I was ever told about the ivory-billed woodpecker was that, for all its impressive size and plumage, seeing it is only part of the story. Hearing it is something else entirely. Until recently, the only place to hear its voice was at the Macaulay Library, a collection of more than 160,000 natural sounds, at Cornell University's Laboratory of Ornithology. Listening to a 70-year-old recording, I tried to imagine what an Arkansas forest or a Louisiana bayou might sound like if it were thick with mated pairs. The honk of the canopy would be mind-bending and relentless, like the petulance of a dozen naughty children hiding in trees with their most blaring toys. The vocalization on record starts with seven sets of two squawks each and dissolves into unstructured but sharp warbling. It's a distinctive, grating sound—the kind you could imagine early settlers reaching for their shotguns to quiet. Without the widespread call and peck of these woodpeckers, the natural soundscape of the southeast has softened. Career ornithologists live for the promise of that sound.

∾Apurva Narechania is a software engineer at Cognia Corporation in New York City. He holds an M.A. in Journalism from New York University.

⑦ **Page Numbers**   84

Periodicals

For the basic format for an article in a periodical, see pp. 256–57. For newspaper and magazine articles, include the section designation and column number, if any, in addition to the date and the inclusive page numbers. For rules on abbreviating journal titles, consult the CSE manual, or ask an instructor to suggest other examples.

8. ARTICLE IN A JOURNAL

CITATION-SEQUENCE AND CITATION-NAME

8. Mahmud K, Vance ML. Human growth hormone and aging. New Engl J Med. 2003;348(2):2256–2257.

NAME-YEAR

Mahmud K, Vance ML. 2003. Human growth hormone and aging. New Engl J Med. 348(2):2256–2257.

9. ARTICLE IN A WEEKLY JOURNAL

CITATION-SEQUENCE AND CITATION-NAME

9. Holden C. Future brightening for depression treatments. Science. 2003 Oct 31:810–813.

NAME-YEAR

Holden C. 2003. Future brightening for depression treatments. Science. Oct 31:810–813.

10. ARTICLE IN A MAGAZINE

CITATION-SEQUENCE AND CITATION-NAME

10. Livio M. Moving right along: the accelerating universe holds secrets to dark energy, the Big Bang, and the ultimate beauty of nature. Astronomy. 2002 Jul:34–39.

NAME-YEAR

Livio M. 2002 Jul. Moving right along: the accelerating universe holds secrets to dark energy, the Big Bang, and the ultimate beauty of nature. Astronomy. 34–39.

11. ARTICLE IN A NEWSPAPER

CITATION-SEQUENCE AND CITATION-NAME

11. Kolata G. Bone diagnosis gives new data but no answers. New York Times (National Ed.). 2003 Sep 28;Sect. 1:1 (col. 1).

NAME-YEAR

Kolata G. 2003 Sep 28. Bone diagnosis gives new data but no answers. New York Times (National Ed.). Sect. 1:1 (col. 1).

Electronic Sources

These examples use the citation-sequence or citation-name system. To adapt them to the name-year system, delete the note number and place the update date immediately after the author's name.

The basic entry for most sources accessed through the Internet should include the following elements:

- *Author.* Give the author's name, if available, last name first, followed by the initial(s) and a period.
- *Title.* For book, journal, and article titles, follow the style for print materials. For all other types of electronic material, reproduce the title that appears on the screen.
- *Medium.* Indicate, in brackets, that the source is not in print format by using designations such as [Internet].
- *Place of publication.* The city usually should be followed by the two-letter abbreviation for state. No state abbreviation is necessary for well-known cities such as New York, Chicago, Boston, and London or for a publisher whose location is part of its name (for example, University of Oklahoma Press). If the city is implied, put the city and

CSE SOURCE MAP: Citing articles from databases

Note that date placement will vary depending on whether you are using the citation-sequence or citation-name format or the name-year format.

(1) **Author.** List all authors' last names first, and use only initials for first and middle names.

(2),(5) **Publication date.** For name-year format, put publication date after author name(s). In citation-sequence or citation-name format, put it after periodical title. Use year only (for journals) or year month day (for other periodicals).

(3) **Article title.** Capitalize first word and proper nouns/adjectives.

(4) **Periodical title.** Capitalize major words. Abbreviate journal titles. Follow with [*Internet*] and a period.

(6) **Date of access.** In brackets, write *cited* and year, month, and day. End with a semicolon.

(7) **Publication information for article.** Give volume number, issue number (in parentheses), a colon, and page numbers. End with a period.

(8) **Name of database.** End with a period.

(9) **Publication information for database.** Include the city, the state abbreviation in parentheses, a colon, the publisher's name, and a period.

(10) **Web address.** Write *Available from* and the brief URL.

(11) **Document number.** Write *Document no.* and identifying number.

A citation for the article on p. 261 would look like this:

Citation-sequence or citation-name format

    (1)   (3)

1. Miller AL. Epidemiology, etiology, and natural treatment of seasonal

                     (4)   (5)   (6)

affective disorder. Altern Med Rev [Internet]. 2005 [cited 2010 25 May];

  (7)   (8)   (9)

10(1):5–13. Academic Search Premier. Ipswich (MA): EBSCO. Available

         (10)   (11)

from http://www.ebscohost.com Document No.: 16514813.

Name-year format

① ② ③

Miller AL. 2005. Epidemiology, etiology, and natural treatment of

④ ⑥

seasonal affective disorder. Altern Med Rev [Internet]. [cited 2010 25

⑦ ⑧ ⑨

May]; 10(1):5–13. Academic Search Premier. Ipswich (MA): EBSCO.

⑩ ⑪

Available from http://www.ebscohost.com Document No.: 16514813.

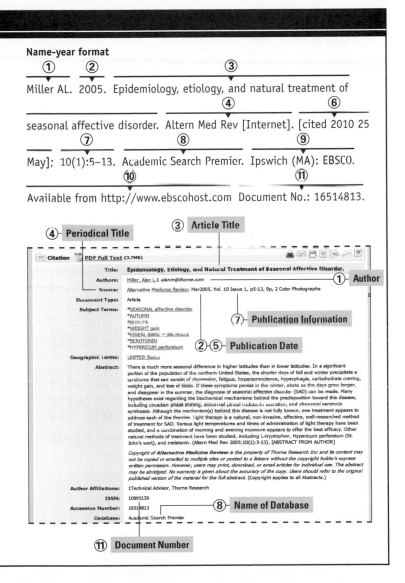

state in brackets. If the city cannot be inferred, use the words *place unknown* in brackets.

- *Publisher.* For Web sites, pages on Web sites, and online databases, include the individual or organization that produces or sponsors the site. If no publisher can be determined, use the words *publisher unknown* in brackets. No publisher is necessary for online journals or journals accessed online.

- *Dates.* Cite three important dates if possible: the date the publication was placed on the Internet or the copyright date; the latest date of any update or revision; and the date the publication was accessed by you.

- *Page, document, volume, and issue numbers.* When citing a portion of a larger work or site, list the inclusive page numbers or document numbers of the specific item being cited. For journals or journal articles, include volume and issue numbers. If exact page numbers are not available, include in brackets the approximate length in computer screens, paragraphs, or bytes: [2 screens], [10 paragraphs], [332K bytes].

- *Address.* Include the URL or other electronic address; use the phrase *Available from:* to introduce the address. Only URLs that end with a slash are followed by a period.

12. MATERIAL FROM AN ONLINE DATABASE

For the basic format for citing an article from a database, see pp. 260–61. (Because CSE does not provide guidelines for citing an article from an online database, this model has been adapted from CSE guidelines for citing an online journal article.)

12. Shilts E. Water wanderers. Can Geographic [Internet]. 2002 [cited 2010 Jan 27]; 122(3):72–77. Academic Search Premier. Ipswich (MA): EBSCO. Available from: http://ebscohost.com Document No.: 6626534.

13. ARTICLE IN AN ONLINE JOURNAL

13. Perez P, Calonge TM. Yeast protein kinase C. J Biochem [Internet]. 2002 Oct [cited 2008 Nov 3];132(4):513–517. Available from: http://edpex104.bcasj.or.jp/jb-pdf/132-4/jb132-4-513.pdf

14. ARTICLE IN AN ONLINE NEWSPAPER

14. Brody JF. Reasons, and remedies, for morning sickness. New York Times Online [Internet]. 2004 Apr 27 [cited 2009 Apr 30]. Available from: http://www.nytimes.com/2004/04/27/health/27BROD.html

15. ONLINE BOOK

15. Patrick TS, Allison JR, Krakow GA. Protected plants of Georgia [Internet]. Social Circle (GA): Georgia Department of Natural Resources; c1995 [cited 2010 Dec 3]. Available from: http://www.georgiawildlife.com/content/displaycontent.asp?txtDocument=89&txtPage=9

To cite a portion of an online book, give the name of the part after the publication information: *Chapter 6, Encouraging germination.* See model 6.

16. WEB SITE

16. Geology and public policy [Internet]. Boulder (CO): Geological Society of America; c2010 [updated 2010 Jun 3; cited 2010 Sep 19]. Available from: http://www.geosociety.org/geopolicy.htm

17. GOVERNMENT WEB SITE

17. Health disparities: reducing health disparities in cancer [Internet]. Atlanta (GA): Centers for Disease Control and Prevention (US); [updated 2010 Apr 5; cited 2010 May 1]. Available from: http://www.cdc.gov /cancer/healthdisparities/basic_info/disparities.htm

A Student Paper, CSE Style

Student Writer

Tara Gupta

The following research proposal by Tara Gupta conforms to the citation-sequence format in the CSE guidelines described in this chapter. Note that these pages have been reproduced in a narrow format to allow for annotation.

Field Measurements of
Photosynthesis and Transpiration
Rates in Dwarf Snapdragon
(*Chaenorrhinum minus* Lange):
An Investigation of Water Stress
Adaptations

Specific and informative title

Tara Gupta

Information centered on title page

Proposal for a
Summer Research
Fellowship
Colgate University
February 25, 2003

Water Stress Adaptations 2

Introduction

Headings
throughout
help organize
the proposal

Dwarf snapdragon (*Chaenorrhinum minus*) is a weedy pioneer plant found growing in central New York during spring and summer. Interestingly, the distribution of this species has been limited almost exclusively to the cinder ballast of railroad tracks[1] and to sterile strips of land along highways[2]. In these harsh environments, characterized by intense sunlight and poor soil water retention, one would expect *C. minus* to exhibit anatomical features similar to those of xeromorphic plants (species adapted to arid habitats).

Introduction
states scientific
issue, gives
background
information

However, this is not the case. T. Gupta and R. Arnold (unpublished) have found that the leaves and stems of *C. minus* are not covered by a thick, waxy cuticle but rather with a thin cuticle that is less effective in inhibiting water loss through diffusion. The root system is not long and thick, capable of reaching deeper, moister soils; instead, it is thin and diffuse, permeating only the topmost (and driest) soil horizon. Moreover, in contrast to many xeromorphic plants, the stomata (pores regulating gas exchange) are not found in sunken crypts or cavities in the epidermis that retard water loss from transpiration.

Documentation
follows
CSE citation-
sequence
format

Despite a lack of these morphological adaptations to water stress, *C. minus* continues to grow and reproduce

Water Stress Adaptations 3

when morning dew has been its only source of water for up to 5 weeks (2002 letter from R. Arnold to me). Such growth involves fixation of carbon by photosynthesis and requires that the stomata be open to admit sufficient carbon dioxide. Given the dry, sunny environment, the time required for adequate carbon fixation must also mean a significant loss of water through transpiration as open stomata exchange carbon dioxide with water. How does *C. minus* balance the need for carbon with the need to conserve water?

Personal communication cited in parentheses within text but not included in references

Purposes of the Proposed Study

The above observations have led me to an exploration of the extent to which *C. minus* is able to photosynthesize under conditions of low water availability. It is my hypothesis that *C. minus* adapts to these conditions by photosynthesizing in the early morning and late afternoon, when leaf and air temperatures are lower and transpirational water loss is reduced. During the middle of the day, its photosynthetic rate may be very low, perhaps even zero, on hot, sunny afternoons. Similar diurnal changes in photosynthetic rate in response to midday water deficits have been described in crop plants[3,4]. There appear to be no comparable studies on noncrop species in their natural habitats.

States purposes and scope of proposed study

Thus, the research proposed here aims to help explain the apparent paradox of an organism that thrives in water-

Significance of study noted

Water Stress Adaptations 4

stressed conditions despite a lack of morphological

Relates proposed research project to future research

adaptations. This summer's work will also serve as a basis for controlled experiments in a plant growth chamber on the individual effects of temperature, light intensity, soil water availability, and other environmental factors on photosynthesis and transpiration rates. These experiments are planned for the coming fall semester.

Methods and Timeline

Briefly describes methodology to be used

Simultaneous measurements of photosynthesis and transpiration rates will indicate the balance *C. minus* has achieved in acquiring the energy it needs while retaining the water available to it. These measurements will be

Provides timeline

taken daily from June 22 to September 7, 2003, at field sites in the Hamilton, NY, area, using an LI-6220 portable photosynthesis system (LICOR, Inc., Lincoln, NE). Basic methodology and use of correction factors will be similar to that described in related studies[5-7]. Data will be collected at regular intervals throughout the daylight hours and will be related to measurements of ambient air temperature, leaf temperature, relative humidity, light intensity, wind velocity, and cloud cover.

Water Stress Adaptations 5

Budget

1	kg soda lime, 4-8 mesh	$70	
	(for absorption of CO_2 in photosynthesis analyzer)		
1	kg anhydrous magnesium perchlorate	$130	
	(used as desiccant for photosynthesis analyzer)		
	SigmaScan software (Jandel Scientific Software, Inc.)	$195	Budget provides itemized details
	(for measurement of leaf areas for which		
	photosynthesis and transpiration rates are to		
	be determined)		
	Estimated 500 miles travel to field sites in own	$140	
	car @ $0.28/mile		
	CO_2 cylinder, 80 days rental @ $0.25/day	$20	
	(for calibration of photosynthesis analyzer)		
	TOTAL REQUEST	$555	

Water Stress Adaptations 6

References

1. Wildrlechner MP. Historical and phenological observations of the spread of *Chaenorrhinum minus* across North America. Can J Bot. 1983;61(1):179–187.

2. Dwarf Snapdragon [Internet]. Olympia (WA): Washington State Noxious Weed Control Board; 2001 [updated 2001 Jul 7; cited 2003 Jan 25]. Available from: http://www.wa.gov /agr/weedboard/weed_info/dwarfsnapdragon.html

3. Boyer JS. Plant productivity and environment. Science. 1982 Nov 6:443–448.

4. Manhas JG, Sukumaran NP. Diurnal changes in net photosynthetic rate in potato in two environments. Potato Res. 1988;31:375–378.

5. Doley DG, Unwin GL, Yates DJ. Spatial and temporal distribution of photosynthesis and transpiration by single leaves in a rainforest tree, *Argyrodendron peralatum*. Aust J Plant Physiol. 1988;15(3):317–326.

6. Kallarackal J, Milburn JA, Baker DA. Water relations of the banana. III. Effects of controlled water stress on water potential, transpiration, photosynthesis and leaf growth. Aust J Plant Physiol. 1990;17(1):79–90.

7. Idso SB, Allen SG, Kimball BA, Choudhury BJ. Problems with porometry: measuring net photosynthesis by leaf chamber techniques. Agron. 1989;81(4):475–479.

Article from government Web site

Article in weekly journal

Article in journal

Includes all published works cited; numbers correspond to order in which sources are first mentioned

8

Research in the Applied Sciences

Resources in the Applied Sciences

GENERAL REFERENCE SOURCES FOR THE APPLIED SCIENCES

Encyclopedia of Physical Science and Technology. Ed. Robert A. Meyers. 3rd ed. 18 vols. Burlington: Academic Press, 2002. Available in print and online. Consists of over seven hundred entries, each approximately twenty pages in length, on topics such as molecular electronics, image-guided surgery, fiber-optic chemical sensors, self-organizing systems, humanoid robots, pharmacokinetics, and superstring theory.

The International Encyclopedia of Science and Technology. Chicago: University of Chicago Press, 2000. Includes over sixty-five hundred entries with graphs, photos, and diagrams; a detailed timeline of the development of science since 2500 BC; and a reference section of tables such as SI units, chemical elements, facts about the earth, lists of constellations, and Nobel Prize winners.

INDEXES AND DATABASES FOR THE APPLIED SCIENCES

Applied Science and Technology Index. New York: Wilson, 1958–. Available in print and online. Formerly *Industrial Arts Index,* 1913–1957. Indexes and abstracts nearly four hundred periodicals, concentrating on

applied science in areas such as computers, construction, electronics, engineering, the environment, energy sources, geology, technology, telecommunications, and many others.

NTIS Database. 1964–. Indexes over two million bibliographic records, and includes full-text reports handled through the National Technical Information Service.

Scientific and Technical Information Sources. Ed. Ching-chin Chen. 2nd ed. Cambridge: MIT Press, 1987. Lists resources available in the pure and applied sciences.

WEB RESOURCES FOR THE APPLIED SCIENCES

EurekAlert
www.eurekalert.org
　Under the sponsorship of the American Association for the Advancement of Science, posts news of scientific and technological research advances; also includes glossaries, dictionaries, and other reference materials for agriculture, computer sciences, environmental studies, and other fields.

Infomine: Scholarly Internet Resource Collections
lib-www.ucr.edu
　Supplies indexed and annotated links to more than one thousand databases and other resources of academic interest in the physical sciences, including engineering, environmental studies, and computer sciences.

LSU Subject Guides
www.lib.lsu.edu/weblio.html
　Provides extensive annotated guides to Web resources in the applied sciences, including agriculture, computer science, environmental studies, food science, human ecology, and other specialized fields.

New Scientist
www.newscientist.com/weblinks
　Supplies engaging news, articles, and blogs, often on specialized topics, in fields including technology, the Internet, and the environment.

Agriculture

GENERAL REFERENCE SOURCES FOR AGRICULTURE

Agriculture Handbooks. U.S. Department of Agriculture. 1950–. Each volume supplies reliable information on a specific topic. (Online at the National Agricultural Library Digital Repository.)

Encyclopedia of Agricultural Science. 4 vols. Burlington: Academic Press, 1994. Contains 210 alphabetically arranged articles, each about ten pages in length, covering subjects such as animal science, soil science, agricultural education, biotechnology, pest management, and water resources; includes tables and illustrations.

Yearbook of Agriculture. U.S. Department of Agriculture, 1895–1979. Supplies chapters on various aspects of the year's topic.

INDEXES AND DATABASES FOR AGRICULTURE

Agriculture: Illustrated Search Strategy and Sources. Ann Arbor: Pierian Press, 1992. Supplies guidance about using print and electronic reference materials.

NAL Catalog (AGRICOLA). Indexes and abstracts sources from periodicals, state and federal publications, and reports covering agriculture and related topics.

WEB RESOURCES FOR AGRICULTURE

Agricultural Research Service: U.S. Department of Agriculture
www.ars.usda.gov
> Supplies news and research information as well as links to major agriculture databases and resources, including the National Agricultural Library.

CRIS: Current Research Information System
cris.csrees.usda.gov
> Under the auspices of the U.S. Department of Agriculture, reports on thousands of current federal and state research projects on agriculture, forestry, food, and nutrition.

National Agricultural Library
www.nal.usda.gov
> Provides its own collection of materials and images on agriculture, and consolidates access to resources through a catalog (AGRICOLA) on animal science, economics, food science, forestry, natural resources, nutrition, range land, and other agriculture-related topics.

(See also the resources listed for the life sciences in Chapter 7.)

Computer Science

GENERAL REFERENCE SOURCES FOR COMPUTER SCIENCE

Dictionary of Computer Science, Engineering, and Technology. Ed. Phillip A. Laplante. Boca Raton: CRC Press, 2001. Provides detailed definitions for over eight thousand terms that cover topics such as telecommunication, information theory, artificial intelligence, programming language, privacy issues, and software and hardware systems.

Dictionary of Computing. Ed. John Daintith and Edmund Wright. 6th ed. New York: Oxford, 2008. Defines over ten thousand terms, concepts, and technologies from various areas of computing, such as software, hardware, networking, mainframes, the Internet, multimedia, and programming.

Encyclopedia of Computer Science. Ed. Anthony Ralston, Edwin D. Reilly, and David Hemmendinger. 4th ed. Hoboken: Wiley, 2003.

McGraw-Hill Encyclopedia of Electronics and Computers. Ed. Sybil P. Parker. New York: McGraw-Hill, 1988. Includes heavily illustrated articles on the design, materials, functioning, and uses of electronic devices.

INDEXES AND DATABASES FOR COMPUTER SCIENCE

ACM Digital Library. 1954–. Includes the full text of all the Association for Computing Machinery's articles and the *Guide to Computing Literature* (1977–1997). Includes citations of articles about data, computation, hardware, software, systems, and applications.

WEB RESOURCES FOR COMPUTER SCIENCE

The Collection of Computer Science Bibliographies
liinwww.ira.uka.de/bibliography/
> Provides access to over fifteen hundred bibliographies on computer technology, programming, and research, with references to articles, reports, and presentations arranged by subject area.

Developer.com
www.developer.com
> Supplies career information, news, graphics, and resources on computer technology and topics such as servers, databases, and Web sites, all oriented to professional computer developers.

Webopedia
www.webopedia.com
> Provides keyword and topical searches on a vast range of terms and topics related to personal computers and computing technology.

The WWW Virtual Library — Computing and Computer Science
vlib.org/Computing
> Includes access to bibliographies, indexes, and a dictionary of computer terminology, as well as resources in specialty areas as diverse as artificial intelligence, telecommunications, computational linguistics, and cryptography.

Engineering

GENERAL REFERENCE SOURCES FOR ENGINEERING

Annual Book of ASTM Standards. West Conshohocken: ASTM International, 1970-. Supplies many volumes, published annually, that detail the specifications, practices, and other guidelines necessary to meet the standards of the American Society for Testing and Materials (ASTM) for products as diverse as plastics, paint, soap, metals and alloys, textiles, and paper.

ASTM Dictionary of Engineering, Science and Technology. West Conshohocken: ASTM International, 2008. Online reference supplies

concise definitions derived from technical committee–developed standards for ASTM terminology.

CRC Handbook of Tables for Applied Engineering Science. Ed. Richard C. Dorf. Boca Raton: CRC Press, 2004; biennial. Provides basic tables and data for the various engineering fields.

Encyclopedia of Materials Science and Engineering. 8 vols. Cambridge: MIT Press, 1986–1993. Supplies entries on the nature and use of fibers, plastics, and other materials.

Handbook of Engineering Fundamentals. New York: Wiley-Interscience, 1990. Provides essential information for the varied fields of engineering, including equations, laws, theorems, properties, and statistical data.

Handbook of Industrial Engineering. Ed. Gavriel Salvendy. 3rd ed. New York: Wiley-Interscience, 2001. Includes formulas and data for industrial engineering.

IEEE 100: The Authoritative Dictionary of IEEE Standards Terms. 7th ed. New York: IEEE, 2000. Supplies authoritative explanations of terms and standards approved by the Institute of Electrical and Electronics Engineers (IEEE).

The Illustrated Dictionary of Electronics. By Stan Gibilisco. New York: McGraw-Hill, 2001. Provides over 27,500 definitions, many with illustrations, of terms in fields that include computers, robotics, lasers, television, radio, and IC technology.

Marks' Standard Handbook for Mechanical Engineers. 11th ed. New York: McGraw-Hill, 2007. Provides essential information for mechanical engineering, including mathematical data, technical standards, and environmental issues.

McGraw-Hill Concise Encyclopedia of Engineering. New York: McGraw-Hill, 2005. Supplies articles on major topics in the many fields of engineering.

Perry's Chemical Engineers' Handbook. Ed. Don W. Green. 8th ed. New York: McGraw-Hill, 2008. Includes essential specific information for the chemical engineer.

Standard Handbook for Civil Engineers. By Jonathan T. Ricketts, M. Kent Loftin, and Frederick S. Merritt. 5th ed. New York: McGraw-Hill,

2004. Supplies fundamental information for civil engineers, including specifications, construction, design, and management.

Standard Handbook for Electrical Engineers. By Donald G. Fink and H. Wayne Beaty. 15th ed. New York: McGraw-Hill, 2006. Includes necessary reference material for the electrical engineer on topics related to the production, use, and conversion of electrical power.

Standard Handbook of Environmental Engineering. By Robert A. Corbitt. 2nd ed. New York: McGraw-Hill, 1999. Supplies essential information about air and water quality, water management, waste disposal, and related topics.

INDEXES AND DATABASES FOR ENGINEERING

Applied Science & Technology Abstracts. New York: Wilson, 1984 . Indexes and abstracts almost eight hundred periodicals in applied sciences. A full-text version is available for 220 periodicals going back to 1997.

Compendex. Hoboken: Elsevier Engineering Information, 1969-. Comprehensive bibliographic database for engineering literature, covering 175 engineering disciplines.

Engineering Index Monthly. 1884-. Formerly *Engineering Index*. Indexes and abstracts periodical articles, books, patents, and some conference papers on engineering.

INSPEC. 1969-. A database containing citations to journals, conference proceedings, books, reports, and dissertations in physics, electrical engineering and electronics, computers, and information technology.

WEB RESOURCES FOR ENGINEERING

ASCE's Civil Engineering Database
cedb.asce.org/
Provides access to over 170,000 bibliographic and abstracted records in civil engineering since 1975.

IEEE Spectrum
spectrum.ieee.org
> The flagship magazine of IEEE, the site offers news, articles, blogs, and resources of the Institute of Electrical and Electronics Engineers.

IEEE Xplore Digital Library
ieeexplore.ieee.org/Xplore/guesthome.jsp
> Provides full-text access to the journals, conference publications, newsletters, and other publications of the IEEE.

Institute of Electrical and Electronics Engineers
www.ieee.org
> Links to member services, related technical societies, search engines, databases, publications, and activities.

Mechanical Design Engineering Resources
www.gearhob.com
> Lists everything from industry associations to research and development sites.

TechXtra: Engineering, Mathematics, and Computing
www.techxtra.ac.uk/
> Provides access to over five hundred free periodicals and documents in engineering, mathematics, and computing.

The WWW Virtual Library — Engineering
vlib.org/Engineering
> Lists links to many relevant sources across engineering fields, including all the engineering virtual libraries, from acoustic engineering to wastewater engineering. Includes information on standards, products, and institutions.

Environmental Studies

GENERAL REFERENCE SOURCES FOR ENVIRONMENTAL STUDIES

A Dictionary of Ecology, Evolution, and Systematics. By Roger Lincoln, Geoff Boxshall, and Paul Clark. 2nd ed. Cambridge: Cambridge University Press, 1998. Defines over eleven thousand concepts, methodologies, and strategies in disciplines such as botany, zoology, bacteriology, mineralogy, and paleontology.

Dictionary of Energy. Ed. Cutler J. Cleveland and Christopher Morris. Amsterdam: Elsevier, 2006. Supplies entries with illustrations defining energy-related terms and drawing on scientific, technological, engineering, and economics viewpoints.

Encyclopedia of Environmental Science. Ed. D. E. Alexander and R. W. Fairbridge. Dordrecht: Kluwer, 2000. Includes over 340 entries on subjects ranging from alkalinity, dams and reservoirs, and ecological modeling in forestry to renewable resources, urban ecology, and volcanoes.

Encyclopedia of Global Warming and Climate Change. Ed. S. George Philander. Los Angeles: Sage, 2008. Covers concepts, historical background, policies, and perspectives from chemists, development experts, political scientists, climatologists, and engineers. Also included are data tables and country profiles.

Encyclopedia of Water Science. Ed. Stanley W. Trimble et al. London: Taylor & Francis, 2003. Covers water-related topics such as use, quality, management, and legislation; includes maps, illustrations, and statistical data.

Facts on File Dictionary of Environmental Science. By Bruce Wyman and L. Harold Stevenson. 3rd ed. New York: Facts on File, 2007. Includes brief entries on key terms in environmental studies and related fields, such as engineering, law, and computer modeling.

INDEXES AND DATABASES FOR ENVIRONMENTAL STUDIES

Ecological Abstracts. Amsterdam: Elsevier, 1974–. Indexes and abstracts articles from over two thousand periodicals and books. Available online as GEOBASE.

Environment Abstracts. Bethesda: ProQuest, 1975–. Supplies access to more than 950 periodicals as well as government reports and conference proceedings on topics such as natural resources, pollution, energy, ecology, and wildlife.

Environmental Periodicals Bibliography. Santa Barbara: Environmental Studies Institute, 1972–. Lists the contents of hundreds of periodicals, including popular publications, on environmental topics such as natural resources, ecology, air quality, and energy.

Pollution Abstracts. Bethesda: CSA, 1970–. Supplies abstracts of articles from journals and nontechnical publications about air, water, and other types of pollution, as well as waste management, sewage treatment, radiation, noise control, and related topics.

WEB RESOURCES FOR ENVIRONMENTAL STUDIES

Center for International Earth Science Information Network
www.ciesin.org
> Provides scientific data, interactive services, guides to major environmental topics, and access to other resources on the global environment and environmental resources, under the auspices of the Earth Institute at Columbia University.

EnviroInfo: Environmental Information Sources
www.deb.uminho.pt/fontes/enviroinfo
> Provides links to many resources useful for environmental studies of air, water, soil, pollution, waste, ecology, legal issues, and other topics.

EnviroLink
www.envirolink.org
> Supplies interactive services, news, and educational and activist information, as well as many links to environmental resources, broadly defined and grouped by category.

National Geophysical Data Center
www.ngdc.noaa.gov
> Consolidates information—including satellite data—for environmental and related studies.

U.S. Environmental Protection Agency (EPA)
www.epa.gov
> Organizes environmental information for various types of users (including citizens, students, and researchers) and by topic (such as news, projects, and publications), including other resources, clearinghouses, and databases.

AIP Style

Writers in the sciences and applied sciences, including those in the fields of physics, applied physics, optics, astrophysics, and acoustics, use the documentation and format style of the American Institute of Physics. Guidelines for citing print and electronic sources may be found in the *AIP Style Manual,* Fourth Edition (1990).

Many journals and fields in the applied sciences use modifications of AIP style or their own preferred methods for documenting sources and formatting papers. The various branches of engineering, for instance, have different requirements for citations. If your instructor does not specify a style, be sure to ask which one is preferred in that field.

AIP Style for In-Text Notes

The AIP recommends using in-text notes—superscript numbers in the text, numbered consecutively—to mark citations of sources. The references to which the superscript numbers refer are then presented in a double-spaced list of notes at the end of the paper, following the same numerical order. A single number and note may refer to several sources as long as all of them are relevant to the point in the text.

The preliminary work by Grever[1] and Martino[2] defined the essential experimental variables. Later studies by Throckworth et al [3] and Wixell[4] have confirmed the validity of this approach.

DIRECTORY TO AIP STYLE FOR A LIST OF NOTES

BOOKS

1. Book by one author, *282*
2. Book by two or three authors, *282*
3. Book by more than three authors, *283*
4. Book by a corporate or group author, *283*
5. Several sections cited from one edited book in one note, *283*

(Continued)

AIP Style for a List of Notes

Books

1. BOOK BY ONE AUTHOR

Supply the author's name, first name first. Use initials only or spell out a name in full, just as it appears on the title page.

[1] J. A. Poppiti, <u>Practical Techniques for Laboratory Analysis</u> (Lewis, Boca Raton, FL, 1994), p. 35.

2. BOOK BY TWO OR THREE AUTHORS

[2] M. Born and E. Wolf, <u>Principles of Optics</u>, 6th ed. (Pergamon, Oxford, 1980), p. 143.

3. BOOK BY MORE THAN THREE AUTHORS

Use *et al.* freely in the text of your paper, but avoid it in the list of notes unless there are three or more authors.

³ Lillian Hoddeson et al., Critical Assembly: A Technical History of Los Alamos During the Oppenheimer Years, 1943–45 (Cambridge University Press, New York, 1993).

4. BOOK BY A CORPORATE OR GROUP AUTHOR

⁴ American National Standards Institute, American National Standard for Human Factors Engineering of Visual Display Terminal Workstations, ANSI/HFS 100-1988 (Human Factors Society, Santa Monica, CA, 1988).

5. SEVERAL SECTIONS CITED FROM ONE EDITED BOOK IN ONE NOTE

⁵ John J. Sarraille and Thomas A. Gentry, in Computer-Mediated Communication and the Online Classroom, edited by Zane L. Berge and Mauri P. Collins (Hampton Press, Cresskill, NJ, 1995), Chap. 9, pp. 137–150; Raleigh C. Muns, ibid., Chap. 10, pp. 151–164.

Periodicals

6. ARTICLE IN A JOURNAL PAGINATED BY VOLUME

⁶ S. J. Lee, K. Imen, and S. D. Allen, J. Appl. Phys. **74**, 7046 (1993).

7. ARTICLE IN A JOURNAL PAGINATED BY ISSUE

Check with your instructor about whether you should include page numbers for an entire article or a specific page reference.

[7] John Reason, Elec. World **207** (7), 33–42 (1993).

8. ARTICLE CITATION INCLUDING TITLE

Check with your instructor about whether you should or should not include article titles.

[8] S. J. Lee, K. Imen, and S. D. Allen, "Shock wave analysis or laser assisted particle removal," J. Appl. Phys. **74**, 7046 (1993).

9. SEVERAL ARTICLES BY THE SAME AUTHOR(S) IN THE SAME JOURNAL

[9] Zhiqiang Wu and P. Paul Ruber, J. Appl. Phys. **74**, 6240 (1993); **71**, 1318 (1992).

10. SEVERAL ARTICLES BY THE SAME AUTHOR(S) IN DIFFERENT JOURNALS

[10] S. M. Gates, J. Phys. Chem. **96**, 10439–10443 (1992); Surface Sci. **195**, 307 (1988).

11. SEVERAL ARTICLES BY DIFFERENT AUTHOR(S) IN THE SAME JOURNAL

Use *ibid.* to show that the articles are "in the same place."

[11] A. C. Kibblewhite and C. Y. Wu, J. Acoust. Soc. Am. **94**, 36 (1993); G. Haralabus et al., ibid. **94**, 3385 (1993).

Electronic Sources

12. COMPUTER PROGRAM

If the author's name is known, add it to the citation.

[12] SuperCalc3 Release 2.1 (Computer Associates, Micro Products Division, San Jose, CA, 1985).

13. INTERNET SOURCE

The *AIP Style Manual* does not provide guidelines for citing source material from the Internet, and different journals published by the AIP follow different guidelines for such sources. Here are examples of citations that have appeared in such journals.

13 M. Steyvers and J. B. Tenenbaum, 2001, preprint, www-psych.stanford.edu/~jbt/.

13 P. Baran, Introduction to Distributed Communications Networks, RM-3420-PR, August 1964, http://www.rand.org/publications/RM/baran.list.html.

Other Sources

14. PERSONAL COMMUNICATION

14 J. Kincaid (private communication).

Acknowledgments

p. 7, (upper left) *Michigan Quarterly Review*; (lower left) Berkeley Electronic Press; (upper right) Reproduced with permission. **p. 8**, Copyright Scientific American, Inc. All rights reserved.; (lower right) Salon.com; **p. 17**, University of North Carolina; **p. 18**, University of North Carolina; **p. 20**, EBSCOhost; **p. 22**, EBSCOhost; **p. 35**, Harvard University/Nieman Reports; **p. 37**, Ungar, Mark. "Prisons and Politics in Contemporary Latin America," *Human Rights Quarterly* 25:4 (2003): 909–10. © 2003 The Johns Hopkins University Press. Reprinted with permission of The Johns Hopkins University Press; **p. 83**, Book cover and copyright and title pages from *Small Wonder: Essays* by Barbara Kingsolver. Copyright © 2002 by Barbara Kingsolver. Reprinted by permission of HarperCollins Publishers; **p. 91**, Douglas Conway, Lucas Marcoplos; **p. 92**, *Columbia Journalism Review*; **p. 97**, EBSCOhost; **p. 101**, Nobelprize.org; **p. 137**, Jacket design by Susan Mitchell. Copyright and title page from *The Metaphysical Club* by Louis Menand. Jacket design © 2001 by Susan Mitchell. Jacket photo of the Fort Sumter Flag courtesy of the National Park Service. Copyright and title pages copyright © 2001 by Farrar, Straus and Giroux, LLC. Reprinted by permission of Farrar, Straus and Giroux, LLC; **p. 145**, EBSCOhost; **p. 147**, Granger Collection, NorthWind Picture Archive; **p. 151**, Courtesy College of Architecture and the Arts, University of Illinois at Chicago; **p. 158**, Courtesy College of Architecture and the Arts, University of Illinois at Chicago; **p. 205**, Palgrave Macmillan; **p. 209**, *The American Scholar*; **p. 213**, EBSCOhost; **p. 217**, Alexander, Meredith. "Thirty Years Later, Stanford Prison Experiment Lives On," Stanford Report (online), August 22, 2001, http://news.stanford.edu/news/2001/august22/prison2-822.html. Photo: Chuck Painter/Stanford News Service; **p.253**, Reprinted by permission of the publisher from *The Diversity of Life* by Edward O. Wilson, Cambridge, Mass.: The Belknap Press of Harvard University Press, Copyright © 1992 by Edward O. Wilson; **p. 257**, *The American Scholar*; **p. 261**, EBSCOhost